EDWARD JAMES 'JIM' CORBETT (b. 1875) was an Anglo-Indian hunter and tracker-turned-conservationist, author and naturalist. After giving up hunting, Corbett played a key role in protecting India's wildlife, especially the endangered Bengal tiger, and used his influence in the provincial government to establish a national reserve for these tigers. The reserve was renamed in 1957 as Jim Corbett National Park in his honour.

Corbett was an avid photographer and after his retirement wrote several books recounting his hunts and experiences. Some of his works that have enjoyed much critical and commercial acclaim are *Man-Eaters of Kumaon* (1944), *The Man-Eating Leopard of Rudraprayag* (1947), *Jungle Lore* (1953) and *The Temple Tiger and More Man-Eaters of Kumaon* (1954).

Jim Corbett died in Kenya in 1955.

The Fortunate Tiger
AND OTHER CLOSE ENCOUNTERS

JIM CORBETT

SPEAKING TIGER PUBLISHING PVT. LTD
4381/4 Ansari Road, Daryaganj,
New Delhi–110002, India

Edition copyright © Speaking Tiger 2016

ISBN: 978-93-85755-48-4

eISBN: 978-93-85755-46-0

10 9 8 7 6 5 4 3 2 1

The moral right of the author has been asserted.

Typeset in Adobe Caslon Pro by Jojy Philip
Printed at Sanat Printers, Kundli

All rights reserved.
No part of this publication may be reproduced,
transmitted, or stored in a retrieval system, in any form or
by any means, electronic, mechanical, photocopying,
recording or otherwise, without the prior
permission of the publisher.

This book is sold subject to the condition that it shall not,
by way of trade or otherwise, be lent, resold, hired out,
or otherwise circulated, without the publisher's
prior consent, in any form of binding or cover
other than that in which it is published.

Contents

Publisher's Note	vii
The First Leopard	1
For Sport	10
The Fortunate Tiger	17
The Muktesar Man-eater	47
The Talla Des Killer	68
The Fish of My Dreams	128
The Scourge of Champawat	135
The Leopard of Panar	163
The Man-eating Tigress of Chowgarh	183
The Chuka Man-eater	237
The Final Man-eater	263

Publisher's Note

The adventures of Jim Corbett, as he stalked and killed maneating felines in the jungles of Kumaon and Garhwal at the turn of the last century, have fired the imaginations of generations of readers for over seven decades. Corbett's almost perfect recall, the tautness of his prose, and his uncanny ability to bring alive the sights and sounds of the jungle keeps readers on the edge of their seats and brings them back for more.

The Fortunate Tiger and Other Close Encounters, which selects eleven of the most compelling shikar stories from across Corbett's oeuvre, will thrill readers of all ages. This is an eternal classic.

The First Leopard

When I was ten years of age I was considered old enough to join the school cadet company of the Naini Tal Volunteer Rifles. Volunteering was very popular and was taken very seriously in India in those days, and all able-bodied boys and men took pride and pleasure in joining the force. There were four cadet companies and one adult company in our battalion with a combined strength of 500 which, for a population of 6,000, meant that every one in twelve was a volunteer.

The Principal of our school of seventy boys was also captain of the school cadet company, which mustered fifty strong. The holder of these dual posts was an ex-army man and it was his burning, and very praiseworthy, ambition to have the best cadet company in the battalion and to satisfy this ambition we small boys suffered, and suffered greatly. Twice a week we drilled on the school playground, and once a week we drilled with the other four companies on the flats, an open stretch of ground at the upper end of the Naini Tal lake.

Our captain never missed, nor did he ever overlook a fault, and all mistakes made on the drill grounds were atoned for after evening school. Taking up a position four feet from his target and wielding a four-foot-long cane, the captain was a marksman of repute who had earned for himself the title of 'Dead Eye Dick'. I do not know if he made private bets with himself, but we small boys laid wagers of marbles, tops, penknives, and even on occasions the biscuit that formed our breakfast, that nine times out of ten our captain could lay his cane along the most painful weal left on the hand by the previous day's or previous week's caning, and the boy—usually a newcomer—who betted against the odds always lost. The cadets of the other three companies hotly disputed our reputation of being the best drilled company, but they did not dispute our claim of our being the best turned-out company. This claim was justified, for before being marched down to drill with the other companies we were subjected to an inspection that detected the minutest particle of dirt under a finger-nail, or speck of dust on the uniform.

Our uniforms—passed down when grown out of—were of dark blue serge of a quality guaranteed to stand hard wear and to chafe every tender part of the skin they came in contact with, and, further, to show every speck of dust. Hot and uncomfortable as the uniform was it was surpassed in discomfort by the helmet that was worn with it. Made of some heavy compressed material, this instrument of torture was armed with a four-inch-long fluted metal spike, the threaded butt end of which projected down inside the helmet for an inch or more. To keep the threaded end from boring into the brain the inner band had to be lined with paper, and when the helmet had been fixed to the head like a vice it was held in that position by a heavy metal chin strap mounted on hard leather. After three hours in the hot sun few of us left the drill ground without a splitting headache which made repetition of lessons prepared the previous night difficult, with the result that the four-foot cane was used more freely on drill days than on any other.

On one of our drill days on the flats the battalion was inspected by a visiting officer of senior rank. After an hour of musketry drill and marching and counter-marching, the battalion was marched up to the Suka Tal (dry lake) rifle range. Here the cadet companies were made to sit down on the hillside while the adult company demonstrated to the visiting officer their prowess with the 450 Martini rifle. The battalion prided itself on having some of the best rifle shots in India in its ranks, and this pride was reflected in every member of the force. The target, standing on a masonry platform, was made of heavy sheet-iron and the experts could tell from the ring of the bullet on the iron sheet whether it had struck the centre of the target or the edge of it.

Each cadet company had its hero in the adult company, and adverse comments against the marksmanship of a selected hero would that morning have resulted in many sanguinary fights, had fighting in uniform not been frowned on. After the scores of the best shots had been announced, the cadets were ordered to fall in and march down from the 500 to the 200 yard range. Here four senior cadets were selected from each company and we juniors were ordered to pile arms and sit down behind the firing point.

Inter-school competition in all forms of sport, and most of all on the rifle range, was very keen and every shot fired that morning by the four competing teams was eagerly watched and fiercely commented on by friend and foe alike. The scores ran close, for the best shots in each company had been selected by the respective company commanders, and there was great jubilation in our ranks when it was announced that our team had come out second in the competition and that we had been beaten by only one point by the school that had three times our membership.

While we—the rank and file—were commenting on the achievements of the recent competitors, the Sergeant-Major was seen to detach himself from the group of officers and instructors standing at the firing point, and come towards us bellowing in a voice that it was claimed could be heard a mile away, 'Corbett, Cadet Corbett!' Heavens! What had I done now that merited punishment? True I had said that the last shot that had put the rival company one point ahead of us had been a fluke, and someone had offered to fight me, but there had been no fight for I did not even know who the challenger was, and here now was that awful Sergeant-Major again bellowing, 'Corbett, Cadet Corbett!' 'Go on.' 'He's calling you.' 'Hurry up or you'll catch it,' was being said on all sides of me; and at last, in a very weak voice, I answered 'Yes sir.' 'Why didn't you answer? Where is your carbine? Fetch it at once,' were rapped out at me all in one breath. Dazed by these commands I stood undecided until a push from behind by a friendly hand and an urgent 'Go on you fool' set me off at a run for my carbine.

On our arrival at the 200-yard range those of us who were not competing had been made to pile arms, and my carbine had been used to lock one of the piles. In my effort now to release my carbine the whole pile of arms clattered to the ground and while I was trying to set the pile up again the Sergeant-Major yelled, 'Leave those carbines you have mucked up alone, and bring yours here.' 'Shoulder arms, right turn, quick march', were the next orders I received. Feeling far worse than any lamb could possibly ever have felt I was led off to the firing point, the Sergeant-Major whispering over his shoulder as we started, 'Don't you dare disgrace me.'

At the firing point the visiting officer asked if I was the youngest cadet in the battalion, and on being told that I was, he said he would like to see me fire a few rounds. The way in which this was said—and the kindly smile that went with it—gave me the feeling that of all the officers and instructors who were standing round, the visiting officer was the only one who realized how alone, and how nervous, a small boy suddenly called upon to perform before a large and imposing gathering can feel.

The 450 Martini carbine the cadets were armed with had the most vicious kick of any small-arms weapon ever made, and the musketry course I had recently been put through had left my shoulder—which was not padded with overmuch flesh—very tender and very painful, and the knowledge that it would now be subjected to further kicks added to my nervousness. However, I would have to go through with it now, and suffer for being the youngest cadet. So on the command of the Sergeant-Major I lay down, picked up one of the five rounds that had been laid down for me, loaded the carbine and raising it very gently to my shoulder took what aim I could and pressed the trigger. No welcome ring came to my anxious ears from the iron target, only a dull thud, and then a quiet voice said, 'All right, Sergeant-Major, I will take over now,' and the visiting officer, in his spotless uniform, came and lay down beside me on the oily drugget. 'Let me have a look at your carbine,' he said, and when I passed it over to him a steady hand carefully adjusted the back-sight to 200 yards, a detail I had omitted to attend to. The carbine was then handed back to me with the injunction to take my time, and each of the following four shots brought a ring from the target. Patting me on the shoulder the visiting officer got to his feet and asked what score I had made and on being told that I had made ten, out of a possible twenty, with the first shot a miss he said, 'Splendid. Very good shooting indeed,' and as he turned to speak to the officers and instructors I went back to my companions, walking on air. But my elation was short lived, for I was greeted with, 'Rotten shot.' 'Disgraced the Company.' 'Could have done better with my eyes closed.' 'Crumbs, did you see that first shot went and hit the 100-yard firing point.' Boys are like that. They just speak their minds without any thought or intention of being cruel or unkind.

The visiting officer who befriended me that day on the Suka Tal rifle range when I was feeling lonely and nervous, later became the nation's hero and ended his career as Field-Marshal Earl Roberts. When I have been tempted, as many times I have been, to hurry over a shot or over a decision, the memory of that quiet voice telling me to take my time has restrained me and I have never ceased being grateful to the great soldier who gave me that advice.

The Sergeant-Major who for many years ruled the Naini Tal Volunteers with a rod of iron, was short and fat with a neck like a bull's and a heart of gold. After our last drill on the flats that term he asked me if I would like to have a rifle. Surprise and delight rendered me speechless; however, no reply appeared to be expected, and he went on to say, 'Come and see me before you leave for the holidays and I will give you a service rifle and all the ammunition you want, provided you promise to keep the rifle clean, and to return me the empties.'

So that winter I went down to Kaladhungi armed with a rifle, and without any anxiety about ammunition. The rifle the good Sergeant-Major had selected for me was dead accurate, and though a 450 rifle firing a heavy bullet may not have been the best type of weapon for a boy to train on, it served my purpose. The bow and arrow had enabled me to penetrate farther into the jungles than the catapult, and the muzzle-loader had enabled me to penetrate farther than the bow and arrow; and now, armed with a rifle, the jungles were open to me to wander in wherever I chose to go...

~

The muzzle-loader had taught me to economize ammunition and now, when I had a rifle, I considered it wasteful to practise on a fixed target, so I practised on jungle fowl and on peafowl, and I can recall only one instance of having spoilt a bird for the table. I never grudged the time spent, or the trouble taken, in stalking a bird and getting a shot, and when I attained sufficient accuracy with the rifle to place the heavy 450 bullet exactly where I wanted to, I gained confidence to hunt in those areas of the jungle into which I previously had been too frightened to go.

One of these areas, known to the family as the Farm Yard, was a dense patch of tree and scrub jungle several miles in extent, and reputed to be 'crawling' with jungle fowl and tigers. Crawling was not an overstatement as far as the jungle fowl were concerned, for nowhere have I seen these birds in greater numbers than in those days in the Farm Yard. The Kota-Kaladhungi road runs for a part of its length through the Farm Yard and it was on this road that the old dak runner, some years later, told me he had seen the pug marks of the 'Bachelor of Powalgarh'.

The First Leopard

I had skirted round the Farm Yard in the bow-and-arrow and muzzle-loader days, but it was not until I was armed with the 450 that I was able to muster sufficient courage to explore this dense tree and scrub jungle. Through the jungle ran a deep and narrow ravine, and up this ravine I was going one evening intent on shooting a bird for the pot, or a pig for our villagers when I heard jungle fowl scratching among the dead leaves in the jungle to my right. Climbing on to a rock in the ravine I sat down, and on cautiously raising my head above the bank saw some twenty to thirty jungle fowl feeding towards me, led by an old cock in full plumage. Selecting the cock for my target, I was waiting with finger on trigger for his head to come in line with a tree—I never fired at a bird until I had a solid background for the bullet to go into—when I heard a heavy animal on the left of the ravine and on turning my head I saw a big leopard bounding down the hill straight towards me. The Kota road here ran across the hill, 200 yards above me, and quite evidently the leopard had taken fright at something on the road and was now making for shelter as fast as he could go. The jungle fowl had also seen the leopard and as they rose with a great flutter of wings, I slewed round on the rock to face the leopard. Failing in the general confusion to see my movement the leopard came straight on, pulling up when he arrived at the very edge of the ravine.

The ravine here was about fifteen feet wide with steep banks twelve feet high on the left, and eight feet high on the right. Near the right bank, and two feet lower than it, was the rock on which I was sitting; the leopard was, therefore, a little above, and the width of the ravine from me. When he pulled up at the edge of the ravine he turned his head to look back the way he had come, thus giving me an opportunity of raising the rifle to my shoulder without the movement being seen by him. Taking careful aim at his chest I pressed the trigger just as he was turning his head to look in my direction. A cloud of smoke from the black-powder cartridge obscured my view and I only caught a fleeting glimpse of the leopard as he passed over my head and landed on the bank behind me, leaving splashes of blood on the rock on which I was sitting, and on my clothes.

With perfect confidence in the rifle, and in my ability to put a bullet exactly where I wanted to, I had counted on killing the leopard outright and was greatly disconcerted now to find that I had only wounded him. That the leopard was badly wounded I could see from the blood, but I lacked the experience to know— from the position of the wound, and the blood— whether the wound was likely to prove fatal or not. Fearing that if I did not follow him immediately he might get away into some inaccessible cave or thicket where it would be impossible for me to find him, I reloaded the rifle and stepping from my rock on to the bank, set off to follow the blood trail.

For a hundred yards the ground was flat, with a few scattered trees and bushes, and beyond this it fell steeply away for fifty yards before again flattening out. On this steep hillside there were many bushes and big rocks, behind any one of which the leopard might have been sheltering. Moving with the utmost caution, and scanning every foot of ground, I had gone half-way down the hillside when from behind a rock, some twenty yards away, I saw the leopard's tail and one hind leg projecting. Not knowing whether the leopard was alive or dead I stood stock still until presently the leg was withdrawn, leaving only the tail visible. The leopard was alive and to get a shot at him I would have to move either to the right or to the left. Having already hit the leopard in the body, and not killed him, I now decided to try his head, so inch by inch I crept to the left until his head came into view. He was lying with his back to the rock, looking away from me. I had not made a sound but the leopard appeared to sense that I was near, and as he was turning his head to look at me I put a bullet into his ear. The range was short, and I had taken my time, and I knew now that the leopard was dead, so going up to him I caught him by the tail and pulled him away from the blood in which he was lying.

It is not possible for me to describe my feelings as I stood looking down at my first leopard. My hands had been steady from the moment I first saw him bounding down the steep hillside and until I pulled him aside to prevent the blood from staining his skin. But now, not only my hands but my whole body was trembling: trembling with fear at the thought of what would have happened if, instead of landing on the bank behind me, the leopard had landed on my head. Trembling with joy at the beautiful animal I had shot, and trembling most of all with anticipation of the pleasure I would have in carrying the news of my great success to those at home who I knew would be as pleased and as proud of my achievement as I was. I could have screamed, shouted, danced, and sung, all at one and the same time. But I did none of these things, I only stood and trembled, for my feelings were too intense to be given expression in the jungle, and could only be relieved by being shared with others.

I had no idea how heavy a leopard was, but I was determined to carry my leopard home; so, laying the rifle down, I ran back to the ravine where there was a bauhinia creeper, and stripping off sufficient of the inner bark to make a strong rope, I returned and tied the fore and the hind legs of the leopard together. Then squatting down I got the legs across my shoulders but found I could not stand up, so I dragged the leopard on to the rock and again tried and found I could not lift it. Realizing that the leopard would have to be left, I hastily broke some branches and, covering it up, set off on my three-mile run for home. There was great excitement and great rejoicing in the home when I arrived with the news that I had shot a leopard, and within a few minutes Maggie and I, accompanied by two hefty servants, were on our way to the Farm Yard to bring home my first leopard.

For Sport

In nature there is no sorrow, and no repining. A bird from a flock, or an animal from a herd, is taken by hawk or by carnivorous beast and those that are left rejoice that their time had not come today, and have no thought of tomorrow. When I was ignorant I tried to rescue birds and young animals caught by hawks or by eagles, and deer caught by carnivorous beasts, but soon found that in trying to rescue one I caused the death of two. For the talons of hawk and eagle, and the teeth and claws of carnivorous beasts, hold poison in the form of decayed flesh or blood, and unless expert treatment is immediately applied—which is not possible in a jungle—only one in a 100 of rescued birds or animals survive, and the killer, being deprived of its prey, immediately finds another victim to satisfy its hunger or the hunger of its young.

It is the function of certain birds and animals to maintain the balance in nature, and in order to carry out this function and at the same time provide themselves with the only food they can assimilate it is necessary for them to kill. This killing is—whenever possible—expeditiously and very expertly performed. From the killer's point of view expeditious killing is necessary to avoid attracting enemies, and I see no reason why it should not also be a provision of nature designed to minimize suffering.

Each species has its own method of killing and the method employed in individual cases depends to a great extent on the relative size of the killer and its victim. For instance, a peregrine falcon that does most of its killing on the ground will, on occasion, take a small bird on the wing and kill and eat it in the air. Again, a tiger that on occasion finds it necessary to hamstring an animal before overpowering and killing it will on another occasion strike down a victim with a single blow.

The jungle folk, *in their natural surroundings*, do not kill wantonly. Killing for sport is, however, occasionally indulged in, and some animals, notably pine-marten, civet cats, and mongoose, will, *in abnormal circumstances*, kill in excess of their needs. Sport has a wide meaning and can be interpreted in many ways. In the two instances I am going to narrate it should be interpreted liberally.

~

When Percy Wyndham was Commissioner of Kumaon he was asked by Sir Harcourt Butler, Governor of the then United Provinces, to provide a python for the recently opened Lucknow Zoo. Wyndham was on his winter tour when he received the request and on arrival at Kaladhungi he asked me if I knew of a python that would be a credit to our jungles and a suitable gift for a commissioner to present to a Governor. It so happened that I did know of such a python, and next day Wyndham and two of his shikaris and I set out on an elephant to look at the python I had in mind. I had known this python for several years and I had no difficulty in guiding the elephant to it.

We found the python lying full stretch on the bed of a shallow stream with an inch or two of gin-clear water flowing over it, and it looked for all the world like a museum specimen in a glass case. When Wyndham saw it he said it was just the kind of python he had hoped to secure, and he ordered the mahout to undo a length of rope from the trappings of the elephant. When this had been done, Wyndham made a noose at one end of the rope and handing it to the shikaris told them to dismount from the elephant and noose the snake. With an exclamation of horror the two men said it would be *quite* impossible for them to do this. 'Don't be frightened,' Wyndham said, adding that if the snake showed any sign of attacking them he would shoot it—he was armed with a heavy rifle. This, however, did not appeal to the men, so turning to me Wyndham asked me if I would like to help them. Very emphatically I assured him there was nothing in all the world that I would like less, so handing his rifle to me he joined the two men on the ground.

I greatly regret that instead of the rifle I did not have a movie camera in my hands to make a record of the following few minutes, for I have never witnessed a more amusing scene. Wyndham's plan was to noose the python's tail and haul it to dry land, and then tie it up so that it could be loaded on to the elephant. When he explained this plan to the two shikaris they handed the noose to Wyndham and said that if he would pass the noose under the snake's tail they would haul on the rope. Wyndham, however, was firm in his opinion that the noosing could be done more expertly by the shikaris. Eventually, after a lot of advancing and retreating and dumb play to avoid alarming the python, all three men entered the water, each attempting to hold the rope as far away from the noose as possible, and very gingerly they approached the python upstream. When they got to within an arm's length of it, and while each was urging the other to take the noose and pass it under the tail, the python raised its head a foot or two out of the water, and started to turn and glide towards them. With a yell of 'Bhago Sahib' ('Run sir') the shikaris splashed out of the water, followed by Wyndham, and all three dashed into the thick brushwood on the side of the stream while the python glided under the roots of a big jamun tree and disappeared from view, and the mahout and I nearly fell off the elephant laughing.

A month later I received a letter from Wyndham informing me he was arriving in Kaladhungi the following day, and that he would like to have another try to capture the python. Geoff Hopkins and a friend of his who had recently arrived from England were with me when I received the letter, and the three of us set off to see if the python was still in the place where I had last seen it. Near the tree under the roots of which the python lived was a sambhar's stamping ground. On this ground, the earth of which had been churned to fine dust by the hooves of generations of sambhar, we found the python lying dead, killed a few minutes before our arrival by a pair of otters.

The method employed by otters in killing python, and also crocodiles, for sport—for I have never known of their using either of these reptiles for food—is to approach, one on either side of their intended victim. When the python or crocodile turns its head to defend itself against the attack of, say, the otter on the right, the otter on the left jumps in—otters are very agile—and takes a bite at the victim's neck as close to its head as possible. Then when the victim turns and tries to defend itself against its assailant on the left the one on the right jumps in and takes a bite. In this way, biting alternately and a little at a time, the neck of the victim is bitten away right down to the bone before it is dispatched, for both python and crocodiles are very tenacious of life.

In the case I am narrating the python measured 17 feet 6 inches in length and 26 inches in girth, and the pair of otters must have run a considerable risk while killing it. Otters, however, are big-hearted animals and quite possibly—like human beings—they value their sport in proportion to the risk involved.

~

The second instance concerns a big bull elephant and a pair of tigers, and unless my theory of 'sport' is accepted I can give no reason for the encounter between the lord and the king and queen of the Indian jungle. The encounter received wide publicity in the Indian press and many letters on the subject were written by renowned sportsmen to the editors of *The Pioneer* and *The Statesman*. The theories advanced for the encounter were: old vendetta, revenge for the killing of a cub, and killing for food. None of the writers of the articles and letters witnessed the encounter, and as a similar case from which deductions might have been made had never been known, the theories remained just theories and proved nothing.

I first heard of the encounter between the elephant and the tigers, which resulted in the death of the elephant, when the Superintendent, Tarai, and Bhabar asked me if it would take 200 gallons of paraffin oil to cremate the body of an elephant. Inquiries at the Superintendent's office in Naini Tal elicited the information that an elephant had been killed by the tigers at Tanakpur on rocky ground where it could not be buried, hence the claim for the cost of cremating it. This information was intensely interesting to me but unfortunately the trail was ten days old, and, further, the evidence had been burnt and heavy rain had obliterated all tracks.

The Naib-Tahsildar of Tanakpur, who had heard but not witnessed the encounter, was a friend of mine and I am indebted to him for the particulars that enable me to narrate the incident.

Tanakpur, terminus of a branch line of the Oudh-Tirhut Railway and a trading centre of considerable importance, is situated on the right bank of the Sarda river where it emerges from the foothills. Thirty years ago the river flowed along the foot of the high bank on which Tanakpur is built, but like all big rivers where they leave the foothills the Sarda keeps making new channels for itself, and at the time these events took place the river was two miles from Tanakpur. Between the main bank, which is about 100 feet high, and the river there were several small channels and on the islands formed by these channels there was moderate to heavy tree, scrub, and grass jungle.

One day two malhas (boatmen) living in Tanakpur went to the Sarda river to net fish. They stayed out longer than they had intended and the sun was setting when they started on their two-mile walk home. On emerging from a dense patch of grass on to the last channel that lay between them and the high bank, they saw two tigers standing on the far side of the channel, which here was about forty yards wide, with a trickle of water in it, and as the tigers were between them and their objective the men crouched down where they were, intending to wait until the tigers moved away. These men had seen tigers on many occasions and were not unduly alarmed. This point is important for when anyone suffers from nerves in a jungle, imagination is liable to play strange tricks. At this stage of the proceedings there was still a little light from the recently set sun, and the full moon having just risen behind the two men the tigers standing on the open ground were in clear view. Presently there was a movement in the grass through which they had just come and out on to their side of the channel, stepped an elephant with big tusks. This tusker was well known in the Tanakpur forests and it had made itself unpopular with the Forest Department owing to its habit of pulling down the pillars supporting the roof of the Chene forest bungalow. It was not, however, a rogue in the sense of molesting human beings.

When the elephant stepped out on to the channel and saw the tigers on the far side it raised its trunk and trumpeted and started to move towards them. The tigers now turned to face the elephant and as it approached them one demonstrated in front of it while the other circled round behind and sprang on its back. Swinging its head round, the elephant tried to get at the tiger on its back with its trunk, and the one in front then sprang on to its head. The elephant was now screaming with rage, while the tigers were giving vent to full-throated roars. When tigers roar with anger it is a very terrifying sound, and since the screaming of the maddened elephant was added to this terrifying sound, it is little wonder that the malhas lost their nerve and, abandoning their nets and catch of fish, sprinted for Tanakpur at their best speed.

In Tanakpur preparations were being made for the evening meal when the sounds of the fight were first heard. Shortly thereafter, when the malhas arrived with the news that an elephant and two tigers were fighting, a few bold spirits went to the edge of the high bank to try to see the fight. When it was realized, however, that the contestants were coming towards them, a stampede took place and in a few minutes every door in Tanakpur was fast closed. Opinions on the duration of the fight differed. Some maintained that it lasted all night, while others maintained that it ended at midnight. Mr Matheson, a retired gentleman whose bungalow was on the high bank immediately above where the fight took place, said it lasted for many hours, and that he had never heard more appalling or terrifying sounds. Gun shots were heard during the night, but it is not clear whether they were fired by the police or by Mr Matheson; anyway, they did not have the desired effect of stopping the fight and driving the animals away.

In the morning the residents of Tanakpur again assembled on the high ground, and at the foot of the 100-foot boulder-strewn bank they saw the elephant lying dead. From the injuries described by the Naib-Tahsildar, it was evident that it had died of loss of blood. No portion of the elephant had been eaten, and no dead or injured tigers were found at the time or subsequently in the vicinity of Tanakpur.

I do not think that the tigers, at the onset, had any intention of killing the elephant. The theory of an old vendetta, anger at the killing of a cub, and killing for food are not convincing. The fact remains, however, that a big bull elephant, carrying tusks weighing ninety pounds, was killed near Tanakpur by two tigers and I am of the opinion that what started as a lark—by a pair of mating tigers when an elephant tried to shoo them out of his way—developed into a real fight. I am also of the opinion that when the second tiger sprang on the elephant's head it clawed out the elephant's eyes and that thereafter the blinded animal dashed about aimlessly until it came to the high bank. Here on the round loose boulders, which afforded no foothold, it was practically anchored and at the mercy of the tigers who—possibly because of injuries received in the fight—showed no mercy.

The Fortunate Tiger

No one who has visited Dabidhura is ever likely to forget the view that is to be obtained from the Rest House built near the summit of 'God's Mountain' by one who, quite evidently, was a lover of scenery. From the veranda of the little three-roomed house, the hill falls steeply away to the valley of the Panar river. Beyond this valley, the hills rise ridge upon ridge until they merge into the eternal snows which, until the advent of aircraft, formed an impenetrable barrier between India and her hungry northern neighbours.

A bridle-road running from Naini Tal, the administrative headquarters of Kumaon, to Loharghat, an outlying subdivision on her eastern border, passes through Dabidhura, and a branch of this road connects Dabidhura with Almora. I was hunting the Panar man-eating leopard—about which I shall tell you later—in the vicinity of this latter road when I was informed by a road overseer, on his way to Almora, that the leopard had killed a man at Dabidhura. So to Dabidhura I went.

The western approach to Dabidhura is up one of the steepest roads in Kumaon. The object the man who designed this road had in view was to get to the top by the shortest route possible, and this he accomplished by dispensing with hairpin bends and running his road straight up the face of the 8,000-foot mountain. After panting up this road on a hot afternoon in April, I was sitting on the veranda of the Rest House drinking gallons of tea and feasting my eyes on the breathtaking view, when the priest of Dabidhura came to see me. When two years previously I had been hunting the Champawat man-eater, I had made friends with this frail old man, who officiated at the little temple nestling in the shadow of the great rock that had made Dabidhura a place of pilgrimage, and for whose presence in that unusual place I shall hazard no guess. When passing the temple a few minutes earlier I had made the customary offering which had been acknowledged by a nod by the old priest who was at his devotions. These devotions finished, the priest crossed the road that runs between the temple and the Rest House and accepting a cigarette sat down on the floor of the veranda with his back against the wall for a comfortable chat. He was a friendly old man with plenty of time on his hands, and as I had done all the walking I wanted to that day, we sat long into the evening chatting and smoking.

From the priest I learnt that I had been misinformed by the road overseer about the man alleged to have been killed at Dabidhura the previous night by the man-eater. The alleged victim, a herdsman on his way from Almora to a village south of Dabidhura, had been the priest's guest the previous night. After the evening meal the herdsman had elected, against the priest's advice, to sleep on the chabutra (platform) of the temple. Round about midnight, when the rock was casting a shadow over the temple, the man-eater crept up and, seizing the man's ankles, attempted to drag him off the platform. Awakening with a yell, the man grabbed a smouldering bit of wood from the nearby fire, and beat off the leopard. His yell brought the priest and several other men to his rescue and the combined force drove the animal away. The man's wounds were not serious, and after they had received rough-and-ready treatment at the hands of the bania, whose shop was near the temple the herdsman continued his journey.

On the evidence of the priest I decided to remain at Dabidhura. The temple and the bania's shop were daily visited by men from the surrounding villages. These men would spread the news of my arrival and—knowing where I was to be found—I would immediately be informed of any kills of human beings, or of animals, that might take place in the area.

As the old priest got up to leave me that evening I asked him if it would be possible for me to get some shooting in the locality, for my men had been without meat for many days and there was none to be purchased at Dabidhura. 'Yes,' he answered, 'there is the temple tiger.' On my assuring him that I had no desire to shoot his tiger he rejoined with a laugh, 'I have no objection, Sahib, to your *trying* to shoot this tiger, but neither you nor anyone else will ever succeed in *killing* it.' And that is how I came to hear of the Dabidhura temple tiger, which provided me with one of the most interesting shikar experiences I have ever had.

~

The morning following my arrival at Dabidhura I went down the Loharghat road to see if I could find any trace of the maneater, or learn anything about it in the village adjoining the road, for the leopard was alleged to have gone in that direction after its attack on the man at the temple. On my return to the Rest House for a late lunch I found a man in conversation with my servant. This man informed me he had learnt from the priest that I wanted to do some shooting and he said he could show me a jarao—the hillman's name for sambhar—with horns as big as the branches of an oak tree. Hill sambar do on occasions grow very fine horns—one had been shot in Kumaon some time previously with horns measuring forty-seven inches—and as a big animal would not only provide my men with meat but would also provide a meat ration for all at Dabidhura, I told the man I would accompany him after lunch.

Some months previously I had been to Calcutta on a short visit, and one morning walked into Manton's, the gunmaker's shop. On a glass showcase near the door was a rifle. I was looking at the weapon when the manager, who was an old friend of mine, came up. He informed me that the rifle, a ·275 by Westley Richards, was a new model which the makers were anxious to introduce on the Indian market for hill shooting. The rifle was a beauty and the manager had little difficulty in persuading me to buy it on the understanding that if it did not suit me I would be at liberty to return it. So when I set out with my village friend that evening to shoot his jarao with horns as big as the branches of an oak tree, I was carrying my brand-new rifle.

To the south of Dabidhura the hill is less steep than it is to the north and we had proceeded in this direction through oak and scrub jungle for about two miles when we came to a grassy knoll with an extensive view of the valley below. Pointing to a small patch of grass—surrounded by dense jungle—on the left-hand side of the valley, my guide informed me that the jarao came out to graze on this patch of grass morning and evening. He further informed me that there was a footpath on the right-hand side of the valley which he used when on his way to or from Dabidhura, and that it was from this path he was accustomed to seeing the jarao. The rifle I was carrying was sighted to 500 yards and guaranteed to be dead accurate, and as the distance between the path and the jarao's feeding ground appeared to be only about 300 yards, I decided to go down the path and wait for a shot.

While we had been talking I had noticed some vultures circling to our left front. On drawing my companion's attention to them he informed me there was a small village in a fold of the hill in that direction and suggested that the vultures were possibly interested in some domestic animal that had died in the village. However, he said we would soon know what had attracted the birds, for our way lay through the village. The 'village' consisted of a single grass hut, a cattle shed, and an acre or so of terraced fields from which the crops had recently been cut. In one of these fields, separated from the hut and cattle shed by a ten-foot wide rainwater channel, vultures were tearing the last shreds of flesh from the skeleton of some large animal. A man walked out of the hut as we approached and, after greeting us, asked where I had come from and when I had arrived. On my telling him that I had come from Naini Tal to try to shoot the man-eating leopard and that I had arrived at

Dabidhura the previous day, he expressed great regret at not having known of my arrival. 'For you could then,' he said, 'have shot the tiger that killed my cow.' He went on to tell me that he had tethered his fifteen head of cattle in the field, on which the vultures were pulling about the skeleton, the previous night, to fertilize it, and that during the night a tiger had come and killed one of the cows. He had no firearms and as there was no one within reach to whom he could appeal to shoot the tiger, he had gone to a village where a man lived who had the contract for collecting hides and skins in that area. This man had removed the hide of the cow two hours before my arrival, and the vultures had then carried out their function. When I asked the man whether he had known that there was a tiger in the locality and, if so, why he had tethered his cattle out in the open at night, he surprised me by saying there had always been a tiger on the Dabidhura hill, but that up to the previous night it had never molested cattle.

As I moved away from the hut the man asked me where I was going and when I told him I was going to try to shoot the jarao on the far side of the valley, he begged me to leave the jarao alone for the present and to shoot the tiger. 'My holding is small and the land poor, as you can see,' he said, 'and if the tiger kills my cows, on which I depend for a living, my family and I will starve.'

While we had been talking, a woman had come up the hill with a gharra of water on her head, followed a little later by a girl carrying a bundle of green grass and a boy carrying a bundle of dry sticks: four people living on an acre or so of poor land and a few pints of milk—for hill cattle give little milk—sold to the bania at Dabidhura. Little wonder, then, that the man was so anxious for me to shoot the tiger.

The vultures had destroyed the kill. This did not matter, however, for there was no heavy cover near the field where the tiger could have lain up and seen the vultures at their work, so he would be almost certain to return, for he had not been disturbed at his feed the previous night. My guide was also keen on my trying to shoot the tiger in preference to his jarao, so, telling the two men to sit down, I set off to try to find out in which direction the tiger had gone, for there were no trees on which I could sit near the field, and it was my intention to intercept the tiger on its way back. The hill was criss-crossed with cattle paths but the ground was too hard to show pug marks, and after circling round the village twice I eventually tried the rainwater channel. Here on the soft damp ground I found the pug marks of a big male tiger. These pug marks showed that the tiger had gone up the channel after his feed, so it was reasonable to assume that he would return the same way. Growing out of the bank, on the same side of the channel as the hut and about thirty yards from it, was a gnarled and stunted oak tree smothered by a wild rose creeper. Laying down the rifle, I stepped from the bank on to the tree, which was leaning out over the channel, and found there was a reasonably comfortable seat on the top of the creeper.

Rejoining the two men at the hut I told them I was going back to the Rest House for my heavy rifle, a double-barrelled ·500 express using modified cordite. My guide very sportingly offered to save me this trouble, so after instructing him I sat down with the villager at the door of his hut and listened to the tales he had to tell of a poor but undaunted man's fight against nature and wild animals, to keep a grass roof above his head. When I asked him why he did not leave this isolated place and try to make a living elsewhere, he said simply, 'This is my home.'

The sun was near setting when I saw two men coming down the hill towards the hut. Neither of them had a rifle, but Bala Singh—one of the best men who ever stepped out of Garhwal...—was carrying a lantern. On reaching me Bala Singh said he had not brought my heavy rifle because the cartridges for it were locked up in my suitcase and I had forgotten to send the key. Well, the tiger would have to be shot with my new rifle, and it could not have a better christening.

~

Before taking my seat on the tree I told the owner of the hut that my success would depend on his keeping his two children, a girl of eight and a boy of six, quiet, and that his wife would have to defer cooking the evening meal until I had shot the tiger, or until I decided the tiger was not coming. My instructions to Bala Singh were to keep the inmates of the hut quiet, light the lantern when I whistled, and then await my further orders.

The vesper songs of the multitude of birds in the valley were hushed as the red glow from the setting sun died off the hills. Twilight deepened and a horned owl hooted on the hill above me. There would be a short period of semi-darkness before the moon rose. The time had now come, and the inmates of the hut were as silent as the dead. I was gripping the rifle and straining my eyes on the ground under me when the tiger, who had avoided passing under my tree, arrived at his kill and was angry at what he found. In a low muttering voice he cursed the vultures who, though they had departed two hours earlier, had left their musky smell on the ground they had fouled. For two, three, possibly four minutes he continued to mutter to himself, and then there was silence. The light was getting stronger. Another few minutes and the moon rose over the brow of the hill, flooding my world with light. The bones picked clean by the vultures were showing white in the moonlight, and nowhere was the tiger to be seen. Moistening my lips, which excitement had dried, I gave a low whistle. Bala Singh was on the alert and I heard him ask the owner of the hut for a light from the fire. Through the crevices of the grass hut I saw a glimmer of light, which grew stronger as the lantern was lit. The light moved across the hut and Bala Singh pulled open the door and stood on the threshold awaiting my further orders. With the exception of that one low whistle, I had made no sound or movement from the time I had taken my seat on the tree. And now, when I looked down, there was the tiger standing below me, in brilliant moonlight, looking over his right shoulder at Bala Singh. The distance between the muzzle of my rifle and the tiger's head was about five feet, and the thought flashed through my mind that the cordite would probably singe his hair. The ivory foresight of my rifle was on the exact spot of the tiger's heart—where I knew my bullet would kill him instantaneously—when I gently pressed the trigger. The trigger gave under the pressure, and nothing happened.

Heavens! How incredibly careless I had been. I distinctly remembered having put a clip of five cartridges in the magazine when I took my seat on the tree, but quite evidently when I pushed the bolt home it had failed to convey a cartridge from the magazine into the chamber, and this I had omitted to observe. Had the rifle been old and worn it might still have been possible to rectify my mistake. But the rifle was new and as I raised the lever to draw back the bolt there was a loud metallic click, and in one bound the tiger was up the bank and out of sight. Turning my head to see how Bala Singh had reacted, I saw him step back into the hut and close the door.

There was now no longer any need for silence and as Bala Singh came up at my call, to help me off the tree, I drew back the bolt of the rifle with the object of unloading the magazine and, as I did so, I noticed that the extractor at the end of the bolt held a cartridge. So the rifle had been loaded after all and the safety-catch off. Why then had the rifle not fired when I pulled the trigger? Too late, I knew the reason. One of the recommendations stressed by Manton's manager when showing me the rifle was that it had a double pull off. Never having handled a rifle with this so-called improvement, I did not know it was necessary, after the initial pull had taken up the slack, to pull the trigger a second time to release the striker. When

I explained the reason for my failure to Bala Singh, he blamed himself, 'for,' said he, 'if I had brought your heavy rifle *and* the suitcase this would not have happened'. I was inclined to agree with him at the time, but as the days went by I was not so sure that even with the heavy rifle I would have been able to kill the tiger that evening.

~

Another long walk next morning, to try to get news of the man-eater, and when I returned to the Rest House I was greeted by a very agitated man who informed me that the tiger had just killed one of his cows. He had been grazing his cattle on the far side of the valley from where I sat the previous evening, when a tiger appeared and killed a red cow that had calved a few days previously. 'And now,' he said, 'the heifer calf will die, for none of my other cows are in milk.'

Luck had been with the tiger the previous evening but his luck could not last indefinitely, and for the killing of this cow he would have to die, for cattle are scarce in the hills and the loss of a milch cow to a poor man was a serious matter. The man had no anxiety about the rest of his small herd, which had stampeded back to his village, so he was willing to wait while I had a meal. At 1 p.m. we set out, the man leading, I on his heels, and two of my men following with material for making a machan.

From an open patch of ground on the hillside my guide pointed out the lay of the land. His cattle had been grazing on a short stretch of grass a quarter of a mile below the ridge, when the tiger, coming up from the direction of the valley, had killed his cow. The rest of the herd had stampeded up the hill and over the ridge to his village, which was on the far side. Our shortest way was across the valley and up the other side, but I did not want to risk disturbing the tiger, so we skirted round the head of the valley to approach from above the spot where the cow had been killed. Between the ridge over which the cattle had stampeded and the spot where they had been grazing, was more or less open tree jungle. The tracks of the running animals had bitten deep into the soft loamy earth, and it was easy to follow these tracks back to where they had started. Here there was a big pool of blood with a drag-mark leading away from it. The drag led across the hill for 200 yards to a deep and well-wooded ravine with a trickle of water in it. Up this ravine the tiger had taken his kill.

The cow had been killed at about 10 a.m. on open ground, and the tiger's first anxiety would have been to remove it to some secluded spot where it would be hidden from prying eyes. So he had dragged it up the ravine and, after depositing it in a place he knew of, he had, as his pug marks showed, gone down the ravine into the valley below. In an area in which human beings and cattle are moving about, it is unwise to predict where a tiger will be lying up, for the slightest disturbance may make him change his position. So, though the pug marks led down the ravine, the three men and I very cautiously followed the drag up the ravine.

Two hundred yards below the ridge along which we had come, rainwater had scooped out a big hole in the hillside. Here the ravine started. The hole, which at the upper end had a sheer drop into it of fifteen feet, had been made many years previously and was now partly overgrown with oak and ash saplings ten to twelve feet tall. Between these saplings and the fifteen-foot drop was a small open space on which the tiger had deposited his kill. I could sympathize with the owner of the cow when he told me with tears in his eyes that the fine animal that lay dead before us had been bred by him and that it was a special favourite. No portion of the animal had been touched, the tiger having evidently brought it here to eat at his leisure.

A place had now to be found in which to sit. There were several big oak trees on either side of the ravine, but none overlooked the kill and all of them were unclimbable. Thirty yards below the kill and on the left-hand side of the ravine was a small stout holly tree. The branches were growing out at right angles to the trunk, and six feet above ground there was a strong enough branch for me to sit on and another on which to rest my feet. The three men protested strongly against my sitting so close to the ground. However, there was no other suitable place for me to sit, so the holly tree it would have to be. Before sending the men away I instructed them to go to the hut where I had been the previous evening, and to wait there until I called to them, or until I joined them. The distance across the valley was about half a mile and though the men would not be able to see either me or the kill, I was able to see the hut through the leaves of the holly tree.

The men left me at 4 p.m. and I settled down on the holly branch for what I anticipated would be a long wait, for the hill faced west and the tiger would probably not be on the move much before sundown. To the left my field of vision—through the holly leaves—extended down the ravine for fifty yards. In front I had a clear view into the ravine, which was about ten feet deep and twenty feet wide, and of the hill facing me on which there were outcrops of rock but no trees. To the right I had a clear view up to the ridge but I could not see the kill, which was hidden by the thick growth of saplings. Behind me was a dense thicket of ringals which extended down to the level of my tree and further helped to mask the kill. The tiger after depositing his kill in the hole, made by rainwater, had gone down the ravine and it was reasonable to assume that when he returned he would come by the same route. So I concentrated all my attention on the ravine, intending to shoot the tiger when he was at right angles to me. That I could kill him at that short range I had no doubt whatsoever and to make quite sure of getting in a second shot, if it was necessary, I cocked both hammers of my rifle.

There were sambhar, kakar, and langur in the jungle and a great number of pheasants, magpies, babblers, thrushes, and jays, all of which call on seeing a member of the cat family, so I thought I would receive ample warning of the tiger's coming. But here I was wrong, for without having heard a single alarm call, I suddenly heard the tiger at his kill. After going down the ravine, possibly for a drink, the tiger had skirted round the thicket of ringals and approached his kill without passing me. This did not worry me unduly for tigers are restless at a kill in daylight, and I felt sure that sooner or later the tiger would show up on the open ground in front of me. He had been eating for about fifteen minutes, tearing off great chunks of flesh, when I caught sight of a bear coming along the crest of the hill from left to right. He was a great big Himalayan black bear, and was strolling along as though it did not matter to him how long he took to get from here to there. Suddenly he stopped, turned facing downhill, and lay flat. After a minute or two he raised his head, snuffed the wind, and again lay flat. The wind, as always in daylight in the hills, was blowing uphill and the bear had got the scent of flesh and blood, mingled with the scent of tiger. I was a little to the right of the kill, so he had not got my scent. Presently he got to his feet and, with the bent legs and body held close to the ground, started to stalk the tiger.

It was a revelation to me in animal stalking to see that bear coming down the hill. He had possibly 200 yards to go and though he was not built for stalking, as tigers and leopards are, he covered the distance as smoothly as a snake and as silently as a shadow. The nearer he got the more cautious he became. I could see the lip of the fifteen-foot drop into the hole, and when the bear got to within a few feet of this spot he drew himself along with belly to ground. Waiting until the tiger was eating with great gusto, the bear very slowly projected his head over the lip of the hole and looked down, and then as slowly drew his head back. Excitement with me had now reached the stage when the whole of my body was trembling, and my mouth and throat were dry.

On two occasions I have seen Himalayan bears walk off with tigers' kills. On both occasions the tigers were not present. And on two occasions I have seen bears walk up to feeding leopards and, after shooing them off, carry the kills away. But on this occasion the tiger—and a big male at that—was present at his kill and, further, he was not an animal to be shooed away like a leopard. At the back of my mind was the thought that surely this bear would not be so foolish as to try to dispossess the king of the jungle of his kill. But that was just what the bear appeared to intend doing, and his opportunity came when the tiger was cracking a bone. Whether the bear had been waiting for this moment I do not know; anyway, while the tiger was crunching the bone, the bear drew himself to the edge and, gathering his feet under him, launched himself into the hole with a mighty scream. The object of the scream I imagine was to intimidate the tiger, but so far from having this effect it appeared to infuriate him, for the bear's mighty scream was answered by an even mightier roar from the tiger.

Fights in the wild are very rare and this is only the second case I know of different species of animals fighting for the sake of fighting and not for the purpose of one using the other as food. I did not see the fight, for the reasons I have given, but I heard every detail of it. Waged in a hollow of restricted area the sound was terrifying and I was thankful that the fight was a straight one between two contestants who were capable of defending themselves, and not a three-cornered one in which I was involved. Time stands still when every drop of blood racing through a rapidly beating heart is tingling with excitement. The fight may have lasted three minutes, or it may have lasted longer. Anyway, when the tiger considered he had administered sufficient chastisement he broke off the engagement and came along the open ground in front of me at a fast gallop, closely followed by the still screaming bear. Just as I was aligning the sights of my rifle on the tiger's left shoulder he turned sharp to the left and leaping the twenty-foot-wide ravine, landed at my feet. While he was still in the air I depressed the muzzle of the rifle and fired, as I thought, straight into his back. My shot was greeted with an angry grunt as the tiger crashed into the ringals behind me. For a few yards he carried on and then there was silence; shot through the heart and died in his tracks, I thought.

A ·500 modified cordite rifle fired anywhere makes a considerable noise, but here, in the ravine, it sounded like a cannon. The detonation, however, had not the least effect on the maddened bear. Following close on the heels of the tiger he did not attempt to leap the ravine, as the tiger had done. Storming down one bank he came up the other straight towards me. I had no wish to shoot an animal that had the courage to drive a tiger off his kill, but to have let that screaming fury come any nearer would have been madness, so, when he was a few feet from me, I put the bullet of the left barrel into his broad forehead. Slowly he slid down the bank on his stomach, until his haunches met the opposite bank.

Where a moment earlier the jungle had resounded with angry strife and the detonations of a heavy rifle, there was now silence, and when my heart had resumed its normal beat, my thoughts turned to a soothing smoke. Laying the rifle across my knees I put both hands into my pockets to feel for the cigarette case and matches. At that moment I caught sight of a movement on my right and, turning my head, saw the tiger unhurriedly cantering along on the open ground over which he had galloped a minute or two earlier and looking not at me, but at his dead enemy.

I know that in relating these events as they occurred, sportsmen will accuse me of rank bad shooting and gross carelessness. I have no defence to make against the accusation of bad shooting, but I do not plead guilty to carelessness. When

I fired, as I thought, into the tiger's back, I was convinced I was delivering a fatal wound, and the angry response followed by the mad rush and sudden cessation of sound were ample justification for thinking the tiger had died in his tracks. My second shot had killed the bear outright so there was no necessity—while I was still on the tree—to reload the rifle before laying it across my knees.

Surprise at seeing the tiger alive and unhurt lost me a second or two, and thereafter I acted quickly. The rifle was of the under-lever model; the lever being held in position by two lugs on the trigger guard. This made the rapid loading of the rifle difficult, and, further, the spare cartridges were in my trousers pocket; easy to get at when standing up, but not so easy when sitting on a thin branch. Whether the tiger knew the bear was dead, or whether he was just keeping an eye on it to avoid a flank attack, I do not know. Anyway, he carried on across the face of the steep hill at a slow canter and had reached a spot forty yards away—which I can best describe as eleven o'clock—and was passing a great slab of rock when, with only one barrel loaded, I put up the rifle and fired. At my shot he reared up, fell over sideways, made a bad landing, scrambled to his feet, and cantered on round the shoulder of the hill with his tail in the air. The nickel-cased soft-nosed bullet with steel base had struck the rock a few inches from the tiger's face and the blow-back had thrown him off his balance but had done him no harm.

After a quiet smoke I stepped down from the holly tree and went to have a look at the bear, who, I found, was even bigger than I had at first thought. His self-sought fight with the tiger had been a very real one, for blood from a number of deep cuts was seeping through the thick fur on his neck and in several places his scalp was torn right down to the bone. These wounds in themselves would have mattered little to a tough animal like a bear, but what did matter and what had annoyed him was the injury to his nose. All males resent being struck on the nose, and not only had the bear been struck on that tender spot but insult had been added to injury by his nose being torn in half. Reason enough for him to have chased the tiger with murder in his eyes, and for him to have ignored the report of my heavy rifle.

There was not sufficient time for me to call up my men to skin the bear, so I set off to collect them at the hut and get back to the Rest House before nightfall, for somewhere in that area there was a man-eater. My men, and the dozen or so villagers who had collected at the hut, were too intent on gazing across the valley to observe my approach, and when I walked in among them, they were dumb with amazement. Bala Singh was the first to recover speech, and when I heard his story I was not surprised that the assembled men had looked at me as one returned from the dead. 'We advised you,' Bala Singh said, 'not to sit so close to the ground, and when we heard your first scream, followed by the tiger's roar, we were convinced that you had been pulled out of the tree and that you were fighting for your life with the tiger. Then, when the tiger stopped roaring and you continued to scream, we thought the tiger was carrying you away. Later we heard two reports from your rifle, followed by a third, and we were greatly mystified, for we could not understand how a man who was being carried away by a tiger could fire his rifle. And while we were consulting with these men what we should do, you suddenly appeared and we became speechless.' To men keyed-up and listening for sounds from where a tiger was being sat up for, the scream of a bear could easily be mistaken for the scream of a human being, for the two are very similar and at a distance would not be distinguishable from one another.

Bala Singh got a cup of tea ready for me while I told the men about the fight they had heard and about the bear I had shot. Bear's fat is greatly valued as a cure for rheumatism, and the men were delighted when I told them I did not want the fat and that they could share it with their friends. Next morning I set out to skin the bear, accompanied by a crowd of men who were anxious not only to get a share of the fat but also to see the animal that had fought a tiger. I have never measured or weighed a bear but have seen quite a few, and the one I skinned that morning was the biggest and the fattest Himalayan bear I have ever seen. When the fat and the other prized parts of the bear had been divided, a very happy throng of men turned their faces to Dabidhura, and the happiest and the most envied of all was Bala Singh who proudly carried, strapped to his back, the bear's skin I had given him.

The tiger did not return to finish his interrupted meal, and by evening the vultures had picked clean the bones of the cow and the bear.

~

Skinning a bear encased in fat is a very messy job, and as I plodded back to the Rest House for a hot bath and a late breakfast I met a very agitated forest guard, whose headquarters were at Dabidhura. He had been at an outlying beat the previous night and on his return to Dabidhura that morning had heard at the bania's shop about the bear I had shot. Being in urgent need of bear's fat for his father, who was crippled with rheumatism, he was hurrying to try to get a share of the fat when he ran into a herd of stampeding cattle, followed by a boy who informed him that a tiger had killed one of his cows. The forest guard had a rough idea where the cattle had been grazing when attacked by the tiger, so while Bala Singh and the other men carried onto Dabidhura I set off with him to try to find the kill. Uphill and downhill we went for two miles or more until we came to a small valley. It was in this valley that the forest guard thought the cow had been killed.

There had been an auction of condemned stores at the Gurkha depot at Almora a few days previously, and my companion had treated himself to a pair of army boots many sizes too big for his feet. In these he had clumped ahead of me until we came to the lip of the valley. Here I made him remove his boots and when I saw the condition of his feet I marvelled that a man who had gone barefoot all his life had, for the sake of vanity, endured such torture. 'I bought big boots,' he told me, 'because I thought they would shrink.'

The boat-shaped valley, some five acres in extent, was like a beautiful park dotted over with giant oak trees. On the side from which I approached it the ground sloped gently down and was free of bushes, but on the far side the hill went up more steeply with a few scattered bushes on it. I stood on the lip of the valley for a few minutes scanning every foot of ground in my field of vision without seeing anything suspicious, and then went down the grassy slope followed by the forest guard, now walking silently on bare feet. As I approached the flat ground on the floor of the valley I saw that the dead leaves and dry twigs over a considerable area had been scratched together, and piled into a great heap. Though no part of the cow was visible I knew that under this pile of dead matter the tiger had hidden his kill, and very foolishly I did not inform my companion of this fact, for he told me later that he did not know that tigers were in the habit of hiding their kills. When a tiger hides his kill it is usually an indication that he does not intend lying up near it, but it is not safe to assume this always. So, though I had scanned the ground before entering the valley, I again stood perfectly still while I had another look.

A little beyond the piled-up leaves and twigs the hill went up at an angle of forty-five degrees, and forty yards up the hillside there was a small clump of bushes. As I was looking at these I saw the tiger, who was lying on a small bit of flat ground with his feet towards me, turn over and present his back to me. I could see part of his head, and a three-inch wide strip of his body from shoulder to hindquarters. A head shot was out of the question, and nothing would be gained by inflicting a flesh wound. I had the whole afternoon and evening before me and as the tiger would be bound to stand up sooner or later, I decided to sit down and wait on events. As I came to this decision I caught sight of a movement on my left, and on turning my head saw a bear coming stealthily up the valley towards the kill, followed by two half-grown cubs. The bear had evidently heard the tiger killing the cow and after giving the tiger time to settle down—as I have done on many occasions—she was now coming to investigate, for unless they have a special reason bears do not move about at midday. Had I been standing on the lip of the valley, instead of a few feet from the kill, I believe I should have witnessed a very interesting sight, for on finding the kill, which with their keen scent they would have had no difficulty in doing, the bears would have started to uncover it. This would have awakened the tiger and I cannot imagine that he would have relinquished his kill without a fight, and the fight would have been worth seeing.

The forest guard, who all this time had been standing quietly behind me seeing nothing but the ground at his feet, now caught sight of the bears and exclaimed in a loud voice, 'Dekko Sahib, bhalu, bhalu.' The tiger was up and away in a flash, but he had some twenty yards of open ground to cover, and as I aligned my sights on him and pressed the trigger the forest guard, under the impression that I was facing in the wrong direction, grabbed my arm and gave it a jerk with the result that my bullet struck a tree a few yards from where I was standing. Losing one's temper anywhere does no good, least of all in a jungle. The forest guard, who did not know what the piled-up leaves implied and who had not seen the tiger, was under the impression that he had saved my life by drawing my attention to the dreaded bears, so there was nothing to be said. Alarmed by my shot the bears lumbered away while my companion urged me with a catch in his throat, 'Maro, maro!' ('Shoot, shoot!').

A very dejected forest guard walked back with me to Dabidhura, and to cheer him up I asked him if he knew of any place where I could shoot a ghooral, for my men were still without meat. Not only did the game little man know of such a place but he also volunteered, blisters and all, to take me to it. So after a cup of tea we set off accompanied by two of my men who, the forest guard said, would be needed to carry back the bag.

From the veranda of the Rest House the hill falls steeply away. Down this hill the forest guard led me for a few hundred yards until we came to a foot-wide ghooral track running across the face of the hill. I now took the lead and had proceeded for about half a mile to the right when, on coming to a rocky ridge, I looked across a deep ravine and saw a ghooral on the far side standing on a projecting rock and looking into space, as all goats including tahr, ibex, and markor have a habit of doing. It was a male ghooral, as I could see from the white disk on its throat, and the distance between us was a shade over 200 yards. Here now was an opportunity not only of procuring meat for my men but also of testing the accuracy of my new rifle. So, lying down, I put up the 200-yard leaf sight and, taking very careful aim, fired. At my shot the ghooral sank down on the rock on which he had been standing, which was very fortunate, for below him was a sheer drop of many hundred feet. A second ghooral, which I had not seen, now ran up the far side of the ravine followed by a small kid, and after standing still and looking back at us several times, carried on round the shoulder of the hill.

While the forest guard and I had a smoke, my two men set off to retrieve the bag. Deprived of his share of the bear's fat the forest guard was made happy by being promised a bit of the ghooral and its skin, which he said he would make into a seat for his father who, owing to age and rheumatism, spent all his days basking in the sun.

~

A visit to the valley early next morning confirmed my suspicion that the tiger would not return to his kill, and that the bears would. Little but the bones were left when the three bears had finished with the kill, and that little was being industriously sought by a solitary king vulture when I arrived on the scene.

The morning was still young so, climbing the hill in the direction in which the tiger had gone the previous day, I went over the ridge and down the far side to the Loharghat road to look for tracks of the man-eating leopard. On my return to the Rest House at midday I was informed of yet another tiger kill. My informant was an intelligent young man who was on his way to Almora to attend a court case and, being unable to spare the time to show me where he had seen the tiger killing a cow, drew a sketch for me on the floor of the veranda with a piece of charcoal. After a combined breakfast and lunch I set out to try to find the kill which—if the young man's sketch was correct—had taken place five miles from where I had fired at the tiger the previous day. The tiger, I found, had come on a small herd of cattle grazing on the banks of the stream flowing down the main valley and, judging from the condition of the soft ground, had experienced some difficulty in pulling down the victim he had selected. Killing a big and vigorous animal weighing six or seven hundred pounds is a strenuous job and a tiger after accomplishing this feat usually takes a breather. On this occasion, however, the tiger had picked up the cow as soon as he had killed it—as the absence of blood indicated—and crossing the stream entered the dense jungle at the foot of the hill.

Yesterday the tiger had covered up his kill at the spot where he had done his killing, but today it appeared to be his intention to remove his kill to as distant a place as possible from the scene of killing. For two miles or more I followed the drag up the steep face of the densely wooded hill to where the tiger, when he had conveyed his heavy burden to within a few hundred yards of the crest, had got one of the cow's hind legs fixed between two oak saplings. With a mighty jerk *uphill*, the tiger tore the leg off a little below the hock, and leaving that fixed between the saplings went on with his kill. The crest of the hill at the point where the tiger arrived with his kill was flat and overgrown with oak saplings a foot or two feet in girth. Under these trees, where there were no bushes or cover of any kind, the tiger left his kill without making any attempt to cover it up.

I had followed the drag slowly, carrying only my rifle and a few cartridges; even so, when I arrived at the crest my shirt was wet and my throat dry. I could imagine, therefore, the thirst that the tiger must have acquired and his desire to quench it. Being in need of a drink myself I set out to find the nearest water, where there was also a possibility of finding the tiger. The ravine in which I had shot the bear was half a mile to the right and had water in it, but there was another ravine closer to the left and I decided to try that first.

I had gone down this ravine for the best part of a mile and had come to a place where it narrowed with steep shaly banks on either side when, on going round a big rock, I saw the tiger lying in front of me at a range of twenty yards. There was a small pool of water at this spot, and lying on a narrow strip of sand between the pool and the right-hand bank was the tiger. Here the ravine took a sharp turn to the right, and part of the tiger was on my side of the turn and part round the bend. He was lying on his left side with his back to the pool and I could see his tail and part of his hind legs. Between me and the sleeping animal was a great mass of dry branches that had been lopped from overhanging trees some time previously to feed buffaloes. It was not possible to negotiate this obstacle without making a noise, nor was it possible to go along either of the steep banks without causing small landslides of shale. So the only thing to do was to sit down and wait for the tiger to give me a shot.

After his great exertion and a good drink, the tiger was sleeping soundly and for half an hour he made no movement. Then he turned on to his right side and a little more of his legs came into view. In this position he lay for a few minutes and then stood up, and withdrew round the bend. With finger on trigger I waited for him to reappear, for his kill was up the hill behind me. Minutes passed and then a kakar a hundred yards away went dashing down the hill barking hysterically, and a little later a sambhar belled. The tiger had gone; why, I did not know, for he had already taken as much exercise as any tiger needed to take, and it was not a case of his having scented me, for tigers have no sense of smell. It did not matter, however, for presently he would return to the kill he had been at such pains to take to the top of the hill, and I would be there to receive him. The water in the pool where the tiger had drunk was ice-cold, and having slaked my thirst I was able to enjoy a long-deferred smoke.

The sun was near setting when I made myself comfortable on an oak tree ten yards to the east and a little to the right of the kill. The tiger would come up the hill from the west and it was not advisable to have the kill directly between us, for tigers have very good eyesight. From my seat on the tree I had a clear view of the valley and of the hills beyond; and when the setting sun, showing as a great ball of fire, was resting on the rim of the earth bathing the world in red, a sambhar belled in the valley below me. The tiger was on the move and there was plenty of time for him to arrive at his kill while there was still sufficient daylight for accurate shooting.

The ball of fire dipped below the horizon; the red glow died of the earth; twilight gave place to darkness; and all was silent in the jungle. The moon was in its third quarter, but the stars—nowhere more brilliant than in the Himalayas—were giving enough light for me to see the kill, which was white. The head of the kill was towards me and if the tiger came now and started to eat at the hindquarters I would not be able to see him, but by aligning my sights on the white kill and then raising the rifle and pressing the trigger, as the kill disappeared from view, there was a fifty-fifty chance of hitting the tiger. But here was no man-eater to be fired at under any conditions. Here was a 'temple' tiger who had never molested human beings and who, though he had killed four head of cattle in four consecutive days, had committed no crime against the jungle code. To kill him outright would benefit those who were suffering from his depredations, but to take an uncertain shot at night with the possibility of only wounding him and leaving him to suffer for hours, or if unrecovered to become a man-eater, was not justifiable in any circumstances.

Light was coming in the east, for the boles of the trees were beginning to cast vague shadows, and then the moon rose, flooding the open patches of the jungle with light. It was then that the tiger came. I could not see him but I knew he had come for I could feel and sense his presence. Was he crouching on the far side of the kill with just his eyes and the top of his head raised over the brow of the hill watching me? No, that was not possible, for from the time I had made myself comfortable on my seat I had become part of the tree and tigers do not go through a jungle scanning, without a reason, every tree they approach. And yet, the tiger was here, and he was looking at me.

There was sufficient light now for me to see clearly, and very carefully I scanned the ground in front of me. Then as I turned my head to the right, to look behind, I saw the tiger. He was sitting on his hunkers in a patch of moonlight, facing the kill, with his head turned looking up at me. When he saw me looking down on him he flattened his ears, and as I made no further movement, his ears regained their upright position. I could imagine him saying to himself, 'Well, you have now seen me, and what are you going to do about it?' There was little I could do about it, for in order to get a shot I would have to turn a half-circle and it would not be possible to do this without alarming the tiger, who was looking at me from a range of fifteen feet. There was, however, just a possibility of my getting a shot from my left shoulder, and this I decided to try to do. The rifle was resting on my knees with the muzzle pointing to the left, and as I lifted it and started turning it to the right the tiger lowered his head and again flattened his ears. In this position he remained as long as I was motionless, but the moment I started to move the rifle again, he was up and away into the shadows behind.

Well, that was that, and the tiger had very definitely won another round. As long as I sat on the tree he would not return, but if I went away he *might* come back and remove the kill; and as he could not eat a whole cow in a night I would have another chance next day.

The question that now faced me was where to spend the night. I had already walked some twenty miles that day and the prospect of doing another eight miles to the Rest House—through forest all the way—did not appeal to me. In any other locality I would have moved away from the kill for two or three hundred yards and slept peacefully on the ground, but in this locality there was a man-eating leopard, and man-eating leopards hunt at night. While sitting on the tree earlier in the evening, I had heard the distant pealing of cattle-bells, coming either from a village or from a cattle-station. I had pin-pointed the sound and I now set out to find where it had come from. Cattle-lifting is unknown in the Himalayas, and throughout Kumaon there are communal cattle-stations situated in the jungles close to the grazing grounds. I traced the bells I had heard to one of these stations, in which there were about a hundred head of cattle in a large open shed surrounded by a strong stockade. The fact that the station was in the depth of the jungle, and unguarded, was proof of the honesty of the hillfolk, and it was also proof that until my arrival cattle in the Dabidhura area had not been molested by tigers.

At night all animals in the jungle are suspicious, and if I was to spend the night under the protection of the inmates of the shed I would have to disarm their very natural suspicion. The tenants of our village at Kaladhungi keep about 900 head of cows and buffaloes, and having been associated with cattle from my earliest childhood I know the language they understand. Moving very slowly and speaking to the cattle I approached the shed, and on reaching the stockade sat down with my back to it to have a smoke. Several cows were standing near the spot where I sat and one of them now advanced and, putting its head through the bars of the stockade, started to lick the back of my head; a friendly gesture, but a wetting one, and here at an altitude of 8,000 feet the nights were cold. Having finished my cigarette, I unloaded my rifle and, covering it with straw, climbed the stockade.

Care was needed in selecting a place on which to sleep, for if there was an alarm during the night and the cattle started milling round it would be unsafe to be caught on the ground. Near the centre of the shed, and close to one of the roof-supports up which I could go if the need arose, there was an open space between two sleeping cows. Stepping over recumbent animals and moving the heads of standing ones to get past them, I lay down between the two that were lying back to back. There was no alarm during the night, so the necessity for me to shin up the roof-support did not arise, and with the warm bodies of the cows to keep off the night chills and with the honey-sweet smell of healthy cattle in my nostrils I slept as one at peace with all the world, tigers and man-eating leopards included.

The sun was just rising next morning when, on hearing voices, I opened my eyes and saw three men, armed with milking pails, staring at me through the bars of the stockade. The water I had drunk at the tiger's pool was all that had passed my lips since breakfast the previous day, and the warm drink of milk the men gave me—after they had recovered from their amazement at finding me asleep with their cattle—was very welcome. Declining the men's invitation to accompany them back to their village for a meal, I thanked them for their board and lodging and, before returning to the Rest House for a bath and a square meal, set off to see where the tiger had taken his kill. To my surprise I found the kill lying just as I had left it, and after covering it over with branches to protect it from vultures and golden-headed eagles I went on to the Rest House.

In no other part of the world, I imagine, are servants as tolerant of the vagaries of their masters as in India. When I returned to the Rest House after an absence of twenty-four hours, no surprise was expressed, and no questions asked. A hot bath was ready, clean clothes laid out, and within a very short time I was sitting down to a breakfast of porridge, scrambled eggs, hot chapatis and honey—the last a present from the old priest—and a dish of tea. Breakfast over, I sat on the grass in front of the Rest House admiring the gorgeous view and making plans. I had set out from my home in Naini Tal with one object, and one object only, to try to shoot the Panar man-eating leopard; and from the night it had tried to drag the herdsman off the temple platform nothing had been heard of it. The priest, the bania, and all the people in near and distant villages that I questioned informed me that there were occasions when for long periods the man-eater seemed to disappear off the face of the earth and they were of the opinion that one of these periods had now started, but no one could say how long it would last. The area over which the man-eater was operating was vast, and in it there were possibly ten to twenty leopards. To find and shoot in that area one particular leopard—that had stopped killing human beings—without knowing where to look for it, was a hopeless job.

My mission as far as the man-eater was concerned had failed, and no useful purpose would be served by my prolonging my stay at Dabidhura. The question of the temple tiger remained. I did not feel that the killing of this tiger was any responsibility of mine; but I did feel, and felt very strongly, that my pursuit of him was inducing him to kill more cattle than he would otherwise have done. Why a male tiger started killing cattle on the day of my arrival at Dabidhura it was not possible to say, and whether he would stop when I went away remained to be seen. Anyway, I had tried my best to shoot him; had paid compensation for the damage he had done to the full extent of my purse; and he had provided me with one of the most interesting jungle experiences I had ever had. So I harboured no resentment against him for having beaten me at every point in the exciting game we had played during the past four days. These four days had been very strenuous for me, so I would rest today and make an early start next morning on the first stage of my journey back to Naini Tal. I had just come to this decision when a voice from behind me said, 'Salaam, Sahib. I have come to tell you that the tiger has killed one of my cows.' One more chance of shooting the tiger, and whether I succeeded or not I would stick to my plan of leaving next morning.

~

Annoyed at the interference of human beings and bears, the tiger had shifted his ground, and this last kill had taken place on the eastern face of the Dabidhura mountain several miles from where I had sat up for him the previous evening. The ground here was undulating, with patches of scrub and a few odd trees dotted here and there; ideal ground for chukor (hill partridge), but the last place in which I would have expected to find a tiger.

Running diagonally across the face of the mountain was a shallow depression. In this depression were patches of dense scrub, interspersed with open glades of short grass. At the edge of one of these glades the cow had been killed, dragged a few yards towards some bushes, and left in the open. On the opposite or downhill side of the glade to the kill, there was a big oak tree. On this tree, the only one for hundreds of yards around, I decided to sit.

While my men warmed a kettle of water for tea I scouted round to see if I could get a shot at the tiger on foot. The tiger I felt sure was lying up somewhere in the depression, but though I searched every foot of it for an hour I saw no sign of him.

The tree that was to provide me with a seat was leaning out towards the glade. Excessive lopping had induced a crop of small branches all along the trunk, which made the tree easy to climb but obscured a view of the trunk from above. Twenty feet up, a single big branch jutted out over the glade, offering the only seat on the tree but not a comfortable one or one easy to reach. At 4 p.m. I sent my men away, instructing them to go to a village farther up the hill and wait for me, for I had no intention of sitting up after sundown.

The kill, as I have said, was lying in the open, ten yards from me and with its hindquarters a yard or so from a dense clump of bushes. I had been in position for an hour and was watching a number of red-whiskered bulbuls feeding on a raspberry bush to my right front, when on turning my eyes to look at the kill I saw the tiger's head projecting beyond the clump of bushes. He was evidently lying down, for his head was close to the ground, and his eyes were fixed on me. Presently a paw was advanced, then another, and then very slowly and with belly to ground the tiger drew himself up to his kill. Here he lay for several minutes without movement. Then, feeling with his mouth, and with his eyes still fixed on me, he bit off the cow's tail, laid it on one side and started to eat. Having eaten nothing since his fight with the bear three days before, he was hungry, and he ate just as man would eat an apple, ignoring the skin and taking great bites of flesh from the hindquarters.

The rifle was across my knees pointing in the direction of the tiger, and all I had to do was to raise it to my shoulder. I would get an opportunity of doing this when he turned his eyes away from me for a brief moment. But the tiger appeared to know his danger, for without taking his eyes off me he ate on steadily and unhurriedly. When he had consumed about fifteen or twenty pounds of flesh, and when the bulbuls had left the raspberry bush and, joined by two black-throated jays, were making a great chattering on the bushes behind him, I thought it was time for me to act. If I raised the rifle very slowly he would probably not notice the movement so, when the birds were chattering their loudest, I started to do this. I had raised the muzzle possibly six inches, when the tiger slid backwards as if drawn back by a powerful spring. With rifle to shoulder and elbows on knees I now waited for the tiger to project his head a second time, and this I felt sure he would presently do. Minutes passed, and then I heard the tiger. He had skirted round the bushes and, approaching from behind, started to claw my tree where the thick growth of small branches on the trunk made it impossible for me to see him. Purring with pleasure the tiger once and again clawed the tree with vigour, while I sat on my branch and rocked with silent laughter.

I know that crows and monkeys have a sense of humour, but until that day I did not know that tigers also possessed this sense. Nor did I know that an animal could have the luck, and the impudence, that particular tiger had. In five days he had killed five cows, four of them in broad daylight. In those five days I had seen him eight times and on four occasions I had pressed a trigger on him. And now, after staring at me for half an hour and eating while doing so, he was clawing the tree on which I was sitting and purring to show his contempt of me.

When telling me of the tiger the old priest said, 'I have no objection, Sahib, to your *trying* to shoot this tiger but neither you nor anyone else will ever succeed in *killing* it.' The tiger was now, in his own way, confirming what the priest had said. Well, the tiger had made the last move in the exciting game we had played without injury to either of us, but I was not going to give him the satisfaction of having the last laugh. Laying down the rifle and cupping my hands I waited until he stopped clawing, and then sent a full-throated shout echoing over the hills which sent him careering down the hill at full speed and brought my men down from the village at a run. 'We saw the tiger running away with his tail in the air,' the men said when they arrived, 'and just see what he has done to the tree.'

Next morning I bade farewell to all my friends at Dabidhura, and assured them I would return when the man-eater got active again.

I visited Dabidhura several times in subsequent years while hunting man-eaters, and I never heard of anyone having killed the temple tiger. So I hope that in the fullness of time this old warrior, like an old soldier, just faded away.

The Muktesar Man-eater

A tiger that thought as highly of the amenities of Muktesar as human beings did, took up her residence in the extensive forests adjoining the small settlement. Here she lived very happily on sambhar, kakar, and wild pig, until she had the misfortune to have an encounter with a porcupine. In this encounter she lost an eye and got some fifty quills, varying in length from one to nine inches, embedded in the arm and under the pad of her right foreleg. Several of these quills after striking a bone had doubled back in the form of a U, the point and the broken-off end being close together. Suppurating sores formed where she endeavoured to extract the quills with her teeth, and while she was lying up in a thick patch of grass, starving and licking her wounds, a woman selected this particular patch of grass to cut as fodder for her cattle. At first the tigress took no notice, but when the woman had cut the grass right up to where she was lying, the tigress struck once, the blow crushing the woman's skull. Death was instantaneous, for, when found the following day, she was grasping her sickle with one hand and holding a tuft of grass, which she was about to cut when struck, with the other. Leaving the woman lying where she had fallen, the tigress limped off for a distance of over a mile and took refuge in a little hollow under a fallen tree. Two days later a man came to chip firewood off this fallen tree, and the tigress who was lying on the far side killed him also. The man fell across the tree, and as he had removed his coat and shirt and the tigress had clawed his back while killing him, it is possible that the sight of blood trickling down his body as he hung across the bole of the tree first gave her the idea that he was something that she could satisfy her hunger with. However that may be, before leaving him she ate a small portion from his back. A day later she killed her third victim deliberately, and without having received any provocation. Thereafter she became an established man-eater.

I heard of the tigress shortly after she started killing human beings, and as there were a number of sportsmen at Muktesar, all of whom were keen on bagging the tigress—who was operating right on their doorsteps—I did not consider it would be sporting of an outsider to meddle in the matter. When the toll of human beings killed by the tigress had risen to twenty-four, however, and the lives of all the people living in the settlement and neighbouring villages were endangered and work at the Institute slowed down, the veterinary officer in charge of the Institute requested the Government to solicit my help.

My task, as I saw it, was not going to be an easy one, for, apart from the fact that my experience of man-eaters was very limited, the extensive ground over which the tigress was operating was not known to me and I therefore had no idea where to look for her.

Accompanied by a servant and two men carrying a roll of bedding and a suitcase, I left Naini Tal at midday and walked ten miles to the Ramgarh Dak Bungalow, where I spent the night. The Dak Bungalow khansama (cook, bottle-washer, and general factotum) was a friend of mine, and when he learnt that I was on my way to Muktesar to try to shoot the man-eater, he warned me to be very careful while negotiating the last two miles into Muktesar for, he said, several people had recently been killed on that stretch of road.

Leaving my men to pack up and follow me I armed myself with a double-barrelled ·500 express rifle using modified cordite, and making a very early start next morning arrived at the junction of the Naini Tal/Almora road with the Muktesar road just as it was getting light. From this point it was necessary to walk warily for I was now in the man-eater's country. Before zigzagging up the face of a very steep hill the road runs for some distance over flat ground on which grows the orange-coloured lily, the round hard seeds of which can be used as shot in a muzzle-loading gun. This was the first time I had ever climbed that hill and I was very interested to see the caves, hollowed out by wind, in the sandstone cliffs overhanging the road. In a gale I imagine these caves must produce some very weird sounds, for they are of different sizes and, while some are shallow, others appear to penetrate deep into the sandstone.

Where the road comes out on a saddle of the hill there is a small area of flat ground flanked on the far side by the Muktesar Post Office, and a small bazaar. The post office was not open at that early hour, but one of the shops was and the shopkeeper very kindly gave me directions to the Dak Bungalow which, he said, was half a mile away on the northern face of the hill. There are two Dak Bungalows at Muktesar, one reserved for government officials and the other for the general public. I did not know this and my shopkeeper friend, mistaking me for a government official, possibly because of the size of my hat, directed me to the wrong one and the khansama in charge of the bungalow, and I, incurred the displeasure of the red tape brigade, the khansama by providing me with breakfast, and I by partaking of it. However, of this I was at the time happily ignorant, and later I made it my business to see that the khansama did not suffer in any way for my mistake.

While I was admiring the superb view of the snowy range, and waiting for breakfast, a party of twelve Europeans passed me carrying service rifles, followed a few minutes later by a sergeant and two men carrying targets and flags. The sergeant, a friendly soul, informed me that the party that had just passed was on its way to the rifle range, and that it was keeping together because of the man-eater. I learnt from the sergeant that the officer in charge of the Institute had received a telegram from the Government the previous day informing him that I was on my way to Muktesar. The sergeant expressed the hope that I would succeed in shooting the man-eater for, he said, conditions in the settlement had become very difficult. No one even in daylight, dared to move about alone, and after dusk everyone had to remain behind locked doors. Many attempts had been made to shoot the man-eater but it had never returned to any of the kills that had been sat over.

After a very good breakfast I instructed the khansama to tell my men when they arrived that I had gone out to try get news of the man-eater, and that I did not know when I would return. Then, picking up my rifle, I went up to the post office to send a telegram to my mother to let her know I had arrived safely.

From the flat ground in front of the post office and the bazaar the southern face of the Muktesar hill falls steeply away, and is cut up by ridges and ravines overgrown with dense brushwood, with a few trees scattered here and there. I was standing on the edge of the hill, looking down into the valley and the well-wooded Ramgarh hills beyond, when I was joined by the Postmaster and several shopkeepers. The Postmaster had dealt with the Government telegram of the previous day, and on seeing my signature on the form I had just handed in, he concluded I was the person referred to in the telegram and his friends and he had now come to offer me their help.

I was very glad of the offer for they were in the best position to see and converse with everyone coming to Muktesar, and as the man-eater was sure to be the main topic of conversation where two or more were gathered together, they would be able to collect information that would be of great value to me. In rural India, the post office and the bania's shop are to village folk what taverns and clubs are to people of other lands, and if information on any particular subject is sought, the post office and the bania's shop are the best places to seek it.

In a fold of the hill to our left front, and about two miles away and a thousand feet below us, was a patch of cultivation. This I was informed was Badri Sah's apple orchard. Badri, son of an old friend of mine, had visited me in Naini Tal some months previously and had offered to put me up in his guest house and to assist me in every way he could to shoot the man-eater. This offer, for the reason already given, I had not accepted. Now, however, as I had come to Muktesar at the request of the Government I decided I would call on Badri and accept his offer to help me, especially as I had just been informed by my companions that the last human kill had taken place in the valley below his orchard.

Thanking all the men who were standing round me, and telling them I would rely on them for further information, I set off down the Dhari road. The day was still young and before calling on Badri there was time to visit some of the villages farther along the hill to the east. There were no milestones along the road, and after I had covered what I considered was about six miles and visited two villages, I turned back. I had retraced my steps for about three miles when I overtook a small girl having difficulties with a bullock. The girl, who was about eight years old, wanted the bullock to go in the direction of Muktesar, while the bullock wanted to go in the opposite direction, and when I arrived on the scene the stage had been reached when neither would do what the other wanted. The bullock was a quiet old beast, and with the girl walking in front holding the rope that was tied round his neck and I walking behind to keep him on the move he gave no further trouble. After we had proceeded a short distance I said:

'We are not stealing Kalwa, are we?' I heard her addressing the black bullock by that name.

'N—o,' she answered indignantly, turning her big brown eyes full on me.

'To whom does he belong?' I next asked.

'To my father,' she said.

'And where are we taking him?'

'To my uncle.'

'And why does uncle want Kalwa?'

'To plough his field.'

'But Kalwa can't plough uncle's field by himself.'

'Of course not,' she said. I was being stupid, but then you could not expect a sahib to know anything about bullocks and ploughing.

'Has uncle only got one bullock?' I next asked.

'Yes,' she said; 'he has only got one bullock now, but he did have two.'

'Where is the other one?' I asked, thinking that it had probably been sold to satisfy a debt.

'The tiger killed it yesterday,' I was told. Here was news indeed, and while I was digesting it we walked on in silence, the girl every now and then looking back at me until she plucked up courage to ask:

'Have you come to shoot the tiger?'

'Yes,' I said, 'I have come to try to shoot the tiger.'

'Then why are you going away from the kill?'

'Because we are taking Kalwa to uncle.' My answer appeared to satisfy the girl, and we plodded on. I had got some very useful information, but I wanted more and presently I said:

'Don't you know that the tiger is a man-eater?'

'Oh, yes,' she said, 'it ate Kunthi's father and Bonshi Singh's mother, and lots of other people.'

'Then why did your father send you with Kalwa? Why did he not come himself?'

'Because he has bhabari bokhar (malaria).'

'Have you no brothers?'

'No. I had a brother but he died long ago.'

'A mother?'

'Yes, I have a mother; she is cooking the food.'

'A sister?'

'No, I have no sister.' So on this small girl had devolved the dangerous task of taking her father's bullock to her uncle, along a road on which men were afraid to walk except when in large parties, and on which in four hours I had not seen another human being.

We had now come to a path up which the girl went, the bullock following, and I bringing up the rear. Presently we came to a field on the far side of which was a small house. As we approached the house the girl called out and told her uncle that she had brought Kalwa.

'All right,' a man's voice answered from the house, 'tie him to the post, Putli, and go home. I am having my food.' So we tied Kalwa to the post and went back to the road. Without the connecting link of Kalwa between us, Putli (dolly) was now shy, and as she would not walk by my side I walked ahead, suiting my pace to hers. We walked in silence for some time and then I said:

'I want to shoot the tiger that killed uncle's bullock but I don't know where the kill is. Will you show me?'

'Oh, yes,' she said eagerly, 'I will show you.'

'Have you seen the kill?' I asked.

'No,' she said, 'I have not seen it, but I heard uncle telling my father where it was.'

'Is it close to the road?'

'I don't know.'

'Was the bullock alone when it was killed?'

'No, it was with the village cattle.'

'Was it killed in the morning or the evening?'

'It was killed in the morning when it was going out to graze with the cows.'

While talking to the girl I was keeping a sharp look-out all round, for the road was bordered on the left by heavy tree jungle, and on the right by dense scrub. We had proceeded for about a mile when we came to a well-used cattle track leading off into the jungle on the left. Here the girl stopped and said it was on this track that her uncle had told her father the bullock had been killed. I had now got all the particulars I needed to enable me to find the kill, and after seeing the girl safely to her home I returned to the cattle track. This track ran across a valley and I had gone along it for about a quarter of a mile when I came upon a spot where cattle had stampeded. Leaving the track, I now went through the jungle, parallel to and about fifty yards below the track. I had only gone a short distance when I came on a drag-mark. This drag-mark went straight down into the valley, and after I had followed it for a few hundred yards I found the bullock, from which only a small portion of the hindquarters had been eaten. It was lying at the foot of a bank about twenty feet high, and some forty feet from the head of a deep ravine. Between the ravine and the kill was a stunted tree, smothered over by a wild rose. This was the only tree within a reasonable distance of the kill on which I could sit with any hope of bagging the tiger, for there was no moon, and if the tiger came after dark—as I felt sure it would—the nearer I was to the kill the better would be my chance of killing the tiger.

It was now 2 p.m. and there was just time for me to call on Badri and ask him for a cup of tea, of which I was in need for I had done a lot of walking since leaving Ramgarh at four o'clock that morning. The road to Badri's orchard takes off close to where the cattle track joins the road, and runs down a steep hill for a mile through dense brushwood. Badri was near his guest house, attending to a damaged apple tree when I arrived, and on hearing the reason for my visit he took me up the guest house which was on a little knoll overlooking the orchard. While we sat on the veranda waiting for the tea and something to eat that Badri had ordered his servant to prepare for me, I told him why I had come to Muktesar, and about the kill the young girl had enabled me to find. When I asked Badri why this kill had not been reported to the sportsmen at Muktesar, he said that owing to the repeated failures of the sportsmen to bag the tiger the village folk had lost confidence in them, and for this reason kills were no longer being reported to them. Badri attributed the failures to the elaborate preparations that had been made to sit over kills. These preparations consisted of clearing the ground near the kills of all abstractions in the way of bushes and small trees, the building of big machans, and the occupation of the machans by several men. Reasons enough for the reputation the tiger had earned of never returning to a kill. Badri was convinced that there was only one tiger in Muktesar district and that it was slightly lame in its right foreleg, but he did not know what had caused the lameness, nor did he know whether the animal was male or female.

Sitting on the veranda with us was a big Airedale terrier. Presently the dog started growling, and looking in the direction in which the dog was facing, we saw a big langur sitting on the ground and holding down the branch of an apple tree, and eating the unripe fruit. Picking up a shotgun that was leaning against the railing of the veranda, Badri loaded it with No. 4 shot and fired. The range was too great for the pellets, assuming any hit it, to do the langur any harm, but the shot had the effect of making it canter up the hill with the dog in hot pursuit. Frightened that the dog might come to grief, I asked Badri to call it back, but he said it would be all right for the dog was always chasing this particular animal, which he said had done a lot of damage to his young trees. The dog was now gaining on the langur, and when it got to within a few yards the langur whipped round, got the dog by the ears, and bit a lump off the side of its head. The wound was a very severe one, and by the time we had finished attending to it my tea and a plate of hot puris was ready for me.

I had told Badri about the tree I intended sitting on, and when I returned to the kill he insisted on going with me accompanied by two men carrying materials for making a small machan. Badri and the two men had lived under the shadow of the man-eater for over a year and had no illusions about it, and when they saw that there were no trees near the kill—with the exception of the one I had selected—in which a machan could be built, they urged me not to sit up that night, on the assumption that the tiger would remove the kill and provide me with a more suitable place to sit up the following night. This was what I myself would have done if the tiger had not been a man-eater, but as it was I was disinclined to miss a chance which might not recur on the morrow, even if it entailed a little risk. There were bears in this forest and if one of them smelt the kill, any hope I had of getting a shot at the tiger would vanish, for Himalayan bears are no respecters of tigers and do not hesitate to appropriate their kills. Climbing into the tree, smothered as it was by the rose bush, was a difficult feat, and after I had made myself as comfortable as the thorn permitted and my rifle had been handed up to me Badri and his men left, promising to return early next morning.

I was facing the hill, with the ravine behind me. I was in clear view of any animal coming down from above, but if the tiger came from below, as I expected, it would not see me until it got to the kill. The bullock, which was white, was lying on its right side with its legs towards me, and at a distance of about fifteen feet. I had taken my seat at 4 p.m. and an hour later a kakar started barking on the side of the ravine 200 yards below me. The tiger was on the move, and having seen it the kakar was standing still and barking. For a long time it barked and then it started to move away, the bark growing fainter and fainter until the sound died away round the shoulder of the hill. This indicated that after coming within sight of the kill, the tiger had lain down. I had expected this to happen after having been told by Badri the reasons for the failures to shoot the tiger over a kill. I knew the tiger would now be lying somewhere nearby with his eyes and ears open, to make quite sure there were no human beings near the kill, before he approached it. Minute succeeded long minute; dusk came; objects on the hill in front of me became indistinct and then faded out. I could still see the kill as a white blur when a stick snapped at the head of the ravine and stealthy steps came towards me, and then stopped immediately below. For a minute or two there was dead silence, and then the tiger lay down on the dry leaves at the foot at the tree.

Heavy clouds had rolled up near sunset and there was now a black canopy overhead blotting out the stars. When the tiger eventually got up and went to the kill, the night could best be described as pitch black. Strain my eyes as I would, I could see nothing of the white bullock, and still less of the tiger. On reaching the kill the tiger started blowing on it. In the Himalayas, and especially in the summer, kills attract hornets, most of which leave as the light fades but those that are too torpid to fly remain, and a tiger—possibly after bitter experience—blows off the hornets adhering to the exposed portion of the flesh before starting to feed. There was no need for me to hurry over my shot for, close though it was, the tiger would not see me unless I attracted its attention by some movement or sound. I can see reasonably well on a dark night by the light of the stars, but there were no stars visible that night nor was there a flicker of lightning in the heavy clouds. The tiger had not moved the kill before starting to eat, so I knew he was lying broadside on to me, on the right-hand side of the kill.

Owing to the attempts that had been made to shoot the tiger I had suspicion that it would not come before dark, and it had been my intention to take what aim I could—by the light of the stars—and then move the muzzle of my rifle sufficiently for my bullet to go a foot or two to the right of the kill. But now that the clouds had rendered my eyes useless, I would have to depend on my ears (my hearing at that time was perfect). Raising the rifle and resting my elbows on my knees, I took careful aim at the sound the tiger was making, and while holding the rifle steady, turned my right ear to the sound, and then back again. My aim was a little too high, so, lowering the muzzle a fraction of an inch, I again turned my head and listened. After I had done this a few times and satisfied myself that I was pointing at the sound, I moved the muzzle a little to the right and pressed the trigger. In two bounds the tiger was up the twenty-foot bank. At the top there was a small bit of flat ground, beyond which the hill went up steeply. I heard the tiger on the dry leaves as far as the flat ground, and then there was silence. This silence could be interpreted to mean either that the tiger had died on reaching the flat ground or that it was unwounded. Keeping the rifle to my shoulder I listened intently for three or four minutes, and as there was no further sound I lowered the rifle. This movement was greeted by a deep growl from the top of the bank. So the tiger was unwounded, and had seen me. My seat on the tree had originally been about ten feet up but, as I had nothing solid to sit on, the rose bush had sagged under my weight and I was now possibly no more than eight feet above ground, with my dangling feet considerably lower. And a little above and some twenty feet from me a tiger that I had every reason to believe was a man-eater was growling deep down in his throat.

The near proximity of a tiger in daylight, even when it has not seen you, causes a disturbance in the blood stream. When the tiger is not an ordinary one, however, but a man-eater and the time is ten o'clock on a dark night, and you know the man-eater is watching you, the disturbance in the blood stream becomes a storm. I maintain that a tiger does not kill beyond its requirements, except under provocation. The tiger that was growling at me already, had a kill that would last it for two or three days, and there was no necessity for it to kill me. Even so, I had an uneasy feeling that on this occasion this particular tiger might prove an exception to the rule. Tigers will at times return to a kill after being fired at, but I knew this one would not do so. I also knew that in spite of my uneasy feeling I was perfectly safe so long as I did not lose my balance—I had nothing to hold on to—or go to sleep and fall off the tree. There was no longer any reason for me to deny myself a smoke, so I took out my cigarette case and as I lit a match I heard the tiger move away from the edge of the bank. Presently it came back and again growled. I had smoked three cigarettes, and the tiger was still with me, when it came on to rain. A few big drops at first and then a heavy downpour. I had put on light clothes when I started from Ramgarh that morning and in a few minutes I was wet to the skin, for there was not a leaf above me to diffuse the raindrops. The tiger, I knew, would have hurried off to shelter under a tree or on the lee of a rock the moment the rain started. The rain came on at 11 p.m.; at 4 a.m. it stopped and the sky cleared. A wind now started to blow, to add to my discomfort, and where I had been cold before I was now frozen. When I get a twinge of rheumatism I remember that night and others like it, and am thankful that it is no more than a twinge.

Badri, good friend that he was, arrived with a man carrying a kettle of hot tea just as the sun was rising. Relieving me of my rifle the two men caught me as I slid off the tree, for my legs were too cramped to function. Then as I lay on the ground and drank the tea they massaged my legs and restored circulation. When I was able to stand, Badri sent his man off to light a fire in the guest house. I had never previously used my ears to direct a bullet and was interested to find that I had missed the tiger's head by only a few inches. The elevation had been all right but I had not moved the muzzle of the rifle far enough to the right, with the result that my bullet had struck the bullock six inches from where the tiger was eating.

The tea and the half-mile walk up to the road took all the creases out of me, and when we started down the mile-long track to Badri's orchard, wet clothes and an empty stomach were my only discomfort. The track ran over red clay which the rain had made very slippery. In this clay were three tracks: Badri's and his man's tracks going up, and the man's tracks going down. For fifty yards there were only these three tracks in the wet clay, and then, where there was a bend in the track, a tigress had jumped down from the bank on the right and gone down the track on the heels of Badri's man. The footprints of the man and the pug marks of the tigress showed that both had been travelling at a fast pace. There was nothing that Badri and I could do, for the man had a twenty-minute start from us, and if he had not reached the safety of the orchard he would long have been beyond any help we could give him. With uneasy thoughts assailing us, we made what speed we could on the slippery ground and were very relieved to find, on coming to a footpath from where the orchard and a number of men working in it were visible, that the tigress had gone down the path while the man had carried on to the orchard. Questioned later, the man said he did not know that he had been followed by the tigress.

While drying my clothes in front of a roaring wood-fire in the guest house, I questioned Badri about the jungle into which the tigress had gone. The path which the tigress had taken, Badri told me, ran down into a deep and densely wooded ravine which extended down the face of a very steep hill, for a mile or more, to where it was met by another ravine coming down from the right. At the junction of the two ravines there was a stream and here there was an open patch of ground which, Badri said, commanded the exit of both ravines. Badri was of the opinion that the tigress would lie up for the day in the ravine into which we had every reason to believe she had gone, and as this appeared to be an ideal place for a beat, we decided to try this method of getting a shot at the tigress, provided we could muster sufficient men to carry out the beat. Govind Singh, Badri's head gardener, was summoned and our plan explained to him. Given until midday, Govind Singh said he could muster a gang of thirty men to do the beat, and in addition carry out his master's orders to gather five maunds (410 pounds) of peas. Badri had an extensive vegetable garden in addition to his apple orchard and the previous evening he had received a telegram informing him that the price of marrowfat peas on the Naini Tal market had jumped to four annas (four pence) a pound. Badri was anxious to take advantage of this good price and his men were gathering the peas to be dispatched by pack pony that night, to arrive in Naini Tal for the early morning market.

After cleaning my rifle and walking round the orchard, I joined Badri at his morning meal—which had been put forward an hour to suit me—and at midday Govind produced his gang of thirty men. It was essential for someone to supervise the pea-pickers, so Badri decided to remain and send Govind to carry out the beat. Govind and the thirty men were local residents and knew the danger to be apprehended from the man-eater. However, after I had told them what I wanted them to do, they expressed their willingness to carry out my instructions. Badri was to give me an hour's start to enable me to search the ravine for the tigress and, if I failed to get a shot, to take up my position on the open ground near the stream. Govind was to divide his men into two parties, take charge of one party himself, and put a reliable man in charge of the other. At the end of the hour Badri was to fire a shot and the two parties were to set off, one on either side of the ravine, rolling rocks down, and shouting and clapping their hands. It all sounded as simple as that, but I had my doubts, for I have seen many beats go wrong.

Going up the track down which I had come that morning, I followed the path that the tigress had taken, only to find after I had gone a short distance that it petered out in a vast expanse of dense brushwood. Forcing my way through for several hundred yards I found that the hillside was cut up by a series of deep ravines and ridges. Going down a ridge which I thought was the right-hand boundary of the ravine to be beaten, I came to a big drop at the bottom of which the ravine on my left met a ravine coming down from the right, and at the junction of the two ravines there was a stream. While I was looking down and wondering where the open ground was on which I was to take my stand, I heard flies buzzing near me and on following the sound found the remains of a cow that had been killed about a week before. The marks on the animal's throat showed that it had been killed by a tiger. The tiger had eaten all of the cow, except a portion of the shoulders, and the neck and head. Without having any particular reason for doing so, I dragged the carcass to the edge and sent it crashing down the steep hill. After rolling for about a hundred yards the carcass fetched up in a little hollow a short distance from the stream. Working round to the left I found an open patch of ground on a ridge about 300 yards from the hollow into which I had rolled the remains of the cow. The ground down here was very different from what I had pictured it to be. There was no place where I could stand to overlook the hillside that was to be beaten, and the tigress might break out anywhere without my seeing her. However, it was then too late to do anything, for Badri had fired the shot that was to let me know the beat had started. Presently, away in the distance, I heard men shouting. For a time I thought the beat was coming my way and then the sounds grew fainter and fainter until they eventually died away. An hour later I again heard the beaters. They were coming down the hill to my right, and when they were on a level with me I shouted to them to stop the beat and join me on the ridge. It was no one's fault that the beat had miscarried, for without knowing the ground and without previous preparation we had tried to beat with a handful of untrained men a vast area of dense brushwood that hundreds of trained men would have found difficult to cope with.

The beaters had had a very strenuous time forcing their way through the brushwood, and while they sat in a bunch removing thorns from their hands and feet and smoking my cigarettes, Govind and I stood facing each other, discussing his suggestion of carrying out a beat on the morrow in which every available man in Muktesar and the surrounding villages would take part. Suddenly, in the middle of a sentence, Govind stopped talking. I could see that something unusual had attracted his attention behind me, for his eyes narrowed and a look of incredulity came over his face. Swinging round I looked in the direction in which he was facing, and there, quietly walking along a field that had gone out of cultivation, was the tigress. She was about 400 yards away on the hill on the far side of the stream, and was coming towards us.

When a tiger is approaching you in the forest—even when you are far from human habitations—thoughts course through your mind of the many things that can go wrong to spoil your chance of getting the shot, or the photograph, you are hoping for. On one occasion I was sitting on a hillside overlooking a game track, waiting for a tiger. The track led to a very sacred jungle shrine known as Baram ka Than, Baram is a jungle God who protects human beings and does not permit the shooting of animals in the area he watches over. The forest in the heart of which this shrine is situated is well stocked with game and is a favourite hunting ground of poachers for miles around, and of sportsmen from all parts of India. Yet, in a lifetime's acquaintance with that forest, I do not know of a single instance of an animal having been shot in the vicinity of the shrine. When therefore I set out that day to shoot a tiger that had been taking toll of our village buffaloes, I selected a spot a mile from Baram's shrine. I was in position, behind a bush, at 4 p.m. and an hour later a sambhar belled in the direction from which I was expecting the tiger. A little later and a little nearer to me a kakar started barking; the tiger was coming along the track near which I was sitting. The jungle was fairly open and consisted mostly of young jamun trees, two to three feet in girth. I caught sight of the tiger—a big male—when he was 200 yards away. He was coming slowly and had reduced the distance between us to a hundred yards when I heard the swish of leaves, and on looking up saw that one of the jamun trees whose branches were interlaced with another was beginning to lean over. Very slowly the tree heeled over until it came in contact with another tree of the same species and of about the same size. For a few moments the second tree supported the weight of the first and then it, too, started to keel over. When the two trees were at an angle of about thirty degrees from the perpendicular, they fetched up against a third and smaller tree. For a moment or two there was a pause, and then all three trees crashed to the ground. While watching the trees, which were only a few yards from me, I had kept an eye on the tiger. At the first sound of the leaves he had come to a halt and when the trees crashed to the ground he turned and, without showing any sign of alarm, went back in the direction from which he had come. What made the occurrence I had witnessed so unusual was that the trees were young and vigorous; that no rain had fallen recently to loosen their roots; that not a breath of air was stirring in the forest; and, finally, that the trees had fallen across the track leading to the shrine when the tiger had only another seventy yards to cover to give me the shot I was waiting for.

The chances of a shot being spoilt are greatly increased when the quarry is in an inhabited area in which parties of men may be travelling from one village to another or going to or from markets, or where shots may be fired to scare away langurs from apple orchards. The tigress still had 300 yards to go to reach the stream, and 200 yards of that was over open ground on which there was not a single tree or bush. The tigress was coming towards us at a slight angle and would see any movement we made, so there was nothing I could do but watch her, and no tigress had ever moved more slowly. She was known to the people of Muktesar as the lame tiger, but I could see no sign of her being lame. The plan that was forming in my head as I watched her was to wait until she entered the scrub jungle, and then run forward and try to get a shot at her either before or after she crossed the stream. Had there been sufficient cover between me and the point the tigress was making for, I would have gone forward as soon as I saw her and tried either to get a shot at her on the open ground or, failing that, to intercept her at the stream. But unfortunately there was not sufficient cover to mask my movements, so I had to wait until the tigress entered the bushes between the open ground and the stream. Telling the men not to move or make a sound until I returned, I set off at a run as the tigress disappeared from view. The hill was steep and as I ran along the contour I came to a wild rose bush which extended up and down the hill for many yards. Through the middle of the bush there was a low tunnel, and as I bent down to run through it my hat was knocked off, and raising my head too soon at the end of the tunnel I was nearly dragged off my feet by the thorns that entered my head. The thorns of these wild roses are curved and very strong and as I was not able to stop myself some embedded themselves and broke off in my head—where my sister Maggie had difficulty in removing them when I got home—while others tore through the flesh. With little trickles of blood running down my face I continued to run until I approached the hollow into which I had rolled the partly eaten kill from the hill above. This hollow was about forty yards long and thirty yards wide. The upper end of it where the kill was lying, the hill above the kill, and the further bank, were overgrown with dense brushwood. The lower half of the hollow and the bank on my side were free of bushes. As I reached the edge of the hollow and peered over, I heard a bone crack. The tigress had reached the hollow before me and, on finding the old kill, was trying to make up for the meal she had been deprived of the previous night.

If after leaving the kill, on which there was very little flesh, the tigress came out on to the open ground I would get a shot at her, but if she went up the hill or up the far bank I would not see her. From the dense brushwood in which I could hear the tigress, a narrow path ran up the bank on my side and passed within a yard to my left; a yard beyond the path, there was a sheer drop of fifty feet into the stream below. I was considering the possibility of driving the tigress out of the brushwood on to the open ground by throwing a stone on to the hill above her, when I heard a sound behind me. On looking round I saw Govind standing behind me with my hat in his hand. At that time no European in India went about without a hat, and having seen mine knocked of by the rose bush Govind had retrieved it and brought it to me. Near us there was a hole in the hill. Putting my finger to my lips I got Govind by the arm and pressed him into the hole. Sitting on his hunkers with his chin resting on his drawn-up knees, hugging my hat, he just fitted into the hole and looked a very miserable object, for he could hear the tigress crunching bones a few yards away. As I straightened up and resumed my position on the edge of the bank, the tigress stopped eating. She had either seen me or, what was more probable, she had not found the old kill to her liking. For a long minute there was no movement or sound, and then I caught sight of her. She had climbed up the opposite bank, and was now going along the top of it towards the hill. At this point there were a number of six-inch-thick poplar saplings, and I could only see the outline of the tigress as she went through them. With the forlorn hope that my bullet would miss the saplings and find the tigress I threw up my rifle and took a hurried shot. At my shot the tigress whipped round, came down the bank, across the hollow, and up the path on my side, as hard as she could go. I did not know, at the time, that my bullet had struck a sapling near her head, and that she was blind of one eye. So what looked like a very determined charge might only have been a frightened animal running away from danger, for in that restricted space she would not have known from which direction the report of my rifle had come. Be that as it may, what I took to be a wounded and a very angry tigress was coming straight at me; so, waiting until she was two yards away, I leant forward and with great good luck managed to put the remaining bullet in the rifle into the hollow where her neck joined her shoulder. The impact of the heavy ·500 bullet deflected her just sufficiently for her to miss my left shoulder, and her impetus carried her over the fifty-foot drop into the stream below, where she landed with a great splash. Taking a step forward I looked over the edge and saw the tigress lying submerged in a pool with her feet in the air, while the water in the pool reddened with her blood.

Govind was still sitting in the hole, and at a sign he joined me. On seeing the tigress he turned and shouted to the men on the ridge, 'The tiger is dead. The tiger is dead.' The thirty men on the ridge now started shouting, and Badri on hearing them got hold of his shot gun and fired off ten rounds. These shots were heard at Muktesar and in the surrounding villages, and presently men from all sides were converging on the stream. Willing hands drew the tigress from the pool, lashed her to a sapling, and carried her in triumph to Badri's orchard. Here she was put down on a bed of straw for all to see, while I went to the guest house for a cup of tea. An hour later by the light of hand lanterns, and with a great crowd of men standing round, among whom were several sportsmen from Muktesar, I skinned the tigress. It was then that I found she was blind of one eye and that she had some fifty porcupine quills, varying in length from one to nine inches, embedded in the arm and under the pad of her right foreleg. By ten o'clock my job was finished, and declining Badri's very kind invitation to spend the night with him I climbed the hill in company with the people who had come down from Muktesar, among whom were my two men carrying the skin. On the open ground in front of the post office the skin was spread out for the Postmaster and his friends to see. At midnight I lay down in the Dak Bungalow reserved for the public, for a few hour's sleep. Four hours later I was on the move again and at midday I was back in my home at Naini Tal after an absence of seventy-two hours.

The shooting of a man-eater gives one a feeling of satisfaction. Satisfaction at having done a job that badly needed doing. Satisfaction at having outmanoeuvred, on his own ground, a very worthy antagonist. And, the greatest satisfaction of all, at having made a small portion of the earth safe for a brave little girl to walk on.

The Talla Des Killer

Nowhere along the foothills of the Himalayas is there a more beautiful setting for a camp than under the Flame of the Forest trees at Bindukhera, when they are in full bloom. If you can picture white tents under a canopy of orange-coloured bloom; a multitude of brilliantly plumaged red and gold minivets, golden orioles, rose-headed parakeets, golden backed woodpeckers, and wire-crested drongos flitting from tree to tree and shaking down the bloom until the ground round the tents resembled a rich orange-coloured carpet; densely wooded foothills in the background topped by ridge upon rising ridge of the Himalayas, and they in turn topped by the eternal snows, then, and only then, will you have some idea of our camp at Bindukhera one February morning in the year 1929.

Bindukhera, which is only a name for the camping ground, is on the western edge of a wide expanse of grassland some twelve miles long and ten miles wide. When Sir Henry Ramsay was king of Kumaon the plain was under intensive cultivation, but at the time of my story there were only three small villages, each with a few acres of cultivation dotted along the banks of the sluggish stream that meanders down the length of the plain. The grass on the plain had been burnt a few weeks before our arrival, leaving islands of varying sizes where the ground was damp and the grass too green to burn. It was on these islands that we hoped to find the game that had brought us to Bindukhera for a week's shooting. I had shot over this ground for ten years and knew every foot of it, so the running of the shoot was left to me.

Shooting from the back of a well-trained elephant on the grasslands of the Tarai is one of the most pleasant forms of sport I know of. No matter how long the day may be, every moment of it is packed with excitement and interest, for in addition to the variety of game to be shot—on a good day I have seen eighteen varieties brought to bag ranging from quail and snipe to leopard and swamp deer—there is a great wealth of bird life to ordinarily be seen when walking through grass on foot.

There were nine guns and five spectators in camp on the first day of our shoot that February morning, and after an early breakfast we mounted our elephants and formed a line, with a pad elephant between every two guns. Taking my position in the centre of the line, with four guns and four pad elephants on either side of me, we set off due south with the flanking gun on the right—fifty yards in advance of the line—to cut off birds that rose out of range of the other guns and were making for the forest on the right. If you are ever given choice of position in a line of elephants on a mixed-game shoot select a flank, but only if you are good with both gun and rifle. Game put up by a line of elephants invariably try to break out at a flank, and one of the most difficult objects to hit is a bird or an animal that has been missed by others.

When the air is crisp and laden with all the sweet scents that are to be smelt in an Indian jungle in the early morning, it goes to head like champagne, and has the same effect on birds, with the result that both guns *and* birds tend to be too quick off the mark. A too eager gun and a wild bird do not produce a heavy bag, and the first few minutes of all glorious days are usually as unproductive as the last few minutes when muscles are tired and eyes strained. Birds were plentiful that morning, and, after the guns had settled down, shooting improved and in our first beat along the edge of the forest we picked up five peafowl, three red jungle fowl, ten black partridges, four grey partridges, two bush quails, and three hares. A good sambhar had been put up but he gained the shelter of the forest before rifles could be got to bear on him.

Where a tongue of forest extended out on to the plain for a few hundred yards, I halted the line. This forest was famous for the number of peafowl and jungle fowl that were always to be found in it, but as the ground was cut up by a number of deep nullahs that made it difficult to maintain a straight line, I decided not to take the elephants through it, for one of the guns was inexperienced and was shooting from the back of an elephant that morning for the first time. It was in this forest— when Wyndham and I some years previously were looking for a tiger—that I saw for the first time a cardinal bat. These beautiful bats, which look like gorgeous butterflies as they flit from cover to cover, are, as far as I know, only to be found in heavy elephant-grass.

After halting the line I made the elephants turn their heads to the east and move off in single file. When the last elephant had cleared the ground over which we had just beaten, I again halted them and made them turn their heads to the north. We were now facing the Himalayas, and hanging in the sky directly in front of us was a brilliantly lit white cloud that looked solid enough for angels to dance on.

The length of a line of seventeen elephants depends on the ground that is being beaten. Where the grass was heavy I shortened the line to a hundred yards, and where it was light I extended it to twice that length. We had beaten up to the north for a mile or so, collecting thirty more birds and a leopard, when a ground owl got up in front of the line. Several guns were raised and lowered when it was realized what the bird was. These ground owls, which live in abandoned pangolin and porcupine burrows, are about twice the size of a partridge, look white on the wing, and have longer legs than the ordinary run of owls. When flushed by a line of elephants they fly low for fifty to a hundred yards before alighting. This I believe they do to allow the line to clear their burrows, for when flushed a second time they invariably fly over the line and back to the spot from where they originally rose. The owl we flushed that morning, however, did not behave as these birds usually do, for after flying fifty to sixty yards in a straight line it suddenly started to gain height by going round and round in short circles. The reason for this was apparent a moment later when a peregrine falcon, flying at great speed, came out of the forest on the left. Unable to regain the shelter of its burrow the owl was now making a desperate effort to keep above the falcon. With rapid wing beats he was spiralling upwards, while the falcon on widespread wings was circling up and up to get above his quarry. All eyes, including those of the mahouts, were now on the exciting flight, so I halted the line.

It is difficult to judge heights when there is nothing to make a comparison with. At a rough guess the two birds had reached a height of a thousand feet, when the owl—still moving in circles—started to edge away towards the big white cloud, and one could imagine the angels suspending their dance and urging it to make one last effort to reach the shelter of their cloud. The falcon was not slow to see the object of this manoeuvre, and he too was now beating the air with his wings and spiralling up in ever-shortening circles. Would the owl make it or would he now, as the falcon approached nearer to him, lose his nerve and plummet down in a vain effort to reach mother earth and the sanctuary of his burrow? Field glasses were now out for those who needed them, and up and down the line excited exclamations—in two languages—were running.

'Oh! He can't make it.'

'Yes he can, he can.'

'Only a little way to go now.'

'But look, look, the falcon is gaining on him.' And then, suddenly, only one bird was to be seen against the cloud. 'Well done! Well done! Shahbash! Shahbash!' The owl had made it, and while hats were being waved and hands were being clapped, the falcon in a long graceful glide came back to the semul tree from which he had started.

The reactions of human beings to any particular event are unpredictable. Fifty-four birds and four animals had been shot that morning—and many more missed—without a qualm or the batting of an eyelid. And now, guns, spectators, and mahouts were unreservedly rejoicing that a ground owl had escaped the talons of a peregrine falcon.

At the northern end of the plain I again turned the line of elephants south, and beat down along the right bank of the stream that provided irrigation water for the three villages. Here on the damp ground the grass was unburnt and heavy, and rifles were got ready, for there were many hog deer and swamp deer in this area, and there was also a possibility of putting up another leopard.

We had gone along the bank of the stream for about a mile, picking up five more peafowl, four cock florican—hens were barred—three snipe, and a hog deer with very good horns when the accidental (please turn your eyes away, Recording Angel) discharge of a heavy high-velocity rifle in the hands of a spectator sitting behind me in my howdah, scorched the inner lining of my left ear and burst the eardrum. For me the rest of that February day was torture. After a sleepless night I excused myself on the plea that I had urgent work to attend to (again, please, Recording Angel) and at dawn, while the camp was asleep, I set out on a twenty-five-mile walk to my home at Kaladhungi.

The doctor at Kaladhungi, a keen young man who had recently completed his medical training, confirmed my fears that my eardrum had been destroyed. A month later we moved up to our summer home at Naini Tal, and at the Ramsay Hospital I received further confirmation of this diagnosis from Colonel Barber, Civil Surgeon of Naini Tal. Days passed, and it became apparent that abscesses were forming in my head. My condition was distressing my two sisters as much as it was distressing me, and as the hospital was unable to do anything to relieve me I decided—much against the wishes of my sisters and the advice of Colonel Barber—to go away.

I have mentioned this 'accident' not with the object of enlisting sympathy but because it has a very important bearing on the story of the Talla Des man-eater which I shall now relate.

~

Bill Baynes and Ham Vivian were Deputy Commissioners of, respectively, Almora and Naini Tal in the year 1929, and both were suffering from man-eaters, the former from the Talla Des man-eating tiger, and the latter from the Chowgarh man-eating tiger.

I had promised Vivian that I would try to shoot his tiger first, but as it had been less active during the winter months than Baynes's, I decided, with Vivian's approval, to try for the other first. The pursuit of this tiger would, I hoped, tide me over my bad time and enable me to adjust myself to my new condition. So to Talla Des I went.

My story concerns the Talla Des tiger, and I have refrained from telling it until … knowing that I had learnt—when a boy and later—how to walk in a jungle and use a rifle, and the credulity of all who were not present in Kumaon at that time would have been strained and this, after my previous stories had been accepted at their face value, was the last thing I desired.

My preparations were soon made and on 4 April I left Naini Tal accompanied by six Garhwalis, among whom were Madho Singh and Ram Singh, a cook named Elahai, and a Brahmin, Ganga Ram, who did odd jobs and was very keen to go with me. Walking the fourteen miles down to Kathgodam we caught the evening train and, travelling through Bareilly and Pilibhit, arrived at noon next day at Tanakpur. Here I was met by the peshkar, who informed me that a boy had been killed the previous day by the Talla Des man-eater, and that under Baynes's orders two young buffaloes—to be used as bait—had been dispatched for me via Champawat to Talla Des. After my men had cooked and eaten their food and I had breakfasted at the dak bungalow, we started off in good heart to try to walk the twenty-four miles to Kaladhunga (not to be confused with Kaladhungi) the same night.

The first twelve miles of the road—through Baramdeo to the foot of the sacred Purnagiri mountain—runs through forest most of the way. At the foot of the mountain the road ends, and there is the choice of two tracks to Kaladhunga. One, the longer, goes steeply up the left-hand side of the mountain to the Purnagiri temples, over a shoulder of the mountain, and down to Kaladhunga. The other track follows the alignment of the tramway line made by Collier when extracting the million cubic feet of sal timber. . . Collier's tramline—where it ran for four miles through the Sarda river gorge—has long since been washed away, but portions of the track he blasted across the perpendicular rock face of the mountain still remain. The going over this portion of the track was very difficult for my heavily laden Garhwalis, and night came on when we were only half-way through the gorge. Finding a suitable place on which to camp for the night was not easy, but after rejecting several places made dangerous by falling stones we eventually found a narrow shelf where the overhanging rock offered a measure of safety. Here we decided to spend the night, and after I had eaten my dinner and while the men were cooking their food with driftwood brought up from the river I undressed and lay down on my camp bed, the only article of camp equipment, excluding a washbasin and a forty-pound tent, that I had brought with me.

The day had been hot and we had covered some sixteen miles since detraining at Tanakpur. I was comfortably tired and was enjoying an after-dinner cigarette, when on the hill on the far side of the river I suddenly saw three lights appear. The forests in Nepal are burnt annually, the burning starting in April. Now, on seeing the lights, I concluded that the wind blowing down the gorge had fanned to flame the smouldering embers in some dead wood. As I idly watched these fires two more appeared a little above them. Presently the left-hand one of these two new fires moved slowly down the hill and merged into the central one of the original three. I now realized that what I had assumed were fires, were not fires but lights, all of a uniform size of about two feet in diameter, burning steadily without a flicker or trace of smoke. When presently more lights appeared, some to the left and others farther up the hill, an explanation to account for them presented itself. A potentate out on shikar had evidently lost some article he valued and had sent men armed with lanterns to search for it. Admittedly a strange explanation, but many strange things happen on the far side of that snow-fed river.

My men were as interested in the lights as I was, and as the river below us flowed without a ripple and the night was still, I asked them if they could hear voices or any other sounds—the distance across was about 150 yards—but they said they could hear nothing. Speculation as to what was happening on the opposite hill was profitless, and as we were tired out after our strenuous day the camp was soon wrapped in slumber. Once during the night a ghooral sneezed in alarm on the cliff above us, and a little later a leopard called.

A long march and a difficult climb lay before us. I had warned my men that we would make an early start, and light was just showing in the east when I was given a cup of hot tea. Breaking camp, when only a few pots and pans had to be put away and a camp bed dismantled, was soon accomplished. As the cook and my Garhwalis streamed off in single file down a goat track into a deep ravine, which in Collier's day had been spanned by an iron bridge, I turned my eyes to the hill on which we had seen the lights. The sun was not far from rising, and distant objects were now clearly visible. From crest to water's edge and from water's edge to crest I scanned every foot of the hill, first with my naked eyes and then with field glasses. Not a sign of any human being could I see, or, reverting to my first theory, was there any smouldering wood, and it only needed a glance to see that the vegetation in this area had not been burnt for a year. The hill was rock from top to bottom, a few stunted trees and bushes growing where roothold had been found in crack or cranny. Where the lights had appeared was a perpendicular rock where no human being, unless suspended from above, could possibly have gone.

Nine days later, my mission to the hill people accomplished, I camped for a night at Kaladhunga. For a lover of nature, or for a keen fisherman, there are few places in Kumaon to compare with Kaladhunga. From the bungalow Collier built when extracting the timber Nepal gave India, the land slopes gently down in a series of benches to the Sarda river. On these benches, where crops grew in the bygone days, there is now a luxuriant growth of grass. Here sambhar and cheetal are to be seen feeding morning and evening, and in the beautiful forests behind the bungalow live leopards and tigers, and a wealth of bird life including peafowl, jungle fowl, and kaleej pheasants. In the big pools and runs below the bungalow some of the best fishing in the Sarda river is to be had, either on a spinning rod with plug bait or on a light rod with salmon fly or fly spoon.

At crack of dawn next morning we left Kaladhunga, Ganga Ram taking the mountain track to Purnagiri and the rest of us the shorter way through the Sarda gorge. Ganga Ram's mission—which would entail an additional ten-miles walk—was to present our thank-offerings to the sacred Purnagiri shrine. Before he left me I instructed him to find out all he could, from the priests who served the shrine, about the lights we had seen when on our way up to Talla Des. When he rejoined me that evening at Tanakpur he gave me the following information, which he had gleaned from the priests and from his own observations.

Purnagiri, dedicated to the worship of the Goddess Bhagbatti and visited each year by tens of thousands of pilgrims, is accessible by two tracks. These, one from Baramdeo and the other from Kaladhunga, meet on the northern face of the mountain a short distance below the crest. At the junction of the tracks is situated the less sacred of the two Purnagiri shrines. The more sacred shrine is higher up and to the left. This holy of holies can only be reached by going along a narrow crack, or fault, running across the face of a more or less perpendicular rock cliff. Nervous people, children, and the aged are carried across the cliff in a basket slung on the back of a hillman. Only those whom the Goddess favours are able to reach the upper shrine; the others are struck blind and have to make their offerings at the lower shrine.

Puja (prayer) at the upper shrine starts at sunrise and ends at midday. After this hour no one is permitted to pass the lower shrine. Near the upper and more sacred shrine is a pinnacle of rock a hundred feet high, the climbing of which is forbidden by the Goddess. In the days of long ago a sadhu, more ambitious than his fellows, climbed the pinnacle with the object of putting himself on an equality with the Goddess. Incensed at his disregard of her orders, the Goddess hurled the sadhu from the pinnacle to the hill on the far side of the snow-fed river. It is this sadhu who, banished for ever from Purnagiri, worships the Goddess 2,000 feet above him by lighting lamps to her. These votive lights only appear at certain times (we saw them on 5 April) and are only visible to favoured people. This favour was accorded to me and to the men with me, because I was on a mission to the hillfolk over whom the Goddess watches.

That in brief was the information regarding the light which Ganga Ram brought back from Purnagiri and imparted to me while we were waiting for our train at Tanakpur. Some weeks later I received a visit from the Rawal (High Priest) of Purnagiri. He had come to see me about an article I had published in a local paper on the subject of the Purnagiri lights, and to congratulate me on being the only European ever to have been privileged to see them. In my article I gave the explanation for the lights as I have given it in these pages, and I added that if my readers were unable to accept this explanation and desired to find one for themselves, they should bear the following points in mind:

The lights did not appear simultaneously.

They were of a uniform size (about two feet in diameter).

They were not affected by wind.

They were able to move from one spot to another.

The High Priest was emphatic that the lights were an established fact which no one could dispute—in this I was in agreement with him for I had seen them for myself—and that no other explanation than the one I had given could be advanced to account for them.

The following year I was fishing the Sarda with Sir Malcolm (now Lord) Hailey, who was Governor of the United Provinces at the time. Sir Malcolm had seen my article and as we approached the gorge he asked me to point out the spot where I had seen the lights. We had four dhimas (fishermen) with us who were piloting the sarnis (inflated skins) on which we were floating down the river from one fishing stand to the next. These men were part of a gang of twenty engaged by a contractor in floating pine sleepers from the high-level forests in Kumaon and Nepal to the boom at Baramdeo. This was a long, difficult, and very dangerous task, calling for great courage and a thorough knowledge of the river and its many hazards.

Below the shelf blasted out of the cliff by Collier, on which my men and I had spent the night when on our way up to Talla Des, was a narrow sandy beach. Here the dhimas at my request brought the sarnis to the bank, and we went ashore. After I had pointed out where the lights had appeared, and traced their movements on the hill, Sir Malcolm said the dhimas could possibly provide an explanation, or at least throw some light on the subject. So he turned to them—he knew the correct approach to make to an Indian when seeking information and could speak the language perfectly—and elicited the following information. Their homes were in the Kangra Valley where they had some cultivation, but not sufficient to support them. They earned their living by floating sleepers down the Sarda river for Thakur Dan Singh Bist. They knew every foot of the river as far down as Baramdeo, for they had been up and down it countless times. They knew this particular gorge very well, for there were backwaters in it that hung up the sleepers and gave them a great deal of trouble. They had never seen anything unusual in this part of the river in the way of lights, or anything else.

As he turned away from the dhimas I asked Sir Malcolm to put one more question to them. Had they in all the years they had been working on the Sarda ever spent a night in the gorge? Their answer to this question was a very emphatic No! Questioned further they said that not only had they never spent a night in the gorge but that they had never heard of anyone else ever having done so. The reason they gave for this was that the gorge was haunted by evil spirits.

Two thousand feet above us a narrow crack, worn smooth by the naked feet of generations upon generations of devotees, ran for fifty yards across a perpendicular rock cliff where there was no handhold of any kind. In spite of the precautions taken by the priests to safeguard the lives of pilgrims, casualties while negotiating that crack were heavy until H. H. The Maharaja of Mysore provided funds a few years ago for a steel cable to be stretched across the face of the cliff, from the lower shrine to the upper.

So there well might be spirits at the foot of that cliff but not, I think, evil ones.

~

Now to get back to my story.

Ganga Ram, who could cover the ground as fast as any man in Kumaon, had stayed back with me to carry my camera, and we caught up with the cook and the six Garhwalis two miles from where we had spent the night. For the next six hours we walked with never a pause, at times through dense forests and at times along the bank of the Sarda river. Our way took us through Kaladhunga and through Chuka to the foot of the mountain, on the far side of which was our objective, the hunting grounds of the Talla Des man-eater. At the foot of the mountain we halted for two hours—to cook and eat our midday meal—before essaying the 4,000-foot climb.

In the afternoon, with the hot April sun blazing down on

our backs and without a single tree to shade us, we started on one of the steepest and most exhausting climbs my men and I had ever undertaken. The so-called road was only a rough track which went straight up the face of the mountain without a single hairpin bend to ease the gradient. After repeated and many halts we arrived at sunset at a little hamlet, a thousand feet from the crest. We had been warned at Chuka to avoid this hamlet, for, being the only inhabited place on the southern face of the mountain, it was visited regularly by the man-eater. However, man-eater or no man-eater, we could go no farther, so to the hamlet—which was a few hundred yards from the track—we went. The two families in the hamlet were delighted to see us and after we had rested and eaten our evening meal, my men were provided with accommodation behind locked doors, while I settled down on my camp bed under a tree that sheltered the tiny spring which provided the two families with drinking water, with a rifle and a lantern to keep me company.

Lying on my bed that night I had ample time to review the situation. Instructions had been issued by Bill Baynes to headmen of villages not to disturb any human or other kills, pending my arrival. The boy the peshkar of Tanakpur had told me about, had been killed on the fourth and it was now the night of the sixth. Since leaving the train at Tanakpur we had not spared ourselves in an effort to try to get to the scene of the killing with as little delay as possible. I knew the tiger would have eaten out his kill before our arrival and that, if he was not disturbed, he would probably remain in the vicinity for a day or two. I had hoped when leaving camp that morning that we would reach our destination in time to tie out one of the young buffaloes, but the climb up from the Sarda had been too much for us. Regrettable as the loss of one day was, it could not be helped, and I could only hope that if the tiger had moved away from the scene of his kill, he had not gone far. One of the disadvantages I had to contend with was that I did not know this part of Kumaon. The tiger had been operating for eight years and had made 150 human kills, so it was reasonable to assume he was working over a very large area. If contact with him was once lost it might be weeks before it could again be made. However, worrying over what the tiger had done, or what he might do, was profitless, so I went to sleep.

I was to make an early start and it was still quite dark when Ganga Ram roused me by lighting the lantern which had gone out during the night. While breakfast was being got ready I had a bath at the spring, and the sun was just rising over the Nepal mountains when, having cleaned and oiled my ·275 Rigby Mauser rifle and put five rounds in the magazine, I was ready to start. Inter-village communication had been interrupted by the man-eater and the two men in the hamlet had not heard about the tiger's last kill, so they were unable to give me any information as to the direction, or the distance, we would have to go. Not knowing when my men would get their next meal I told them to have a good one now and to follow me when they were ready, keeping close together and selecting open places to sit down in when they wanted to rest.

Rejoining the track up which we had laboured the previous evening, I halted for a spell to admire the view. Below me the valley of the Sarda was veiled in shadow and a wisp of mist showed where the river wound in and out through the foothills to emerge at Tanakpur. Beyond Tanakpur the eye could follow the river as a gleaming silver ribbon, until lost to sight on the horizon. Chuka was in shadow and partly obscured by mist, but I could see the path winding up to Thak, every foot of which I was to know when hunting the Thak man-eater ten years later. Thak village, gifted hundreds of years ago by the Chand Rajas of Kumaon to the priests who see the Purnagiri shrines, was bathed in the morning sun, as was also the pinnacle of Purnagiri.

Twenty-five years have come and gone since I turned away from that view to complete the last stage of my journey to Talla

Des—a long period, in which much has happened. But time does not efface events graven deep on memory's tablets, and the events of the five days I spent hunting the man-eating tiger of Talla Des are as clear-cut and fresh in my memory today as they were twenty-five years ago.

On the far side of the hill I found the track that I was on joined a quite good forest road some six feet wide, running east and west. Here I was faced with a dilemma, for there were no villages in sight and I did not know in which direction to go. Eventually, on the assumption that the road to the east could only take me out of my way as far as the Sarda, I decided to try it first.

Given the option of selecting my own time and place for a walk anywhere, I would unhesitatingly select a morning in early April on the northern face of a well-wooded hill in the Himalayas. In April all Nature is at her best; deciduous trees are putting out new leaves, each of a different shade of green or bronze; early violets, buttercups, and rhododendrons are giving way to later primulas, larkspurs, and orchids; and the birds—thrushes, babblers, minivets, tits, and a host of others—that migrated to the foothills for the winter are back on their nesting grounds and vie with each other in their joyous mating songs. Walking carefree and at ease in a forest in which there is no danger, only those objects and sounds which please the senses are looked at and listened to with any degree of attention, and all the other less-arresting sights and sounds blend together to form a pleasing whole. When there is danger from a man-eating tiger, however, the carefree feeling gives way to intense awareness.

Danger not only adds zest to all forms of sport, it also tends to sharpen the faculties and to bring into focus all that is to be seen and heard in a forest. Danger that is understood, and which you are prepared to face, does not detract in any way from pleasure. The bank of violets does not lose any of its beauty because the rock beyond it may shelter a hungry tiger, and the song of the black-headed sibia, poured out from the topmost branch of an oak tree, is none the less pleasing because a scimitar-babbler at the foot of the tree is warning the jungle folk of the presence of danger.

Fear may not be a heritage to some fortunate few, but I am not of their number. After a lifelong acquaintance with wild life I am no less afraid of a tiger's teeth and claws today than I was the day that a tiger shooed Magog and me out of the jungle in which he wanted to sleep. But to counter that fear and hold it in check I now have the experience that I lacked in those early years. Where formerly I looked for danger all round me and was afraid of every sound I heard, I now knew where to look for danger, and what sounds to ignore or pay special attention to. And, further, where there was uncertainty where a bullet would go, there was now a measure of certainty that it would go in the direction I wanted it to. Experience engenders confidence, and without these two very important assets the hunting of a man-eating tiger on foot, and alone, would be a very unpleasant way of committing suicide.

The forest road I was walking on that April morning ran through an area in which a man-eating tiger was operating and had been used by the tiger frequently, as was evident from the scratch marks on it. In addition to these marks, none of which was fresh enough to show the pug marks of the tiger which had made them, there were many tracks of leopard, sambhar, bear, kakar, and pig. Of birds there were many varieties, and of flowers there was great profusion, the most beautiful of which was the white butterfly orchid. These orchids hang down in showers and veil the branch or the trunk of the tree to which their roots are attached. One of the most artistic nests I have ever seen was that of a Himalayan black bear, made in a tree on which orchids were growing. A big oak tree had snapped off, either by weight of snow or in a storm, some forty feet above ground. Where the break had taken place a ring of branches, the thickness of a man's arm, had sprouted out at right angles to the trunk. Here moss had grown and in the moss butterfly orchids had found root-hold. It was here among these orchids that a bear had made its nest by bending over and pressing down the branches on to the broken-off tree trunk. The trees selected by bears in which to make their nests are of the variety whose branches will bend without snapping. The nests have nothing to do with family affairs and I have seen them at altitudes of 2,000 to 8,000 feet. At the lower altitudes, to which bears descend during the winter months to feed on wild plums and honey, the nests give protection from ants and flies, and at the higher altitudes they enable the animals to bask undisturbed in the sun.

When a road is interesting its length does not register on one's consciousness. I had been walking for about an hour when the forest ended and I came out on a grassy ridge overlooking a village. My approach over the open ground was observed, and when I reached the village the whole population appeared to have turned out to greet me. I often wonder whether in any other part of the world a stranger whose business was not known, arriving unexpectedly at a remote village, would be assured of the same welcome and hospitality as he would receive at any village throughout the length and breadth of Kumaon. I was possibly the first white man who had ever approached that village alone and on foot, and yet, by the time I reached the assembled people, a square of carpet had been produced, a morha (rush seat) placed on it, and I had hardly sat down before a brass vessel containing milk was placed in my hands. A lifelong association with the hillfolk enables me to understand the different dialects that are spoken in Kumaon and, what is just as important, to follow their every thought. As I had arrived armed with a rifle it was taken for granted that I had come to rid them of the man-eater, but what was puzzling them was my arrival on foot at that early hour when the nearest bungalow at which I could have spent the night was thirty miles away.

Cigarettes, passed round while I was drinking the milk, loosened tongues, and after I had answered the many questions put to me I put a few of my own. The name of the village, I learnt, was Tamali. The village had suffered for many years from the man-eater. Some said eight years and others said ten, but all were agreed that the man-eater had made its appearance the year that Bachi Singh had cut off his toes while splitting wood with an axe, and Dan Singh's black bullock, for which he had paid thirty rupees, had fallen down the hill and got killed. The last person killed at Tamali by the man-eater had been Kundan's mother. She had been killed on the twentieth day of the previous month (March), while working with other women in a field below the village. No one knew whether the tiger was a male or a female, but all knew it was a very big animal, the fear of which was now so great that the outlying fields were no longer being cultivated and no one was willing to go to Tanakpur to get the food that was needed for the village. The tiger was never absent from Tamali for long, and if I stayed with them, which they begged me to do, I would have a better chance of shooting it than anywhere else in Talla Des.

To leave people who place implicit trust in you to the tender mercies of a man-eater is not easy. However, my reason for doing so was accepted, and, after I had assured the fifty or more people gathered round me that I would return to Tamali at the first opportunity, I bade them goodbye and set off to try to find the village where the last kill had taken place.

At the point where the track from the hamlet met the forest road I removed the sign I had placed on the road to indicate to my men that I had gone east, and replaced it on the road to the west, and, to ensure that there would be no mistake, I put a 'road closed' sign on the road to the east. The two signs I have mentioned are known throughout the hills, and, though I had not told my men that I would use them, I knew they would understand that I had laid them and would interpret them correctly. The first sign consists of a small branch laid in the middle of the road, held in position with a stone or bit of wood, with the leaves pointing in the direction in which it is intended that the person following should go. The second sign consists of two branches crossed, in the form of an X.

The road to the west was level most of the way and ran through a forest of giant oak trees standing knee-deep in bracken and maidenhair fern. Where there were openings in this forest there were magnificent views of hills upon rising hills backed by the snowy range extending to east and west as far as the eye could see.

~

After going for some four miles due west the forest road turned to the north and crossed the head of a valley. Flowing down the valley was a crystal-clear stream which had its birth in the dense oak forest on the hill that towered above me on my left. Crossing the stream on stepping-stones, and going up a short rise, I came out on an open stretch of ground on the far side of which was a village. Some girls coming down from the village on their way to the stream caught sight of me as I came out on the open ground, and they called out in great excitement, 'The Sahib has come! The Sahib has come!' The cry was caught up from house to house and before I reached the village I was surrounded by an excited throng of men, women, and children.

From the headman I learnt that the name of the village was Talla Kote. That a patwari had arrived two days previously (5 April) from Champawat, to meet me and to tell all the people in the district that a sahib was coming from Naini Tal to try to shoot the man-eater. That shortly after the arrival of the patwari a woman of the village had been killed by the man-eater, and that in obedience to orders received from the Deputy Commissioner, Almora, the kill had not been disturbed. And finally, that in anticipation of my arrival a party of men had been sent that morning to look for the kill and, if there was anything left of it, to put up a machan for me. While the headman was giving me this information the party, numbering some thirty men, returned. These men told me that they had searched the ground where the tiger had eaten its kill and that all they had been able to find were the woman's teeth. Even her clothes, they said, were missing. When I asked where the kill had taken place, a lad of about seventeen who was with the party of men said that if I would accompany him to the other side of the village he would point out to me where his mother had been killed by the man-eater. With the lad leading and the throng of men, women, and children following me, we went through the village to a narrow saddle some fifty yards long connecting two hills. This saddle was the apex of two great valleys. The one on the left, or western side, swept down towards the Ladhya river; the one on the right fell steeply away and down ten or fifteen miles to the Kali river. Halting on the saddle the lad turned and faced the valley on the right. The left-hand or northern side of this valley was under short grass with an odd bush scattered here and there, and the right-hand side was under dense scrub and tree jungle. Pointing to a bush on the grassy side 800 to 1000 yards away and a 1000 to 1,500 feet below us, the lad said his mother had been killed near it while cutting grass in company with several other women. Then pointing to an oak tree in the ravine, the branches of which had been broken by langurs, he said it was under that tree that they had found the remains of his mother. Of the tiger, he said, neither he nor any of the party of men with him had seen or heard anything, but that when they were on their way down the hill they had heard first a ghooral, and then a little later, a langur calling.

   A ghooral and a langur calling. Ghooral do occasionally call on seeing human beings, but not langurs. Both will call on seeing a tiger, however. Was it possible that the tiger had lingered near the scene of its kill and on being disturbed by the party of men had moved off and been seen, first by the ghooral, and then by the langur? While I was speculating on this point, and making a mental map of the whole country that stretched before me, the patwari, who had been having his food when I arrived, joined me. Questioned about the two young buffaloes for which I had asked Baynes, the patwari said he had started out with them from Champawat and that he had left them at a village ten miles from Talla Kote, where a boy had been killed by the man-eater on 4 April within sight of the village. As there was no one on the spot to deal with the man-eater, the body had been recovered, and after a report of the occurrence had been sent to Champawat, from where it had been telegraphed to Tanakpur for my information, he had given orders for the body of the boy to be cremated.

My men had not yet arrived from the hamlet where we spent the night, so, after instructing the headman to have my tent pitched on the open ground near the stream, I decided to go down and have a look at the ground where the tiger had eaten his kill, with the object of finding out if the man-eater was male or female, and if the latter, whether she had cubs. This part of Kumaon was, as I have already said, unknown to me, and when I asked the headman if he could tell me the easiest way to get down into the valley the lad, who had pointed out to me where his mother had been killed and eaten, stepped forward and said very eagerly, 'I will come with you, Sahib, and show you the way.'

The courage of people living in an area in which there is danger from a man-eater, and the trust they are willing to place in absolute strangers, has always been a marvel to me. The lad, whose name I learnt was Dungar Singh, was yet another example of that courage and trust. For years Dungar Singh had lived in fear of the man-eater and only an hour previously he had seen the pitiful remains of his mother. And yet, alone and unarmed, he was willing to accompany an absolute stranger into an area in which he had every reason to believe—from the alarm call of a ghooral and a langur—that the killer of his mother was lurking. True, he had only recently visited that area, but on that occasion he had been accompanied by thirty of his friends, and in numbers there was safety.

There was no way down the steep hillside from the saddle, so Dungar Singh led me back through the village to where there was a goat track. As we went down through scattered bushes I told him that my hearing was defective, that if he wanted to draw my attention to any particular thing to stop and point to it, and that if he wanted to communicate with me to come close and whisper into my right ear. We had gone about 400 yards when Dungar Singh stopped and looked back. Turning round and looking in the same direction, I saw the patwari followed by a man carrying a shotgun hurrying down the hill after us. Thinking they had important information for me, I awaited their arrival and was disappointed to find that all the patwari wanted was to accompany me with his gun-bearer. This, very reluctantly, I permitted him to do for neither he nor his gun-bearer—both of whom were wearing heavy boots—looked like men who could move in a jungle without making considerable noise.

We had gone another 400 yards through dense scrub jungle, when we came out on a clearing a few yards square. Here, where the goat track divided, one arm going towards a deep ravine on the left while the other followed the contour of the hill to the right, Dungar Singh stopped, and pointing in the direction of the ravine whispered that it was down there that the tiger had eaten his mother. As I did not wish the ground on which I wanted to look for pug marks to be disturbed by booted men, I told Dungar Singh to stay on the open ground with the two men, while I went down alone into the ravine. As I stopped talking Dungar Singh whipped round and looked up the hill. When I looked in the same direction I saw a crowd of men standing on the saddle of the hill where I had stood a little while before. With a hand stretched out towards us to ensure silence, and the other cupped to his ear, Dungar Singh was intently listening, occasionally nodding his head. Then with a final nod he turned to me and whispered. 'My brother says to tell you that in the wyran field below you, there is something red lying in the sun.'

A wyran field is one that has gone out of cultivation, and below us on such a field there was something red lying in the sun. Maybe the red object was only a bit of dry bracken, or a kakar or young sambhar, but it might be a tiger. Anyway, I was not going to risk spoiling what might turn out to be a heaven-sent chance. So, handing my rifle to Dungar Singh, I took the patwari and his man, each by an arm, and led them to a medlar tree growing near by. Unloading the patwari's gun and laying it under a bush, I told the two men to climb the tree and on pain of death to remain quietly in it until I ordered them to come down. I do not think any two men ever climbed into a tree more gladly and from the way they clung to the branches after they had climbed as high as it was safe to go, it was evident that their views on man-eater hunting had undergone a drastic change since they followed me from the village.

The goat track to the right led on to a terraced field which had long been out of cultivation, and on which there was a luxuriant growth of oat grass. This field, about a hundred yards long, was ten feet wide at my end and thirty feet wide at the other, where it terminated on a ridge. For fifty yards the field was straight and then it curved to the left. As Dungar Singh saw me looking at it, he said that from the farther end we would be able to see down on to the wyran field on which his brother had seen the red object. Bending down and keeping to the inner edge of the field we crept along until we came to the far end. Here we lay down, and, crawling on hands and knees to the edge of the field, parted the grass and looked down.

Below us was a small valley with, on the far side, a steep grassy slope fringed on the side farthest from us by a dense growth of oak saplings. Beyond the saplings was the deep ravine in which the man-eater had eaten Dungar Singh's mother. The grassy slope was about thirty yards wide and below it was a rock cliff which, judging from the trees growing at the foot, was from eighty to a hundred feet high. On the near side of the slope was a terraced field, a hundred yards long and some ten yards wide. The field, which was in a straight line with us, had a small patch of short emerald-green grass at our end. On the remainder was a dense growth of an aromatic type of weed which grows to a height of four or five feet and has leaves like chrysanthemums, the undersides of which are white. Lying in brilliant sunlight on the patch of grass, and about ten feet apart, were two tigers.

The nearer tiger had its back to us with its head towards the hill, and the farther one had its stomach to us with its tail towards the hill. Both were fast asleep. The nearer offered the better shot, but I was afraid that on hearing the smack of the bullet the farther one would go straight down the hill into dense cover, in the direction in which its head was pointing. Whereas if I fired at the farther one first, the smack of the bullet—not to be confused with the crack of the rifle—would either drive the nearer one up the hill where there was less cover or else drive it towards me. So I decided to take the farther one first. The distance was approximately 120 yards, and the angle of fire was not so steep that any allowance had to be made for the lift of the bullet, a point which has to be kept in mind when shooting downhill on the Himalayas. Resting the back of my hand on the edge of the field, to form a cushion, and holding the rifle steady, I took careful aim at where I thought the animal's heart would be and gently pressed the trigger. The tiger never moved a muscle, but the other one was up like a flash and in one bound landed on a five-foot-high bank of earth that divided the field from a rainwater channel. Here the second tiger stood, broadside on to me, looking back over its right shoulder at its companion. At my shot it reared up and fell over backwards into the rainwater channel, and out of sight.

After my second shot I saw a movement in the aromatic weeds which started close to where the dead tiger was lying. A big animal was going at full gallop straight along the field. Having started from so close to where the two tigers had been lying, this third animal could only be another tiger. I could not see the animal, but I could follow its movements by the parting of the weeds, the leaves of which were white on the underside. Flicking up the 200-yard leaf-sight I waited for the animal to break cover. Presently out on to the grassy slope dashed a tiger. I now noticed that the slope the tiger was on curved to the right, in the same way as the field I was lying on curved to the left. As the tiger was keeping to the contour of the hill this curve in the slope enabled me to get a near-broadside shot at it.

I have seen animals fall over at a shot, and I have seen them crumple up, but I have never seen an animal fall as convincingly dead as that tiger fell at my shot. For a few moments it lay motionless and then it started to slide down, feet foremost, gaining momentum as it went. Directly below it, and within a few feet of the brink of the rock cliff, was an oak sapling eight to ten inches thick. The tiger struck this sapling with its stomach and came to rest with its head and forelegs hanging down on one side and its tail and hindlegs hanging down on the other. With rifle to shoulder and finger on trigger I waited, but there was not so much as a quiver in the tiger. Getting to my feet I beckoned to the patwari, who from his seat on the medlar tree had obtained a grandstand view of the whole proceedings. Dungar Singh, who had lain near me breathing in short gasps, was now dancing with excitement and from the way he was glancing at the tigers and then up at the crowd of people on the saddle, I knew he was thinking of the tale he would have to tell that night and for many moons thereafter.

When I saw the two tigers lying asleep I concluded that the man-eater had found a mate, but later, when my third shot flushed a third tiger, I knew I was dealing with a tigress and her two cubs. Which of the three was the mother and which the cubs it was not possible to say, for all three looked about the same size when I had viewed them over the sights of my rifle. That one of the three was the man-eater of Talla Des there could be no question, for tigers are scarce in the hills, and these three tigers had been shot close to where a human being had recently been killed and eaten. The cubs had died for the sins of their mother. They had undoubtedly eaten the human flesh their mother had provided for them from the time they were weaned; this, however, did not mean that when they left the protection of their mother they would have become man-eaters themselves. For in spite of all that has been said … I still maintain that the cubs of man-eating tigers—in that part of India about which I am writing—do not become man-eaters simply because they have eaten human flesh when young.

Sitting on the edge of the field with my feet dangling down and the rifle resting on my knees, I handed cigarettes to my companions and told them I would go and have a look at the tiger that had fallen into the rainwater channel, after we had finished our smoke. That I would find the tiger dead I had no doubt whatsoever; even so, nothing would be lost by waiting a few minutes, if for no other reason than to give myself a little time to rejoice over the marvellous luck I had met with. Within an hour of my arrival at Talla Des I had, quite by accident, got in touch with a man-eater that had terrorized an area of many hundreds of square miles for eight years, and in a matter of a few seconds had shot dead the man-eater and her two cubs. To the intense pleasure that all sportsmen feel at having held a rifle steady when every drop of blood in one's body is pounding with excitement, was added the pleasure and relief of knowing that there would be no necessity to follow up a wounded animal, a contingency that has to be faced when hunting tigers on foot.

My men would not ascribe my good fortune to luck. To avoid the possibility of failure they had consulted the old priest at the temple in Naini Tal and he had selected the propitious day for us to start on our journey to Talla Des, and evil omens when we started had been absent. My success would not be ascribed to good luck, therefore; nor, if I had failed to shoot the tigers, would my failure have been ascribed to bad luck, for no matter how well aimed a bullet might be it could do no harm to an animal whose time to die had not come. The superstitions of those whom I have been associated with on shikar have always been of interest to me. Being myself unwilling to begin a journey on a Friday, I am not inclined to laugh at a hillman's rooted aversion to begin a journey to the north on Tuesday or Wednesday, to the south on Thursday, to the east on Monday or Saturday, or to the west on Sunday or Friday. To permit those who accompany one on a dangerous mission to select the day for the start of the journey is a small matter, but it makes all the difference between having cheerful and contented companions and companions who are oppressed by a feeling of impending disaster.

The four of us sitting on the edge of the field had nearly finished our cigarettes, when I noticed that the tiger that was resting against the oak sapling was beginning to move. The blood from the body had evidently drained into the forward end of the animal, making that end heavier than the tail end, and it was now slowly slipping down head foremost. Once it was clear of the sapling the tiger glissaded down the grassy slope, and over the brink of the rock cliff. As it fell through space I threw up the rifle and fired. I fired that shot on the spur of the moment to give expression to my joy at the success of my mission to Talla Des, and also, I am ashamed to admit, to demonstrate that there was nothing—not even a tiger falling through space—that I could not hit on a day like this. A moment after the tiger disappeared among the tree tops, there was a rending of branches, followed by a dull and heavy thud. Whether or not I had hit the falling tiger did not matter, but what did matter was that the men of the village would have farther to carry it now than if it had remained on the slope.

My cigarette finished, I told my companions to sit still while I went down to look at the tiger in the rainwater channel. The hill was very steep and I had climbed down some fifty feet when Dungar Singh called out in a very agitated voice. 'Look, Sahib, look. There goes the tiger.' With my thoughts on the tiger below me, I sat down and raised my rifle to meet the charge I thought was coming. On seeing my preparations, the lad called out, 'Not here, but there, Sahib, there.' Relieved of the necessity of guarding my front I turned my head and looked at Dungar Singh and saw he was pointing across the main valley to the lower slopes of the hill on which his mother had been killed. At first I could see nothing, and then I caught sight of a tiger going diagonally up towards a ridge that ran out from the main hill. The tiger was very lame and could only take three or four steps at a time, and on its right shoulder was a big patch of blood. The patch of blood showed it was the tiger that had crashed through the trees, for the tiger that had fallen into the rainwater channel had been shot in the left shoulder.

Growing on the hill close to where I was sitting was a slender pine sapling. Putting up the 300-yard leaf-sight I got a firm grip of the sapling with my left hand and resting the rifle on my wrist took a careful and an unhurried shot. The distance was close on 400 yards and the tiger was on a slightly higher elevation than I was, so, taking a very full sight, I waited until it again came to a stand and then gently pressed the trigger. The bullet appeared to take an incredibly long time to cover the distance, but at last I saw a little puff of dust and at the same moment the tiger lurched forward, and then carried on with its slow walk. I had taken a little too full a sight, and the bullet had gone a shade too high. I now had the range to a nicety and all that I needed to kill the tiger was one more cartridge; the cartridge I had foolishly flung away when the tiger was falling through the air. With an empty rifle in my hands, I watched the tiger slowly and painfully climb to the ridge, hesitate for a few moments, and then disappear from view.

Sportsmen who have never shot in the Himalayas will question my wisdom in having armed myself with a light ·275 rifle, and only carrying five rounds of ammunition. My reasons for having done so were:

(a) The rifle was one I had used for over twenty years, and with which I was familiar.
(b) It was light to carry, accurate, and sighted up to 300 yards.
(c) I had been told by Colonel Barber to avoid using a heavy rifle, and not to fire more shots than were necessary with a light one.

With regard to ammunition, I had not set out that morning to shoot tigers but to find the village where the last human kill had taken place and, if I had the time, to tie out a young buffalo as bait. As it turned out, both the light rifle and the five rounds would have served my purpose if I had not thrown away that vital round.

My men arrived at the village in time to join the crowd on the saddle, and to witness the whole proceedings. They knew that the five rounds in the magazine of the rifle were all the ammunition I had with me, and when after my fifth shot they saw the wounded tiger disappear over the ridge, Madho Singh came tearing down the hill with a fresh supply of ammunition.

The tiger on the patch of green grass, and the tiger in the rainwater channel—which I found lying dead where it had fallen—were both nearly full-grown, and the one that had got away wounded was quite evidently their mother, the man-eater of Talla Des. Leaving Madho Singh and Dungar Singh to make arrangements for the cubs to be carried up to the village, I set out alone to try to get in touch with the wounded tigress. From the bed of bracken on to which she had fallen after crashing through the trees, I followed a light blood-trail to where she had been standing when I fired my last shot. Here I found a few cut hairs clipped from her back by my bullet, and a little extra blood which had flowed from her wound when she lurched forward on hearing my bullet strike the ground above her. From this spot to the ridge there was only an occasional drop of blood, and on the short stiff grass beyond the ridge I lost the trail. Close by was a dense patch of scrub, a hundred yards wide, extending up the side of a steep hill for 300 yards, and I suspected that the tigress had taken shelter in this scrub. But as night was now closing in and there was not sufficient light for accurate shooting, I decided to return to the village and leave the searching of the scrub until the following day.

~

The next morning was spent in skinning the cubs and in pegging out their skins with the six-inch nails I had brought with me from Naini Tal. While I was performing this task at least a hundred vultures alighted on the trees fringing the open ground on which my tent was pitched. It was these that brought to light the missing clothes of the man-eater's victim, for the cubs had torn the blood-soaked garments into strips and swallowed them.

The men of the village sat round me while I was skinning the cubs and I told them I wanted them to assist my Garhwalis in beating out the patch of scrub in which I thought the wounded tigress had taken shelter. This they were very willing to do. At about midday we set off, the men going through the village and along the saddle to the top of the hill above the cover, while I went down the goat track into the valley and up to the ridge over which I had followed the tigress the previous evening. At the lower edge of the scrub there was an enormous boulder—from which I was visible to the men at the top of the hill—I waved my hat as a signal for them to start the beat. To avoid the risk of anyone getting mauled, I had instructed the men to stay on the top of the hill and, after clapping their hands and shooting, to roll rocks down the hillside into the scrub I have spoken of. One kakar and a few kaleej pheasants came out of the bushes, but nothing else. When the rocks had searched out every foot of the ground, I again waved my hat as a signal for the men to stop the beat and return to the village.

When the men had gone I searched the cover, but without any hope of finding the tigress. As I watched her going up the hill the previous evening I could see that she was suffering from a very painful wound, and when I examined the blood where she had lurched forward, I knew the wound was a surface one and not internal. Why then had the tigress fallen to my bullet as if poleaxed, and why had she hung suspended from the oak sapling for a matter of ten to fifteen minutes without showing any signs of life? To these questions I could not at the time nor can I now find any reasonable answer. Later I found my soft-nose, nickel-encased bullet firmly fixed in the ball-and-socket joint of the right shoulder. When the flight of a high-velocity bullet is arrested by impact with a bone the resulting shock to an animal is very considerable. Even so, a tiger is a heavy animal with a tremendous amount of vitality, and why a light ·275 bullet should knock such an animal flat and render it unconscious for ten or fifteen minutes is to me inexplicable.

Returning to the ridge, I stood and surveyed the country. The ridge appeared to be many miles long and divided two valleys. The valley to the left at the upper end of which was the patch of scrub was open grass country, while the valley to the right at the upper end of which the tigers had eaten the woman had dense tree and scrub jungle on the right-hand side, and a steep shaly slope edging in a rock cliff on the left.

Sitting down on a rock on the ridge to have a quiet smoke, I reviewed the events of the previous evening, and came to the following conclusions:

(a) From the time the tigress fell to my shot to the time she crashed through the trees, she had been unconscious.
(b) Her fall, cushioned by the trees and the bed of bracken, had restored consciousness but had left her dazed.
(c) In this dazed condition she had just followed her nose and on coming up against the hill she had climbed it without knowing where she was going.

The question that now faced me was: How far and in what direction had the tigress gone? Walking downhill with an injured leg is far more painful than walking uphill and as soon as the tigress recovered from her dazed condition she would stop going downhill and would make for cover in which to nurse her injury. To get to cover she would have to cross the ridge, so the obvious thing was to try to find out if she had done so. The task of finding if a soft-footed animal had crossed a ridge many miles long would have been a hopeless one if the ridge had not had a knife-edge. Running along the top was a game track, with an ideal surface for recording the passages of all the animals that used it. On the left of the track was a grassy slope and on the right a steep shale scree ending in a sheer drop into the ravine below.

Finishing my smoke I set off along the game track on which I found the tracks of ghooral, sarao, sambhar, langur, porcupine, and the pug marks of a male leopard. The farther I went the more despondent I grew, for I knew that if I did not find the tigress's pug marks on this track there was little hope of my ever seeing her again. I had gone about a mile along the ridge, disturbing two ghooral who bounded away down the grassy slope to the left, when I found the pug marks of the tigress, and a spot of dry blood. Quite evidently, after disappearing from my view over the ridge the previous evening, the tigress had gone straight down the grassy slope until she recovered form her dazed condition and then had kept to the contour of the hill, which brought her to the game track. For half a mile I followed her pug marks to where the shale scree narrowed to about fifteen yards. Here the tigress attempted to go down the scree, evidently with the intention of gaining the shelter of the jungle on the far side of the ravine. Whether her injured leg failed her or whether dizziness overcame her, I do not know; anyway, after falling forward and sliding head-foremost for a few yards she turned round and with legs widespread clawed the ground in a desperate but vain effort to avoid going over the sheer drop into the ravine below. I am as sure-footed as a goat, but that scree was far too difficult for me to attempt to negotiate, so I carried on along the track for a few hundred yards until I came to a rift in the hill. Down this rift I climbed into the ravine.

As I walked up the thirty-yard-wide ravine I noted that the rock cliff below the shale scree was from sixty to eighty feet high. No animal, I was convinced, could fall that distance on to rocks without being killed. On approaching the spot where the tigress had fallen I was overjoyed to see the white underside of a big animal. My joy, however, was short lived, for I found the animal was a sarao and not the tigress. The sarao had evidently been lying asleep on a narrow ledge near the top of the cliff and, on being awakened by hearing, and possibly scenting, the tigress above him, had lost his nerve and jumped down, breaking his neck on the rocks at the foot of the cliff. Close to where the sarao had fallen there was a small patch of loose sand. On this the tigress had landed without doing herself any harm beyond tearing open the wound in her shoulder. Ignoring the dead sarao, within a yard of which she passed, the tigress crossed the ravine, leaving a well-defined blood trail. The bank on the right-hand side of the ravine was only a few feet high, and several times the tigress tried but failed to climb it. I knew now that I would find her in the first bit of cover she could reach. But my luck was out. For some time heavy clouds had been massing overhead, and before I found where the tigress had left the ravine a deluge of rain came on, washing out the blood trail. The evening was now well advanced and as I had a long and a difficult way to go, I turned and made for camp.

Luck plays an important part in all sport, and the tigress had—so far—had her full share of it. First, instead of lying out in the open with her cubs where I would have been able to recognize her for what she was, she was lying out of sight in thick cover. Then, the flight of my bullet had been arrested by striking the one bone that was capable of preventing it from inflicting a fatal wound. Later the tigress had twice fallen down a rock cliff, where she would undoubtedly have been killed had her fall in the one case not been cushioned by branches and a bed of bracken and in the other by a soft patch of sand. And finally, when I was only a hundred yards from where she was lying up, the rain came down and washed out the blood trail. However, I too had had a measure of luck, for my fear that the tigress would wander away down the greasy slope where I would lose touch with her had not been realized, and, further, I knew now where to look for her.

~

Next morning I returned to the ravine, accompanied by my six Garhwalis. Throughout Kumaon the flesh of sarao is considered a great delicacy, and as the young animal that had broken its neck was in prime condition, it would provide a very welcome meat ration for my men. Leaving the men to skin the sarao, I went to the spot from where I had turned back the previous evening. Here I found that two deep and narrow ravines ran up the face of the hill on the right. As it was possible that the tigress had gone up one of these, I tried the nearer one first only to find, after I had gone up it for a few hundred yards, that the sides were too steep for any tiger to climb, and that it ended in what in the monsoon rains must have been a thirty-foot-high waterfall. Returning to my starting point I called out to the men, who were about fifty yards away up the main ravine, to light a fire and boil a kettle of water for my tea. I then turned to examine the second ravine and as I did so I noticed a well-used game track coming down the hill on the left-hand side. On the game track I found the pug marks of the tigress, partly obliterated by the rain of the previous evening. Close to where I was standing was a big rock. On approaching this rock I saw that there was a little depression on the far side. The dead leaves in the depression had been flattened down, and on them were big clots of blood. After her fall into the ravine—which may have been forty hours earlier—the tigress had come to this spot and had only moved off on hearing me call to the men to boil the kettle for tea.

Owing to differences in temperament it is not possible to predict what a wounded tiger will do when approached by a human being on foot, nor is it possible to fix a period during which a wounded tiger can be considered as being dangerous—that is liable to charge when disturbed. I have seen a tiger with an inch-long cut in a hind pad, received while running away, charge full out from a distance of a hundred yards five minutes after receiving the wound; and I have seen a tiger that had been nursing a very painful jaw wound for many hours allow an approach to within a few feet without making any attempt to attack. Where a wounded man-eating tiger is concerned the situation is a little complicated, for, apart from not knowing whether the wounded animal will attack on being approached, there is the possibility—when the wound is not an internal one—of its attacking to provide itself with food. Tigers, except when wounded or when man-eaters, are on the whole very good-tempered. Were this not so it would not be possible for thousands of people to work as they do in tiger-infested jungles, nor would it have been possible for people like me to have wandered for years through the jungles on foot without coming to any harm. Occasionally a tiger will object to too close an approach to its cubs or to a kill that it is guarding. The objection invariably takes the form of growling, and if this does not prove effective it is followed by short rushes accompanied by terrifying roars. If these warnings are disregarded, the blame for any injury inflicted rests entirely with the intruder. The following experience with which I met some years ago is a good example of my assertion that tigers are good-tempered. My sister Maggie and I were fishing one evening on the Boar river three miles from our home at Kaladhungi. I had caught two small mahseer and was sitting on a rock smoking when Geoff Hopkins, who later became Conservator of Forests, Uttar Pradesh, turned up on his elephant. He was expecting friends, and being short of meat he had gone out with a ·240 rook-rifle to try to shoot a kakar or a peafowl. I had caught all the fish we needed, so we fell in with Geoff's suggestion that we should accompany him and help him to find the game he was looking for. Mounting the elephant we crossed the river and I directed the mahout to a part of the jungle where kakar and peafowl were to be found. We were going through short grass and plum jungle when I caught sight of a dead cheetal lying under a tree. Stopping the elephant I slipped to the ground and went to see what had killed the cheetal. She was an old hind that had been dead for twenty-four hours, and as I could find no marks of injury on her I concluded that she had died of snakebite. As I turned to rejoin the elephant I saw a drop of fresh blood on a leaf. The shape of the drop of blood showed that the animal from which it had come had been moving away from the dead cheetal. Looking a little farther in the direction in which the splash from the blood indicated the animal had gone, I saw another spot of blood. Puzzled by this fresh blood-trail I set off to see where it led to, and signalled to the elephant to follow me. After going over short grass for sixty or seventy yards the trail led towards a line of thick bushes some five feet high. Going up to the bushes where the trail ended I stretched out both arms—I had left my rod on the elephant—and parted the bushes wide, and there under my outstretched hands was a cheetal stag with horns in velvet, and lying facing me and eating the stag was a tiger. As I parted the bushes the tiger looked up and the expression on its face said, as clearly as any words, 'Well, I'll be damned!' Which was exactly what I was saying to myself. Fortunately I was so surprised that I remained perfectly still—possibly because my heart had stopped beating—and after looking straight into my face for a moment the tiger, who was close enough to have stretched out a paw and stroked my head, rose, turned, and sprang into the bushes behind him all in one smooth graceful movement. The tiger had killed the stag among the plum bushes shortly before our arrival, and in taking it to cover he went past the dead hind, leaving the blood trail that I followed. The three on the elephant did not see the tiger until he was in the air, when the mahout exclaimed with horror, 'Khabardar, Sahib. Sher hai.' He was telling me that it was a tiger and to be careful.

 Rejoining my men I drank a cup of tea while they cut up the sarao into convenient bits to carry, and returned with them to the depression in which I had found the clots of blood. All six men had been out on shikar with me on many occasions, and on seeing the quantity of blood they were of the opinion that the tigress had a body wound which would prove fatal in a matter of hours. On this point we were not in agreement, for I knew the wound was a superficial one from which the tigress, given time, would recover, and that the longer she lived the more difficult it would be to get in touch with her.

If you can imagine a deep and narrow ravine running up the face of a steep hill with the ground on the right sloping towards the ravine and well wooded but free of undergrowth, and the ground on the left-hand side of the ravine sloping upwards and covered with dense patches of ringal (stunted bamboo), bracken, and brushwood of all kinds, you will have some idea of the country my men and I worked over for the rest of that day.

My plan was for the men to go up on the right-hand side of the ravine, to keep me in sight by climbing into the highest trees they could find, and, if they wished to attract my attention, to whistle—hillmen, like some boys, are very good at whistling through their teeth. They would be in no danger from the tigress, for there was no cover on their side, and all of them were expert tree-climbers. The tracks of the tigress after she left the depression near the big rock showed that she had gone up the hill on the left-hand side of the ravine. Up this hill I now started to follow her.

I have emphasized elsewhere that jungle lore is not a science that can be learnt from textbooks, but that it can be absorbed a little at a time, and that the absorption process can go on indefinitely. The same applies to tracking. Tracking, because of its infinite variations, is one of the most interesting forms of sport I know and it can, at times, be also the most exciting. There are two generally accepted methods of tracking. One, following a trail on which there is blood, and the other, following a trail on which there is no blood. In addition to these two methods I have also at times been able to find a wounded animal by following blowflies, or by following meat-eating birds. Of the two generally accepted methods, following a blood-trail is the more sure way of finding a wounded animal. But as wounds do not always bleed, wounded animals have at times to be tracked by their footprints or by the disturbance to vegetation caused by their passage. Tracking can be easy or difficult according to the nature of the ground, and also according to whether the animal being tracked has hard hooves or soft pads. When the tigress left the depression—on hearing me calling to my men—her wound had stopped bleeding and the slight discharge that was coming from the wound owing to its having turned septic was not sufficient to enable me to follow her, so I had to resort to tracking her by her footprints and by disturbed vegetation. This, on the ground I was on, would not be difficult, but it would be slow, and time was on the side of the tigress. For the longer the trail the better the chances would be of her recovering from her wound and the less chance there would be of my finding her, for the strain of the past few days was now beginning to tell on me.

For the first hundred yards the trail led through knee-high bracken. Here tracking was easy, for the tigress had kept to a more or less straight line. Beyond the bracken was a dense thicket of ringal. I felt sure the tigress would be lying up in this thicket, but unless she charged there was little hope of my getting a shot at her, for it was not possible to move silently through the matted ringals. When I was half-way through the thicket a kakar started barking. The tigress was on the move, but instead of going straight up the hill she had gone out on the left, apparently on to open ground, for the kakar was standing still and barking. Retracing my steps I worked round to the left but found no open ground in that direction, nor did I appear to be getting any nearer the barking deer. The kakar, soon after, stopped barking and a number of kaleej pheasants started chattering. The tigress was still on the move, but, turn my head as I would, I could not locate the sound.

Pin-pointing, that is fixing the exact direction and distance of all sounds heard, is a jungle accomplishment which I have reduced to a fine art and of which I am very proud. Now, for the first time, I realized with a shock that my accident had deprived me of this accomplishment and that no longer would I be able to depend on my ears for safety and for the pleasure of listening intimately to the jungle folk whose language it had taken me years to learn. Had my remaining ear been sound it would not have mattered so much, but unfortunately the drum of that ear also had been injured by a gun 'accident' many years previously. Well, there was nothing that could be done about it now, and handicapped though I was I was not going to admit at this stage of the proceedings that any tiger, man-eater or other, had any advantage over me when we were competing for each other's lives under conditions that favoured neither side.

Returning to the bracken, I started to try to find the tigress, depending on my eyes only. The jungle appeared to be well stocked with game, and I repeatedly heard sambhar, kakar, and langur giving their alarm calls, and more than once I heard pheasants, jays, and white-capped laughing thrush mobbing the tigress. Paying no attention to these sounds, which ordinarily I would have listened for eagerly, I tracked the tigress foot by foot as, resting frequently, she made her way up the hill, at times in a straight line and at times zigzagging from cover to cover. Near the top of the hill was a stretch of short stiff grass about a hundred yards wide. Beyond this open ground were two patches of dense brushwood divided by a narrow lane which ran up to the top of the hill. On the short stiff grass I lost the tracks. The tigress knew she was being closely followed and would therefore expose herself as little as possible. The patch of brushwood to my right front was thirty yards nearer than the patch to the left, so I decided to try it first. When I was within a yard or two of the cover I heard a dry stick snap under the weight of some heavy animal. I was positive on this occasion that the sound had come from the left, so I turned and went to the patch of brushwood from which the sound appeared to have come. This was the second mistake I made that day—the first was calling to my men to boil the kettle for tea—for my men told me later that I crossed the open stretch of ground on the heels of the tigress, and that when I turned and walked away to the left she was lying on an open bit of ground a few yards inside the bushes, evidently waiting for me.

Finding no trace of the tigress in the brushwood on the left I came back to the open ground, and, on hearing my men whistling, looked in the direction in which I expected them to be. They had climbed to the top of a tree a few hundred yards to my right, and when I lifted my hand to indicate that I had seen them, they waved me up, up, up, and then down, down, down. They were letting me know that the tigress had climbed to the top of the hill, and that she had gone down on the far side. Making what speed I could I went up the narrow lane and on reaching the top found an open hillside. On this the grass had been burnt recently, and in the ashes, which were still damp from the rain of the previous evening, I found the pug marks of the tigress. The hill sloped gently down to a stream, the one that I had crossed several miles higher up on the day of my arrival at Talla Kote. After lying down and quenching her thirst the tigress had crossed the stream and gone up into the thick jungle beyond. It was now getting late, so I retraced my steps to the top of the hill and beckoned to my men to join me.

From the big rock where I took up the tracks of the tigress to the stream where I left them was only some four miles, and it had taken me seven hours to cover the distance. Though it had ended in failure the day had been an interesting and exciting one. Not only for me who, while doing the tracking, had to avoid being ambushed by a wounded man-eating tiger, but also for my Garhwalis who by climbing trees had kept both the tigress and myself in view most of the time. And it had been a long day also, for we had started at daylight, and it was 8 p.m. when we got back to camp.

~

The following morning while my men were having their food I attended to the skins, re-pegging them on fresh ground and rubbing wood ashes and powdered alum on the damp parts. Tiger skins need a lot of care, for if every particle of fat is not removed and the lips, ears, and pads properly treated, the hair slips, ruining the skin. A little before midday I was ready to start, and accompanied by four of my men—I left the other two men in camp to attend to the sarao's skin—I set out for the place where I had stopped tracking the tigress the previous evening.

The Valley through which the stream flowed was wide and comparatively flat, and ran from west to east. On the left-hand side of the valley was the hill on the far side of which I had followed the tigress the previous day, and on the right-hand side was the hill along which ran the road to Tanakpur. Before the advent of the man-eater the valley between these two hills had been extensively grazed over by the cattle of Talla Kote, and in consequence the ground was criss-crossed by a maze of cattle paths, and cut up with narrow eroded water-channels. Dotted about the valley were open glades of varying sizes surrounded by dense scrub and tree jungle. Good ground on which to hunt sambhar, kakar, and bear, all of whose tracks were to be seen on the cattle paths, but not the ground one would select on which to hunt a man-eating tiger. The hill on the left commanded an extensive view of the valley, so I spaced my men in trees along the crest at intervals of 200 yards to keep a look-out and to be on hand in case they were needed. I then went down to the spot where I had left the tracks of the tigress the previous evening.

I had wounded the tigress on 7 April, and it was now the 10th. As a general rule a tiger is not considered to be dangerous—that is, liable to charge at sight—twenty-four hours after being wounded. A lot depends on the nature of the wound, however, and on the temper of the wounded individuals. Twenty-four hours after receiving a light flesh wound a tiger usually moves away on being approached, whereas a tiger with a painful body-wound might continue to be dangerous for several days. I did not know the nature of the wound the tigress was suffering from, and as she had made no attempt to attack me the previous day I believed I could now ignore the fact that she was wounded and look upon her only as a man-eater, and a very hungry man-eater at that, for she had eaten nothing since killing the woman whom she had shared with the cubs.

Where the tigress had crossed the stream there was a channel, three feet wide and two feet deep, washed out by rainwater. Up this channel, which was bordered by dense brushwood, the tigress had gone. Following her tracks I came to a cattle path. Here she had left the channel and gone along the path to the right. Three hundred yards along was a tree with heavy foliage and under this tree the tigress had lain all night. Her wound had troubled her and she had tossed about, but on the leaves on which she had been lying there was neither blood nor any discharge from her wound. From this point on I followed her fresh tracks, taking every precaution not to walk into an ambush. By evening I had tracked her for several miles along cattle paths, water channels, and game tracks, without having set eyes on so much as the tip of the her tail. At sunset I collected my men, and as we returned to camp they told me they had been able to follow the movements of the tigress through the jungle by the animals and birds that had called at her, but that they too had seen nothing of her.

When hunting unwounded man-eating tigers the greatest danger, when walking into the wind, is of an attack from behind, and to a lesser extent from either side. When the wind is from behind, the danger is from either side. In the same way, if the wind is blowing from the right the danger is from the left and from behind, and if blowing from the left the danger is from the right and from behind. In none of these cases is there any appreciable danger of an attack from the front, for in my experience all unwounded tigers, whether man-eaters or not, are disinclined to make a head-on attack. Under normal conditions man-eating tigers limit the range of their attack to the distance they can spring, and for this reason they are more difficult to cope with than wounded tigers, who invariably launch an attack from a little distance, maybe only ten or twenty yards, but possibly as much as a hundred yards. This means that whereas the former have to be dealt with in a matter of split seconds, the latter give one time to raise a rifle and align the sights. In either case it means rapid shooting and a fervent prayer that an ounce or two of lead will stop a few hundred pounds of muscle and bone.

In the case of the tigress I was hunting, I knew that her wound would not admit of her springing and that if I kept out of her reach I would be comparatively safe. The possibility that she had recovered from her wound in the four days that had elapsed since I had last seen her had, however, to be taken into account. When therefore I started out alone on the morning of 11 April to take up the tracks where I had left them the previous evening, I resolved to keep clear of any rock, bush, tree, or other object behind which the tigress might be lying up in wait for me.

She had been moving the previous evening in the direction of the Tanakpur road. I again found where she had spent the night, this time on a soft bed of dry grass, and from this point I followed her fresh tracks. Avoiding dense cover—possibly because she could not move through it silently—she was keeping to water channels and game tracks and it became apparent that she was not moving about aimlessly but was looking for something to kill and eat. Presently, in one of these water channels she found and killed a few-weeks-old kakar. She had come on the young deer as it was lying asleep in the sun on a bed of sand, and had eaten every scrap of it, rejecting nothing but the tiny hooves. I was now only a minute or two behind her, and knowing that the morsel would have done no more than whet her appetite, I redoubled my precautions. In places the channels and game tracks to which the tigress was keeping twisted and turned and ran through dense cover or past rocks. Had my condition been normal I would have followed on her footsteps and possibly been able to catch up with her, but unfortunately I was far from normal. The swelling on my head, face, and neck, had now increased to such proportions that I was no longer able to move my head up or down or from side to side, and my left eye was closed. However, I still had one good eye, fortunately my right one, and I could still hear a little.

During the whole of that day I followed the tigress without seeing her and without, I believe, her seeing me. Where she had gone along water channels, game tracks, or cattle paths that ran through dense cover I skirted round the cover and picked up her pug marks on the far side. Not knowing the ground was a very great handicap, for not only did it necessitate walking more miles than I need have done, but it also prevented my anticipating the movements of the tigress and ambushing her. When I finally gave up the chase for the day, the tigress was moving up the valley in the direction of the village.

Back in camp I realized that the 'bad time' I had foreseen and dreaded was approaching. Electric shocks were stabbing through the enormous abscess, and the hammer blows were increasing in intensity. Sleepless nights and a diet of tea had made a coward of me, and I could not face the prospect of sitting on my bed through another long night, racked with pain and waiting for something, I knew not what, to happen. I had come to Talla Des to try to rid the hill people of the terror that menaced them and to tide over my bad time, and all that I had accomplished so far was to make their condition worse. Deprived of the ability to secure her natural prey, the tigress, who in eight years had only killed 150 people would now, unless she recovered from her wound, look to her easiest prey—human beings—to provide her with most of the food she needed. There was therefore an account to be settled between the tigress and myself, and that night was as suitable a time as any to settle it.

Calling for a cup of tea—made hill-fashion with milk—which served me as dinner, I drank it while standing in the moonlight. Then, calling my eight men together, I instructed them to wait for me in the village until the following evening, and if I did not return by then to pack up my things and start early the next morning for Naini Tal. Having done this I picked up my rifle from where I put it on my bed, and headed down the valley. My men, all of whom had been with me for years, said not a word either to ask me where I was going or to try to dissuade me from going. They just stood silent in a group and watched me walk away. Maybe the glint I saw on their cheeks was only imagination, or maybe it was only the reflection of the moon. Anyway, when I looked back not a man had moved. They were just standing in a group as I had left them.

~

One of my most pleasant recollections—of the days when I was young—are the moonlight walks along forest roads that ten or a dozen of us used to take during the winter months, and the high teas we consumed on our return home. These walks tended to dispel all the fears that assail a human being in a forest at night, and, further, they made us familiar with the sounds to be heard in a forest by night. Later, years of experience added to my confidence and to my knowledge. When therefore I left my camp on the night of 11 April—in brilliant moonlight—to try conclusions with the Talla Des man-eating tigress, I did not set out with any feeling of inferiority on what might appear to have been a suicidal quest.

I have been interested in tigers from as far back as I can remember, and having spent most of my life in an area in which they were plentiful I have had ample opportunities of observing them. My ambition when I was very young was to see a tiger, just that, and no more. Later my ambition was to shoot a tiger, and this I accomplished on foot with an old army rifle which I bought for fifty rupees from a seafaring man, who I am inclined to think had stolen it and converted it into a sporting rifle. Later still, it was my ambition to photograph a tiger. In the course of time all three of these ambitions were fulfilled. It was while trying to photograph tigers that I learnt the little I know about them. Having been favoured by Government with the 'freedom of the forests', a favour which I very greatly appreciate and which I shared with only one other sportsman in India, I was able to move about without let or hindrance in those forests in which tigers were most plentiful. Watching tigers for days or weeks on end, and on one occasion for four and a half months, I was able to learn a little about their habits and in particular their method of approaching and of killing their victims. A tiger does not run down its prey; it either lies in wait or stalks it. In either case contact with its victim is made by a single spring, or by a rush of a few yards followed by a spring. If therefore an animal avoids passing within striking distance of a tiger, avoids being stalked, and reacts instantly to danger whether conveyed by sight, scent, or by hearing, it has a reasonable chance of living to an old age. Civilization has deprived human beings of the keen sense of scent and hearing enjoyed by animals, and when a human being is menaced by a man-eating tiger he has to depend for his safety almost entirely on sight. When restlessness and pain compelled me to be on the move that night, I was handicapped to the extent that I only had one effective eye. But against this handicap was the knowledge that the tigress could do me no harm if I kept out of her reach, whereas I could kill her at a distance. My instructions therefore to my men to go back to Naini Tal if I failed to return by the following evening were not given since I feared there was a possibility of my becoming unconscious and unable to defend myself.

One of the advantages of making detailed mental maps of ground covered is that finding the way back to any given spot presents no difficulty. Picking up the pug marks of my quarry where I had left them, I resumed my tracking, which was now only possible on game tracks and on cattle paths, to which the tigress was, fortunately, keeping. Sambhar and kakar had now come out to the open glades, some to feed and others for protection, and though I could not pin-point their alarm calls they let me know when the tigress was on the move and gave me a rough idea of the direction in which she was moving.

On a narrow, winding cattle path running through dense cover I left the pug marks of the tigress and worked around through scattered brushwood to try to pick them up on the far side. The way round was longer than I had anticipated, and I eventually came out on an open stretch of ground with short grass and dotted about with big oak trees. Here I came to a halt in the shadow of a big tree. Presently, by a movement of this shadow, I realized that the tree above me was tenanted by a troop of langurs. I had covered a lot of ground during the eighteen hours I had been on my feet that day, and here now was a safe place for me to rest awhile, for the langurs above would give warning of danger. Sitting with my back against the tree and facing the cover round which I had skirted, I had been resting for half an hour when an old langur gave his alarm call; the tigress had come out into the open and the langur had caught sight of her. Presently I too, caught sight of the tigress just as she started to lie down.

She was a hundred yards to my right and ten yards from the cover, and she lay down broadside on to me with her head turned looking up at the calling langur.

I have had a lot of practice in night shooting, for during the winter months I assisted our tenants at Kaladhungi to protect their crops against marauding animals such as pig and deer. On a clear moonlit night I can usually count on hitting an animal up to a range of about a hundred yards. Like most people who have taught themselves to shoot, I keep both eyes open when shooting. This enables me to keep the target in view with one eye, while aligning the sights of the rifle with the other. At any other time I would have waited for the tigress to stand up and then fired at her, but unfortunately my left eye was now closed and a hundred yards was too far to risk a shot with only one eye. On the two previous nights the tigress had lain in the one spot and had possibly slept most of the night, and she might do the same now. If she lay right down on her side—she was now lying on her stomach with her head up—and went to sleep I could either go back to the cattle path on which I had left her pug marks and follow her tracks to the edge of the cover and get to within ten yards of her, or I could creep up to her over the open ground until I got close enough to make sure of my shot. Anyway, for the present I could do nothing but sit perfectly still until the tigress made up her mind what she was going to do.

For a long time, possibly half an hour or a little longer, the tigress lay in one position, occasionally moving her head from side to side, while the old langur in a sleepy voice continued to give his alarm call. Finally she got to her feet and very slowly and very painfully started to walk away to my right. Directly in the line in which she was going there was an open ravine ten to fifteen feet deep and twenty to twenty-five yards wide, which I had crossed lower down when coming to the spot where I now was. When the tigress had increased the distance between us to 150 yards, and the chances of her seeing me had decreased, I started to follow her. Slipping from tree to tree, and moving a little faster than she, I reduced her lead to fifty yards by the time she reached the edge of the ravine. She was now in range, but was standing in shadow, and her tail end was a very small mark to fire at. For a long and anxious minute she stood in the one position and then, having made up her mind to cross the ravine, very gently went over the edge.

As the tigress disappeared from view I bent down and ran forward on silent feet. Bending my head down and running was a very stupid mistake for me to have made, and I had only run a few yards when I was overcome by vertigo. Near me were two oak saplings, a few feet apart and with inter-laced branches. Laying down my rifle I climbed up the saplings to a height of ten or twelve feet. Here I found a branch to sit on, another for my feet, and yet other small branches for me to rest against. Crossing my arms on the branches in front of me, I laid my head on them, and at that moment the abscess burst, not into my brain as I feared it would, but out through my nose and left ear.

'No greater happiness can man know, than the sudden cessation of great pain,' was said by someone who had suffered and suffered greatly, and who knew the happiness of sudden relief. It was round about midnight when relief came to me, and the grey light was just beginning to show in the east when I raised my head from my crossed arms. Cramp in my legs resulting from my having sat on a thin branch for four hours had roused me, and for a little while I did not know where I was or what had happened to me. Realization was not long in coming. The great swelling on my head, face, and neck had gone and with it had gone the pain. I could now move my head as I liked, my left eye was open, and I could swallow without discomfort. I had lost an opportunity of shooting the tigress, but what did that matter now, for I was over my bad time and no matter where or how for the tigress went I would follow her, and sooner or later I would surely get another chance.

When I last saw the tigress she was heading in the direction of the village. Swinging down from the saplings, up which I had climbed with such difficulty, I retrieved my rifle and headed in the same direction. At the stream I stopped and washed and cleaned myself and my clothes as best I could. My men had not spent the night in the village as I had instructed them to, but had sat round a fire near my tent keeping a kettle of water on the boil. As, dripping with water, they saw me coming towards them they sprang up with a glad cry of 'Sahib! Sahib! You have come back, and you are well.' 'Yes,' I answered, 'I have come back, and I am now well.' When an Indian gives his loyalty, he gives it unstintingly and without counting the cost. When we arrived at Talla Kote the headman put two rooms at the disposal of my men, for it was dangerous to sleep anywhere except behind locked doors. On this my bad night, and fully alive to the danger, my men had sat out in the open in case they could be of any help to me, and to keep a kettle on the boil for my tea—if I should return. I cannot remember if I drank the tea, but I can remember my shoes being drawn off by willing hands, and a rug spread over me as I lay down on my bed.

Hours and hours of peaceful sleep, and then a dream. Someone was urgently calling me, and someone was as urgently saying I must not be disturbed. Over and over again the dream was repeated with slight variations, but with no less urgency, until the words penetrated through the fog of sleep and became a reality. 'You *must* wake him or he will be very angry.' And the rejoinder, 'We will *not* wake him for he is very tired.' Ganga Ram was the last speaker, so I called out and told him to bring the man to me. In a minute my tent was besieged by an excited throng of men and boys all eager to tell me that the man-eater had just killed six goats on the far side of the village. While pulling on my shoes I looked over the throng and on seeing Dungar Singh, the lad who was with me when I shot the cubs, I asked him if he knew where the goats had been killed and if he could take me to the spot. 'Yes, yes,' he answered eagerly, 'I know where they were killed and I can take you there.' Telling the headman to keep the crowd back, I armed myself with my ·275 rifle and, accompanied by Dungar Singh, set off through the village.

My sleep had refreshed me, and as there was now no need for me to put my feet down gently—to avoid jarring my head—I was able, for the first time in weeks, to walk freely and without discomfort.

~

The day I arrived at Talla Kote, Dungar Singh, the lad who was with me now, had taken me through the village to a narrow saddle from where there was an extensive view into two valleys. The valley to the right fell steeply away in the direction of the Kali river. At the upper end of this valley I had shot the cubs and wounded the tigress. The other valley, the one to the left, was less steep and from the saddle a goat track ran down into it. It was in this valley that the goats had been killed. Down the goat track the lad now started to run, with me close on his heels. After winding down over steep and broken ground for five or six hundred yards, the track crossed a stream and then continued down the valley on the left bank. Close to where the track crossed the stream there was an open bit of comparatively flat ground. Running from left to right across this open ground was a low ridge of rock, on the far side of which was a little hollow, and lying in the hollow were three goats.

On the way down the hill the lad had told me that round about midday a large flock of goats in charge of ten or fifteen boys was feeding in the hollow, when a tiger—which they suspected was the man-eater—suddenly appeared among them and struck down six goats. On seeing the tiger the boys started yelling and were joined by some men collecting firewood near by. In the general confusion of goats dashing about and human beings yelling, the tiger moved off and no one appeared to have seen in which direction it went. Grabbing hold of three dead goats the men and boys dashed back to the village to give me the news, leaving three goats with broken backs in the hollow.

That the killer of the goats was the wounded man-eater there could be no question, for when I last saw her the previous night she was going straight towards the village. Further, my men told me that an hour or so before my return to camp a kakar had barked near the stream, a hundred yards from where they were sitting, and thinking that the animal had barked on seeing me they had built up the fire. It was fortunate that they had done so, for I later found the pug marks of the tigress where she had skirted round the fire and had then gone through the village, obviously with the object of securing a human victim. Having failed in her quest she had evidently taken cover near the village, and at the first opportunity of securing food had struck down the goats. This she had done in a matter of seconds, while suffering from a wound that made her limp badly.

As I was not familiar with the ground, I asked Dungar Singh in which direction he thought the tigress had gone. Pointing down the valley he said she had probably gone in that direction, for there was heavy jungle farther down. While I was questioning him about this jungle, with the idea of going down and looking for the tigress, a kaleej pheasant started chattering. On hearing this the lad turned round and looked up the hill, giving me an indication of the direction in which the bird was calling. To our left the hill went up steeply, and growing on it were a few bushes and stunted trees. I knew the tigress would not have attempted to climb this hill, and on seeing me looking at it Dungar Singh said the pheasant was not calling on the hill but in a ravine round the shoulder of it. As we were not within sight of the pheasant, there was only one thing that could have alarmed it, and that was the tigress. Telling Dungar Singh to leave me and run back to the village as fast as he could go, I covered his retreat with my rifle until I considered he was clear of the danger zone and then turned round to look for a suitable place in which to sit.

The only trees in this part of the valley were enormous pines which, as they had no branches for thirty or forty feet, it would be quite impossible to climb. So of necessity I would have to sit on the ground. This would be all right during daylight, but if the tigress delayed her return until nightfall, and preferred human flesh to mutton, I would need a lot of luck to carry me through the hour or two of darkness before the moon rose.

On the low ridge running from left to right on the near side of the hollow was a big flat rock. Near it was another and smaller one. By sitting on this smaller rock I found I could shelter behind the bigger, exposing only my head to the side from which I expected the tigress to come. So here I decided to sit. In front of me was a hollow some forty yards in width with a twenty-foot-high bank on the far side. Above this bank was a ten- to twenty-yard wide flat stretch of ground sloping down to the right. Beyond this the hill went up steeply. The three goats in the hollow, which were alive when the boys and men ran away, were now dead. When striking them down the tigress had ripped the skin on the back of one of them.

The kaleej pheasant had now stopped chattering, and I speculated as to whether it had called at the tigress as she was going up the ravine after the lad and I had arrived or whether it had called on seeing the tigress coming back. In the one case it would mean a long wait for me, and in the other a short one. I had taken up my position at 2 p.m., and half an hour later a pair of blue Himalayan magpies came up the valley. These beautiful birds, which do a lot of destruction in the nesting season among tits and other small birds, have an uncanny instinct for finding in a jungle anything that is dead. I heard the magpies long before I saw them, for they are very vocal. On catching sight of the goats they stopped chattering and very cautiously approached. After several false alarms they alighted on the goat with the ripped back and started to feed. For some time a king vulture had been quartering the sky, and now, on seeing the magpies on the goat, he came sailing down and landed as lightly as a feather on the dead branch of a pine tree. These king vultures with their white shirt-fronts, black coats, and red heads and legs, are always the first of the vultures to find a kill. Being smaller than other vultures it is essential for them to be first at the table, for when the others arrive they have to take a back seat.

I welcomed the vulture's coming, for he would provide me with information I lacked. From his perch high up on the pine tree he had an extensive view, and if he came down and joined the magpies it would mean that the tigress had gone, whereas if he remained where he was it would mean that she was lying up somewhere close by. For the next half hour the scene remained unchanged—the magpies continued to feed, and the vulture sat on the dead branch—and then the sun was blotted out by heavy rain-clouds. Shortly after, the kaleej pheasant started chattering again and the magpies flew screaming down the valley. The tigress was coming, and here, sooner than I had expected, was the chance of shooting her that I had lost the previous night when overcome by vertigo.

A few light bushes on the shoulder of the hill partly obstructed my view in the direction of the ravine, and presently through these bushes I saw the tigress. She was coming, very slowly, along the flat bit of ground above the twenty-foot-high bank and was looking straight towards me. With only head exposed and my soft hat pulled down to my eyes, I knew she would not notice me if I made no movement. So, with the rifle resting on the flat rock, I sat perfectly still. When she had come opposite to me the tigress sat down, with the bole of a big pine tree directly between us. I could see her head on one side of the tree and her tail and part of her hindquarters on the other. Here she sat for minutes, snapping at the flies that, attracted by her wound, were tormenting her.

~

Eight years previously, when the tigress was a comparatively young animal, she had been seriously injured in an encounter with a porcupine. At the time she received this injury she may have had cubs, and unable for the time being to secure her natural prey to feed herself in order to nourish her cubs, she had taken to killing human beings. In doing this she had committed no crime against the laws of Nature. She was a carnivorous animal, and flesh, whether human or animal, was the only food she could assimilate. Under stress of circumstances an animal, and a human being also, will eat food that under normal conditions they are averse to eating. From the fact that during the whole of her man-eating career the tigress had only killed 150 human beings—fewer than twenty a year—I am inclined to think that she only resorted to this easily procured form of food when she had cubs and when, owing to her injury, she was unable to get the requisite amount of natural food needed to support herself and her family.

The people of Talla Des had suffered and suffered grievously from the tigress, and for the suffering she had inflicted she was now paying in full. To put her out of her misery I several times aligned the sights of my rifle on her head, but the light, owing to the heavy clouds, was not good enough for me to make sure of hitting a comparatively small object at sixty yards.

Eventually the tigress stood up, took three steps and then stood broadside on to me, looking down at the goats. With my elbows resting on the flat rock I took careful aim at the spot where I thought her heart would be, pressed the trigger, and saw a spurt of dust go up on the hill on the far side of her. On seeing the dust the thought flashed through my mind that not only had I missed the tigress's heart, but that I had missed the whole animal. And yet, after my careful aim, that could not be. What undoubtedly had happened was that my bullet had gone clean through her without meeting any resistance. At my shot the tigress sprang forward, raced over the flat ground like a very frightened but unwounded animal, and before I could get in another shot, disappeared from view.

Mad with myself for not having killed the tigress when she had given me such a good shot, I was determined now that she would not escape from me. Jumping down from the rock, I sprinted across the hollow, up the twenty-foot bank and along the flat ground until I came to the spot where the tigress had disappeared. Here I found there was a steep forty-foot drop down a loose shale scree. Down this the tigress had gone in great bounds. Afraid to do the same for fear of spraining my ankles, I sat down on my heels and tobogganed to the bottom. At the foot of the scree was a well-used footpath, along which I felt sure the tigress had gone, though the surface was too hard to show pug marks. To the right of the path was a boulder-strewn stream, the one that Dungar Singh and I had crossed farther up, and flanking the stream was a steep grassy hill. To the left of the path was a hill with a few pine trees growing on it. The path for some distance was straight, and I had run along it for fifty or more yards when I heard a ghooral give its alarm sneeze. There was only one place where the ghooral could be and that was on the grassy hill to my right. Thinking that the tigress had possibly crossed the stream and gone up this hill, I pulled up to see if I could see her. As I did so, I thought I heard men shouting. Turning around, I looked up in the direction of the village and saw a crowd of men standing on the saddle of the hill. On seeing me look around they shouted again and waved me on, straight along the path. In a moment I was on the run again, and on turning a corner found fresh blood on the path.

The skin of animals is loose. When an animal that is standing still is hit in the body by a bullet and it dashes away at full speed, the hole made in the skin does not coincide with the hole in the flesh, with the result that, as long as the animal is running at speed, little if any blood flows from the wound. When, however, the animal slows down and the two holes come closer together, blood flows and continues to flow more freely the slower the animal goes. When there is any uncertainty as to whether an animal that has been fired at has been hit or not, the point can be very easily cleared up by going to the exact spot where the animal was when fired at, and looking for cut hairs. These will indicate that the animal was hit, whereas the absence of such hairs will show that it was clean missed.

After going round the corner the tigress had slowed down, but she was still running, as I could see from the blood splashes, and in order to catch up with her I put on a spurt. I had not gone very far when I came to a spur jutting out from the hill on my left. Here the path bent back at a very acute angle, and not being able to stop myself, and there being nothing for me to seize hold of on the hillside, I went over the edge of the narrow path all standing. Ten to fifteen feet below was a small rhododendron sapling, and below the sapling a sheer drop into a dark and evil-looking ravine where the stream, turning at right angles, had cut away the toe of the hill. As I passed the sapling with my heels cutting furrows in the soft earth, I gripped it under my right arm. The sapling, fortunately, was not uprooted, and though it bent it did not break. Easing myself round very gently, I started to kick footholds in the soft loamy hill-face which had a luxuriant growth of maidenhair fern.

The opportunity of catching up with the tigress had gone, but I now had a well-defined blood-trail to follow, so there was no longer any need for me to hurry. The footpath which at first had run north now ran west along the north face of a steep and well-wooded hill. When I had gone for another 200 yards along the path, I came to flat ground on a shoulder of the hill. This was the limit I would have expected a tiger shot through the body to have travelled, so I approached the flat ground, on which there was a heavy growth of bracken and scattered bushes, very cautiously.

A tiger that has made up its mind to avenge an injury is the most terrifying animal to be met with in an Indian jungle. The tigress had a very recent injury to avenge and she had demonstrated—by striking down six goats and by springing and dashing away when I fired at her—that the leg wound she had received five days before was no handicap to rapid movement. I felt sure, therefore, that as soon as she became aware that I was following her and she considered that I was within her reach, she would launch an all-out attack on me, which I would possibly have to meet with a single bullet. Drawing back the bolt of the rifle, I examined the cartridge very carefully and satisfied that it was one of a fresh lot I had recently got from Manton in Calcutta, I replaced it in the chamber, put back the bolt, and threw off the safety catch.

The path ran through the bracken, which was waist high and which met over it. The blood trail led along the path into the bracken, and the tigress might be lying up on the path or on the right or the left-hand side of it. So I approached the bracken foot by foot and looking straight ahead for, on these occasions, it is unwise to keep turning the head, when I was within three yards of the bracken I saw a movement a yard from the path on the right. It was the tigress gathering herself together for a spring. Wounded and starving though she was, she was game to fight it out. Her spring, however, was never launched, for, as she rose, my first bullet raked her from end to end, and the second bullet broke her neck.

Days of pain and strain on an empty stomach left me now trembling in every limb, and I had great difficulty in reaching the spot where the path bent back at an acute angle and where, but for the chance dropping of a rhododendron seed, I would have ended my life on the rocks, below.

The entire population of the village, plus my own men, were gathered on the saddle of the hill and on either side of it, and I had hardly raised my hat to wave when, shouting at the top of their voices, the men and boys came swarming down. My six Garhwalis were the first to arrive. Congratulations over, the tigress was lashed to a pole and six of the proudest Garhwalis in Kumaon carried the Talla Des man-eater in triumph to Talla Kote village. Here the tigress was laid down on a bed of straw for the women and children to see, while I went back to my tent for my first solid meal in many weeks. An hour later with a crowd of people around me, I skinned the tigress.

My first bullet, a ·275 soft-nose with split nickel case fired on 7 April, was bushed and firmly fixed in the ball-and-socket joint of the tigress's right shoulder. The second and third bullets, fired as she was falling through the air and climbing up the hill, had missed her. The fourth, fired on 12 April, had gone clean through without striking any bones, and the fifth and sixth had killed her. From her right foreleg and shoulder I found some twenty porcupine quills, ranging in length from two to six inches, which were firmly embedded in muscle and were undoubtedly the cause of the tigress's having become a man-eater.

I spent the following day in partly drying the skin, and three days later I was safely back in my home with my bad time behind me. Baynes very kindly sent for Dungar Singh and his brother, and at a public function at Almora thanked them for the help they had given me and presented them with my token of gratitude.

A week after my return to Naini Tal, Sir Malcolm Hailey gave me an introduction to Colonel Dick, an ear specialist, who treated me for three months in his hospital in Lahore and restored my hearing sufficiently for me to associate with my fellow men without embarrassment, and gave me back the joy of hearing music and the song of birds.

The Fish of My Dreams

I was returning one day towards the latter end of March, after visiting a village on the Kedarnath pilgrim route, when, as I approached a spot where the road runs close alongside the Mandakini river, and where there is a water fall ten to twelve feet high, I saw a number of men sitting on the rock at the head of the fall on the far side of the river, armed with a triangular net attached to a long bamboo pole. The roar of the water prevented conversation, so leaving the road I sat down on the rocks on my side of the fall, to have a rest and a smoke—for I had walked far that day—and to see what the men were doing.

Presently one of the men got to his feet, and as he pointed down excitedly into the foaming white water at the foot of the fall, two of his companions manning the long pole held the triangular net close to the fall. A large shoal of mahseer fish, varying in size from five to fifty pounds, were attempting to leap the fall. One of these fish, about ten pounds in weight, leapt clear of the fall and when falling back was expertly caught in the net. After the fish had been extracted and placed in a basket, the net was again held out close to the fall. I watched the sport for about an hour, during which time the men caught four fish, all about the same size—ten pounds.

On my previous visit to Rudraprayag I had been informed by the chowkidar in charge of the Inspection Bungalow that there was good fishing in the spring—before the snow-water came down—in both the Alaknanda and Mandakini rivers, so I had come armed on this my second visit with a fourteen-foot split cane salmon rod, a silex reel with 250 yards of line, a few stout traces, and an assortment of home-made brass spoons varying in size from one to two inches.

The following morning—as no news had come in of the man-eater—I set off for the waterfall with my rod and tackle.

No fish were leaping the fall as they had been doing the previous day, and the men on the far side of the river were sitting in a group round a small fire smoking a hookah which was passing from hand to hand. They watched me with interest.

Below the waterfall was a pool thirty to forty yards wide,

flanked on both sides by a wall of rock, and about 200 yards long, 100 yards of which was visible from where I stood at the head of the pool. The water in this beautiful and imposing pool was crystal-clear.

The rock face at the head of the pool rose sheer up out of the water to a height of twelve feet, and after keeping at this height for twenty yards, sloped gradually upwards to a height of a hundred feet. It was not possible to get down to water level anywhere on my side of the pool, nor would it be possible, or profitable, to follow a fish—assuming that I hooked one—along the bank, for at the top of the high ground there were trees and bushes, and at the tail of the pool the river cascaded down in a foaming torrent to its junction with the Alaknanda. To land a fish in this pool would be a difficult and a hazardous task, but the crossing of that bridge could be deferred until the fish had been hooked—and I had not yet put together my rod.

On my side of the pool the water—shot through with millions of small bubbles—was deep, and from about half-way across a shingle bottom was showing, over which four to six feet of water was flowing. Above this shingle bottom, every stone and pebble of which was visible in the clear water, a number of fish, ranging in size from three to ten pounds, were slowly moving upstream.

As I watched these fish, standing on the rocks twelve feet above the water with a two-inch spoon mounted with a single strong treble hook in my hand, a flight of fingerlings flashed out of the deep water and went skimming over the shingle bottom, hotly pursued by three big mahseer. Using the good salmon rod as friend Hardy had never intended that it should be used—and as it had been used on many previous occasions—I slung the spoon out, and in my eagerness over-estimated the distance, with the result that the spoon struck the rock on the far side of the pool, about two feet above the water. The falling of the spoon into the water coincided with the arrival of the fingerlings at the rock, and the spoon had hardly touched the water, when it was taken by the leading mahseer.

Striking with a long line from an elevated position entails a very heavy strain, but my good rod stood the strain, and the strong treble hook was firmly fixed in the mahseer's mouth. For a moment or two the fish did not appear to realize what had happened as, standing perpendicularly in the water with his white belly towards me, he shook his head from side to side, and then, possibly frightened by the dangling spoon striking against his head, he gave a mighty splash and went tearing downstream, scattering in all directions the smaller fish that were lying on the shingle bottom.

In his first run the mahseer ripped a hundred yards of line off the reel, and after a moment's check carried on for another fifty yards. There was plenty of line still on the reel, but the fish had now gone round the bend and was getting dangerously near the tail of the pool. Alternately easing and tightening the strain on the line, I eventually succeeded in turning his head upstream, and having done so, very gently pulled him round the bend, into the hundred yards of water I was overlooking.

Just below me a projection of rock had formed a backwater, and into this backwater the fish, after half an hour's game fight, permitted himself to be drawn.

I had now very definitely reached my bridge and had just regretfully decided that, as there was no way of crossing it, the fish would have to be cut adrift, when a shadow fell across the rock beside me. Peering over the rock into the backwater, the new arrival remarked that it was a very big fish, and in the same breath asked what I was going to do about it. When I told him that it would not be possible to draw the fish up the face of the rock, and that therefore the only thing to do was to cut it free, he said, 'Wait, Sahib, I will fetch my brother.' His brother—a long and lanky stripling with dancing eyes—had quite evidently been cleaning out a cow shed when summoned, so telling him to go upstream and wash himself lest he should slip on the smooth rock, I held council with the elder man.

Starting from where we were standing, a crack, a few inches wide, ran irregularly down the face of the rock, ending a foot above the water in a ledge some six inches wide. The plan we finally agreed on was that the stripling—who presently returned with his arms and legs glistening with water—should go down to the ledge, while the elder brother went down the crack far enough to get hold of the stripling's left hand, while I lay on the rock holding the elder brother's other hand. Before embarking on the plan I asked the brothers whether they knew how to handle a fish and whether they could swim, and received the laughing answer that they had handled fish and swum in the river from childhood.

The snag in the plan was that I could not hold the rod and at the same time make a link in the chain. However, some risk had to be taken, so I put the rod down and held the line in my hand, and when the brothers had taken up position I sprawled on the rock and, reaching down, got hold of the elder brother's hand. Then very gently I drew the fish towards the rock, holding the line alternately with my left hand and with my teeth. There was no question that the stripling knew how to handle a fish, for before the fish had touched the rock, he had inserted his thumb into one side of the gills and his fingers into the other, getting a firm grip on the fish's throat. Up to this point the fish had been quite amenable, but on having its throat seized, it lashed out, and for seconds it appeared that the three of us would go headlong into the river.

Both brothers were bare-footed, and when I had been relieved of the necessity of holding the line and was able to help with both hands, they turned and, facing the rock, worked their way up with their toes, while I pulled lustily from on top.

When the fish at last had been safely landed, I asked the brothers if they ate fish, and on receiving their eager answer that they most certainly did, when they could get any, I told them I would give them the fish we had just landed—a mahseer in grand condition weighing a little over thirty pounds—if they would help me to land another fish for my men. To this they very readily agreed.

The treble had bitten deep into the leathery underlip of the mahseer, and as I cut it out, the brothers watched interestedly. When the hook was free, they asked if they might have a look at it. Three hooks in one, such a thing had never been seen in their village. The bit of bent brass of course acted as a sinker. With what were the hooks baited? Why should fish want to eat brass? And was it really brass, or some kind of hardened bait? When the spoon, and the trace with its three swivels, had been commented on and marvelled at, I made the brothers sit down and watch while I set about catching the second fish.

The biggest fish in the pool were at the foot of the fall, but here in the foaming white water, in addition to mahseer were some very big goonch, a fish that takes a spoon of dead bait very readily, and which is responsible for 90 per cent of the tackle lost in our hill rivers through its annoying habit of diving to the bottom of the pool when hooked and getting its head under a rock from where it is always difficult, and often impossible, to dislodge it.

No better spot than the place from where I had made my first cast was available, so here I again took up my position, with rod in hand and spoon held ready for casting.

The fish on the shingle bottom had been disturbed while I was playing the mahseer and by our subsequent movements on the face of the rock but were now beginning to return, and presently an exclamation from the brothers, and an excited pointing of fingers, drew my attention to a big fish downstream where the shingle bottom ended and the deep water began. Before I was able to make a cast, the fish turned and disappeared in the deep water, but a little later it reappeared, and as it came into the shallow water I made a cast, but owing to the line being wet the cast fell short. The second cast was beautifully placed and beautifully timed, the spoon striking the water exactly where I wanted it to. Waiting for a second to give the spoon time to sink, I started to wind in the line, giving the spoon just the right amount of spin, and as I drew it along in little jerks, the mahseer shot forward, and next moment, with the hook firmly fixed in his mouth, jumped clean out of the water, fell back with a great splash, and went madly downstream, much to the excitement of the spectators, for the men on the far bank had been watching the proceedings as intently as the brothers.

As the reel spun round and the line paid out, the brothers—now standing one on either side of me—urged me not to let the fish go down the run at the trail of the pool. Easier said than done, for it is not possible to stop the first mad rush of a mahseer of any size without risking certain break, or the tearing away of the hook-hold. Our luck was in, or else the fish feared the run, for when there was less than fifty yards of line on the reel he checked, and though he continued to fight gamely he was eventually drawn round the bend, and into the little backwater at the foot of the rock.

The landing of this second fish was not as difficult as the landing of the first had been, for we each knew our places on the rock and exactly what to do.

Both fish were the same length, but the second was a little heavier than the first, and while the elder brother set off in triumph for his village with his fish carried over his shoulder—threaded on a grass cable he had made—the stripling begged to be allowed to accompany me back to the Inspection Bungalow, and to carry both my fish and my rod. Having in the days of long ago been a boy myself, and having had a brother who fished, there was no need for the stripling when making his request to have said, 'If you will let me carry both the fish and the rod, and will walk a little distance behind me, Sahib, all the people who see me on the road, and in the bazaar, will think that I have caught this great fish, the like of which they have never seen.'

The Scourge of Champawat

I was shooting with Eddie Knowles in Malani when I first heard of the tiger which later received official recognition as the 'Champawat man-eater'.

Eddie, who will long be remembered in this province as a sportsman *par excellence* and the possessor of an inexhaustible fund of shikar yarns, was one of those few, and very fortunate, individuals who possess the best of everything in life. His rifle was without equal in accuracy and striking power, and while one of his brothers was the best gunshot in India, another brother was the best tennis player in the Indian Army. When therefore Eddie informed me that his brother-in-law, the best shikari in the world, had been deputed by the Government to shoot the Champawat man-eater, it was safe to assume that a very definite period had been put to the animal's activities.

The tiger, however, for some inexplicable reason, did not die, and was causing the Government a great deal of anxiety when I visited Naini Tal four years later. Rewards were offered, special shikaris employed, and parties of Gurkhas sent out from the depot in Almora. Yet, in spite of these measures, the toll of the human victims continued to mount alarmingly.

The tigress, for such the animal turned out to be, had arrived in Kumaon as a full-fledged man-eater, from Nepal, from whence she had been driven out by a body of armed Nepalese after she had killed 200 human beings, and during the four years she had been operating in Kumaon had added 234 to this number.

This is how matters stood, when shortly after my arrival in Naini Tal I received a visit from Berthoud. Berthoud, who was

Deputy Commissioner of the Naini Tal at that time, and who after his tragic death now lies buried in an obscure grave in Haldwani, was a man who was loved and respected by all who knew him, and it is not surprising therefore that when he told me of the trouble the man-eater was giving the people of his district, and the anxiety it was causing him, he took my promise with him that I would start for Champawat immediately on receipt of news of the next human kill.

Two conditions I made, however: one that the Government rewards be cancelled, and the other, that the special shikaris, and regulars from Almora, be withdrawn. My reasons for making these conditions need no explanation for I am sure all sportsmen share my aversion to being classed as a reward-hunter and are as anxious as I am to avoid the risk of being accidentally shot. These conditions were agreed to, and a week later Berthoud paid me an early morning visit and informed me that news had been brought in during the night by runners that a woman had been killed by the man-eater at Pali, a village between Dabidhura and Dhunaghat.

In anticipation of a start at short notice, I had engaged six men to carry my camp kit, and leaving after breakfast, we did a march the first day of seventeen miles to Dhari. Breakfasting at Mornaula next morning, we spent the night at Dabidhura, and arrived at Pali the following evening, five days after the woman had been killed.

The people of the village, numbering some fifty men, women and children, were in a state of abject terror, and though the sun was still up when I arrived, I found the entire population inside their homes behind locked doors, and it was not until my men had made a fire in the courtyard and I was sitting down to a cup of tea that a door here and there was cautiously opened, and the frightened inmates emerged.

I was informed that for five days no one had gone beyond their own doorsteps—the insanitary condition of the courtyard testified to the truth of this statement—that food was running short, and that the people would starve if the tiger was not killed or driven away.

That the tiger was still in the vicinity was apparent. For three nights it had been heard calling on the road, distant a hundred yards from the houses, and that very day it had been seen on the cultivated land at the lower end of the village.

The Headman of the village very willingly placed a room at my disposal, but as there were eight of us to share it, and the only door it possessed opened on to the insanitary courtyard, I elected to spend the night in the open.

After a scratch meal which had to do duty for dinner, I saw my men safely shut into the room and myself took up a position on the side of the road, with my back to the tree. The villagers said the tiger was in the habit of perambulating along this road, and as the moon was at the full I thought there was a chance of getting a shot—provided I saw it first.

I had spent many nights in the jungle looking for game, but this was the first time I had ever spent a night looking for a man-eater. The length of road immediately in front of me was brilliantly lit by the moon, but to the right and left the overhanging trees cast dark shadows, and when the night wind agitated the branches and the shadows moved, I saw a dozen tigers advancing on me, and bitterly regretted the impulse that had induced me to place myself at the man-eater's mercy. I lacked the courage to return to the village and admit I was too frightened to carry out my self-imposed task, and with teeth chattering, as much from fear as from cold, I sat out the long night. As the grey dawn was lighting up the snowy range which I was facing, I rested my head on my drawn-up knees, and it was in this position my men an hour later found me—fast asleep; of the tiger I had neither heard nor seen anything.

Back in the village I tried to get the men—who I could see were very surprised I had survived the night—to take me to the places where the people of the village had from time to time been killed, but this they were unwilling to do. From the courtyard they pointed out the direction in which the kills had taken place; the last kill—the one that had brought me to the spot—I was told, had taken place round the shoulder of the hill to the west of the village. The women and girls, some twenty in number, who had been out collecting oak leaves for the cattle when the unfortunate woman had been killed, were eager to give me details of the occurrence. It appeared that the party had set out two hours before midday and, after going half a mile, had climbed into trees to cut leaves. The victim and two other women had selected a tree growing on the edge of a ravine, which I subsequently found was about four feet deep and ten to twelve feet wide. Having cut all the leaves she needed, the woman was climbing down from the tree when the tiger, who had approached unseen, stood up on its hind legs and caught her by the foot. Her hold was torn from the branch she was letting herself down by, and, pulling her into the ravine, the tiger released her foot, and while she was struggling to rise, caught her by the throat. After killing her it sprang up the side of the ravine and disappeared with her into some heavy undergrowth.

All this had taken place a few feet from the two women on the tree, and had been witnessed by the entire party. As soon as the tiger and its victim were out of sight, the terror-stricken women and girls ran back to the village. The men had just come in for their midday meal and, when all were assembled and armed with drums, metal cooking-pots—anything in fact that would produce a noise—the rescue party set off, the men leading and the women bringing up the rear.

Arrived at the ravine in which the woman had been killed, the very important question of 'what next?' was being debated when the tiger interrupted the proceedings by emitting a loud roar from the bushes thirty yards away. As one man the party turned and fled helter-skelter back to the village. When breath had been regained, accusations were made against one another of having been the first to run and cause the stampede. Words ran high until it was suggested that if no one was afraid and all were as brave as they claimed to be, why not go back and rescue the woman without loss of more time? The suggestion was adopted, and three times the party got as far as the ravine. On the third occasion the one man who was armed with a gun fired it off, and brought the tiger roaring out of the bushes; after this the attempted rescue was very wisely abandoned. On my asking the gun man why he had not discharged his piece into the bushes instead of up into the air, he said the tiger was already greatly enraged and that if by any mischance he had hit it, it would undoubtedly have killed him.

For three hours that morning I walked round the village looking for tracks and hoping, and at the same time dreading, to meet the tiger. At one place in the dark heavily wooded ravine, while I was skirting some bushes, a covey of kaleej pheasants fluttered screaming out of them, and I thought my heart had stopped beating for good.

My men had cleared a spot under a walnut tree for my meals, and after breakfast the Headman of the village asked me to mount guard while the wheat crop was being cut. He said that if the crop was not harvested in my presence, it would not be harvested at all, for the people were too frightened to leave their homes. Half an hour later the entire population of the village, assisted by my men, were hard at work while I stood on guard with a loaded rifle. By evening the crop from five large fields had been gathered, leaving only two small patches close to the houses, which the Headman said he would have no difficulty in dealing with the next day.

The sanitary condition of the village had been much improved, and a second room for my exclusive use was placed at my disposal; and that night, with thorn bushes securely wedged in the doorway to admit ventilation and exclude the man-eater, I made up for the sleep I had lost the previous night.

My presence was beginning to put new heart into the people and they were moving about more freely, but I had not yet gained their confidence sufficiently to renew my request of being shown round the jungle, to which I attached some importance. These people knew every foot of the ground for miles round, and could, if they wished, show me where I was most likely to find the tiger, or in any case, where I could see its pug marks. That the man-eater was a tiger was an established fact, but it was not known whether the animal was young or old, a male or a female, and this information, which I believed would help me to get in touch with it, I could only ascertain by examining its pug marks.

After an early tea that morning, I announced that I wanted meat for my men and asked the villagers if they could direct me to where I could shoot a ghooral. The village was situated on the top of a long ridge running east and west, and just below the road on which I had spent the night the hill fell steeply away to the north in a series of grassy slopes; on these slopes I was told ghooral were plentiful, and several men volunteered to show me over the ground. I was careful not to show my pleasure at this offer and, selecting three men, I set out, telling the Headman that if I found the ghooral as plentiful as he said they were, I would shoot two for the village in addition to shooting one for my men.

Crossing the road we went down a very steep ridge, keeping a sharp look-out to right and left, but saw nothing. Half a mile down the hill the ravines converged, and from their junction here was a good view of the rocky and grass-covered slope to the right. I had been sitting for some minutes, scanning the slope, with my back to a solitary pine which grew at this spot, when a movement high up on the hill caught my eye. When the movement was repeated I saw it was a ghooral flapping its ears; the animal was standing in grass and only its head was visible. The men had not seen the movement, and as the head was now stationary and blended in with its surroundings it was not possible to point it out to them. Giving them a general idea of the animal's positions I made them sit down and watch while I took a shot. I was armed with an old Martini Henry rifle, a weapon that atoned for its vicious kick by being dead accurate—up to any range. The distance was as near 200 yards as made no matter and, lying down and resting the rifle on a convenient pine root, I took careful aim, and fired.

The smoke from the black powder cartridge obscured my view and the men said nothing had happened and that I had probably fired at the rock, or a bunch of dead leaves. Retaining my position I reloaded the rifle and presently saw the grass, a little below where I had fired, moving, and the hind quarters of the ghooral appeared. When the whole animal was free of the grass it started to roll over and over, gaining momentum as it came down the steep hill. When it was half-way down it disappeared into heavy grass, and disturbed two ghooral that had been lying up there. Sneezing their alarm call, the two animals dashed out of the grass and went bounding up the hill. The range was shorter now, and, adjusting the leaf sight, I waited until the bigger of the two slowed down and put a bullet through its back, and as the other one turned, and made off diagonally across the hill, I shot it through the shoulder.

On occasions one is privileged to accomplish the seemingly impossible. Lying in an uncomfortable position and shooting up to an angle of sixty degrees at a range of 200 yards at the small white mark on the ghooral's throat, there did not appear to be one chance in a million of the shot coming off, and yet the heavy lead bullet driven by black powder had not been deflected by a hair's breadth and had gone true to its mark, killing the animal instantaneously. Again, on the steep hillside which was broken up by small ravines and jutting rocks, the dead animal had slipped and rolled straight to the spot where its two companions were lying up; and before it had cleared the patch of grass the two companions in their turn were slipping and rolling down the hill. As the three dead animals landed in the ravine in front of us it was amusing to observe the surprise and delight of the men who never before had seen a rifle in action. All thought of the man-eater was for the time being forgotten as they scrambled down into the ravine to retrieve the bag.

The expedition was a great success in more ways than one; for in addition to providing a ration of meat for everyone, it gained me the confidence of the entire village. Shikar yarns, as everyone knows, never lose anything in repetition, and while the ghooral were being skinned and divided up, the three men who had accompanied me gave full rein to their imagination, and from where I sat in the open, having breakfast, I could hear the exclamations of the assembled crowd when they were told that the ghooral had been shot at a range of over a mile, and that the magic bullets used had not only killed the animals—like that—but had also drawn them to the sahib's feet.

After the midday meal the Headman asked me where I wanted to go, and how many men I wished to take with me. From the eager throng of men who pressed round I selected two of my late companions, and with them to guide me set off to visit the scene of the last human tragedy.

The people of our hills are Hindus and cremate their dead, and when one of their number had been carried off by a man-eater it is incumbent on the relatives to recover some portion of the body for cremation even if it be only a few splinters of bone. In the case of this woman the cremation ceremony was yet to be performed, and as we started out, the relatives requested us to bring back any portion of the body we might find.

From early boyhood I have made a hobby of reading, and interpreting jungle signs. In the present case I had the account of the eye-witnesses who were present when the woman was killed, but eye-witnesses are not always reliable, whereas jungle signs are a true record of all that has transpired. On arrival at the spot a glance at the ground showed me that the tiger could only have approached the tree one way, without being seen, and that was up the ravine. Entering the ravine a hundred yards below the tree, and working up, I found the pug marks of the tiger in some fine earth that had sifted down between two big rocks; these pug marks showed the animal to be a tigress, a little past her prime. Further up the ravine, and some ten yards from the tree, the tigress had lain down behind a rock, presumably to wait for the woman to climb down from the tree. The victim had been the first to cut all the leaves she needed, and as she was letting herself down by a branch some two inches in diameter the tigress had crept forward and, standing up on her hind legs, had caught the woman by the foot and pulled her down into the ravine. The branch showed the desperation with which the unfortunate woman had clung to it, for adhering to the rough oak bark where the branch, and eventually the leaves, had slipped through her grasp were strands of skin which had been torn from the palms of her hands and fingers. Where the tigress had killed the woman there were signs of a struggle and a big patch of dried blood; from here the blood trail, now dry but distinctly visible, led across the ravine and up the opposite bank. Following the blood trail from where it left the ravine we found the place in the bushes where the tigress had eaten her kill.

It is a popular belief that man-eaters do not eat the head, hands, and feet of the human victims. This is incorrect. Man-eaters, if not disturbed, eat everything—including the blood-soaked clothes, as I found on one occasion…

On the present occasion we found the woman's clothes, and a few pieces of bone which we wrapped up in the clean cloth we had brought for the purpose. Pitifully little as these remains were, they would suffice for the cremation ceremony which would ensure the ashes of the high-caste woman reaching Mother Ganges.

After tea I visited the scene of yet another tragedy. Separated from the main village by the public road was a small holding of a few acres. The owner of this holding had built himself a hut on the hillside just above the road. The man's wife, and the mother of his two children, a boy and a girl aged four and six respectively, was the younger of two sisters. These two sisters were out cutting grass one day on the hill above the hut when the tigress suddenly appeared and carried off the elder sister. For a hundred yards the younger woman ran after the tigress brandishing her sickle and screaming at the tigress to let her sister go, and take her instead. This incredible act of heroism was witnessed by the people in the main village. After carrying the dead woman for a hundred yards the tigress put her down and turned on her pursuer. With a loud roar it sprang at the brave woman who, turning, raced down the hillside, across the road, and into the village, evidently with the intention of telling the people what they, unknown to her, had already witnessed. The woman's incoherent noises were at the time attributed to loss of breath, fear, and excitement, and it was not until the rescue party that had set out with all speed had returned, unsuccessful, that it was found the woman had lost her power of speech. I was told this tale in the village, and when I climbed the path to the two-roomed hut where the woman was engaged in washing clothes, she had then been dumb a twelvemonth.

Except for a strained look in her eyes the dumb woman appeared to be quite normal and, when I stopped to speak to her and tell her I had come to try and shoot the tiger that had killed her sister, she put her hands together and stooping down touched my feet, making me feel a wretched impostor. True, I had come with the avowed object of shooting the man-eater, but with an animal that had the reputation of never killing twice in the same locality, never returning to a kill, and whose domain extended over an area of many hundred square miles, the chance of my accomplishing my object was about as good as finding a needle in two haystacks.

Plans in plenty I had made way back in Naini Tal; one I had already tried and wild horses would not induce me to try it again, and the others—now that I was on the ground—were just as unattractive. Further there was no one I could ask for advice, for this was the first man-eater that had ever been known in Kumaon; and yet something would have to be done. So for the next three days I wandered through the jungles from sunrise to sunset, visiting all the places for miles round where the villagers told me there was a chance of my seeing the tigress.

I would like to interrupt my tale here for a few minutes to refute a rumour current throughout the hills that on this, and on several subsequent occasions, I assumed the dress of a hill woman and, going into the jungle, attracted the man-eaters to myself and killed them with either a sickle or an axe. All I have ever done in the matter of alteration of dress has been to borrow a sari and with it draped round me cut grass, or climbed into trees and cut leaves, and in no case has the ruse proved successful; though on two occasions—to my knowledge—man-eaters have stalked the tree I was on, taking cover, on one occasion behind a rock and on the other behind a fallen tree, and giving me no opportunity of shooting them.

To continue. As the tigress now appeared to have left this locality I decided, much to the regret of the people of Pali, to move to Champawat fifteen miles due east of Pali. Making an early start, I breakfasted at Dhunaghat, and completed the journey to Champawat by sunset. The roads in this area were considered very unsafe, and men only moved from village to village or to the bazaars in large parties. After leaving Dhunaghat, my party of eight was added to by men from villages adjoining the road, and we arrived at Champawat thirty strong. Some of the men who joined me had been in a party of twenty men who had visited Champawat two months earlier, and they told me the following very pitiful story.

'The road for a few miles on this side of Champawat runs along the south face of the hill, parallel to, and about fifty yards above the valley. Two months ago a party of twenty of us men were on our way to the bazaar at Champawat, and as we were going along this length of the road at about midday, we were startled by hearing the agonized cries of a human being coming from the valley below. Huddled together on the edge of the road we cowered in fright as these cries drew nearer and nearer, and presently into view came a tiger, carrying a naked woman. The woman's hair was trailing on the ground on one side of the tiger, and her feet on the other—the tiger was holding her by the small of the back—and she was beating her chest and calling alternately on God and man to help her. Fifty yards from, and in clear view of us, the tiger passed with its burden, and when the cries had died away in the distance we continued on our way.'

'And you twenty men did nothing?'

'No, Sahib, we did nothing for we were afraid, and what can men do when they are afraid? And further, even if we had been able to rescue the woman without angering the tiger and bringing misfortune on ourselves, it would have availed the woman nothing, for she was covered with blood and would of a surety have died of her wounds.'

I subsequently learnt that the victim belonged to a village near Champawat, and that she had been carried off by the tiger while collecting dry sticks. Her companions had run back to the village and raised an alarm, and just as a rescue party was starting, the twenty frightened men arrived. As these men knew the direction in which the tiger had gone with its victim, they joined the party, and can best carry on the story.

'We were fifty or sixty strong when we set out to rescue the woman, and several of the party were armed with guns. A furlong from where the sticks collected by the woman were lying, and from where she had been carried off, we found her torn clothes. Thereafter the men started beating their drums and firing off their guns, and in this way we proceeded for more than a mile right up to the head of the valley, where we found the woman, who was little more than a girl, lying dead on a great slab of rock. Beyond licking off all the blood and making her body clean the tiger had not touched her, and, there being no woman in our party, we men averted our faces as we wrapped her body in the loincloths which one and another gave, for she looked as she lay on her back as one who sleeps, and would waken in shame when touched.'

With experiences such as these to tell and retell through the long night watches behind fast-shut doors, it is little wonder that the character and outlook on life of people living year after year in a man-eater country should change, and that one coming from the outside should feel that he had stepped right into a world of stark realities and the rule of the tooth and claw, which forced man in the reign of the sabre-toothed tiger to shelter in dark caverns. I was young and unexperienced in those far-off Champawat days, but, even so, the conviction I came to after a brief sojourn in that stricken land, that there is no more terrible thing than to live and have one's being under the shadow of a man-eater, has been strengthened by thirty-two years' subsequent experience.

The Tahsildar of Champawat, to whom I had been given letters of introduction, paid me a visit that night at the Dak Bungalow where I was putting up, and suggested I should move next day to a bungalow a few miles away, in the vicinity of which many human beings had been killed.

Early next morning, accompanied by the Tahsildar, I set out for the bungalow, and while I was having breakfast on the verandah two men arrived with news that a cow had been killed by a tiger in a village ten miles away. The Tahsildar excused himself to attend to some urgent work at Champawat, and said he would return to the bungalow in the evening and stay the night with me. My guides were good walkers, and as the track went downhill most of the way we covered the ten miles in record time. Arrived at the village I was taken to a cattleshed in which I found a week-old calf, killed and partly eaten by a leopard. Not having the time or the inclination to shoot the leopard I rewarded my guides, and retraced my steps to the bungalow. Here I found the Tahsildar had not returned, and as there was still an hour or more of daylight left I went out with the chowkidar of the bungalow to look at a place where he informed me a tiger was in the habit of drinking; this place I found to be the head of the spring which supplied the garden with irrigation water. In the soft earth round the spring were tiger pug marks several days old, but these tracks were quite different from the pug marks I had seen, and carefully examined, in the ravine in which the woman from Pali village had been killed.

On returning to the bungalow I found the Tahsildar was back, and as we sat on the verandah I told him of my day's experience. Expressing regret at my having had to go so far on a wild-goose chase, he rose, saying that as he had a long way to go he must start at once. This announcement caused me no little surprise, for twice that day he had said he would stay the night with me. It was not the question of his staying the night that concerned me, but the risk he was taking; however, he was deaf to all my arguments and, as he stepped off the verandah into the dark night, with only one man following him carrying a smoky lantern which gave a mere glimmer of light, to do a walk of four miles in a locality in which men only moved in large parties in daylight, I took off my hat to a very brave man. Having watched him out of sight I turned and entered the bungalow.

I have a tale to tell of that bungalow but I will not tell it here, for this is a book of jungle stories, and tales 'beyond the laws of nature' do not consort well with such stories.

~

I spent the following morning in going round the very extensive fruit orchard and tea garden and in having a bath at the spring, and at about midday the Tahsildar, much to my relief, returned safely from Champawat.

I was standing talking to him while looking down a long sloping hill with a village surrounded by cultivated land in the distance, when I saw a man leave the village and start up the hill in our direction. As the man drew nearer I saw he was alternately running and walking, and was quite evidently the bearer of important news. Telling the Tahsildar I would return in a few minutes, I set off at a run down the hill, and when the man saw me coming he sat down to take breath. As soon as I was near enough to hear him he called out, 'Come quickly, Sahib, the man-eater has just killed a girl.' 'Sit still,' I called back, and turning, ran up to the bungalow. I passed the news on to the Tahsildar while I was getting a rifle and some cartridges, and asked him to follow me down to the village.

The man who had come for me was one of those exasperating individuals whose legs and tongue cannot function at the same time. When he opened his mouth he stopped dead, and when he started to run his mouth closed; so telling him to shut his mouth and lead the way, we ran in silence down the hill.

At the village an excited crowd of men, women, and children awaited us and, as usually happens on these occasions, all started to talk at the same time. One man was vainly trying to quieten the babel. I led him aside and asked him to tell me what had happened. Pointing to some scattered oak trees on a gentle slope a furlong or so from the village, he said a dozen people were collecting dry sticks under the trees when a tiger suddenly appeared and caught one of their number, a girl sixteen or seventeen years of age. The rest of the parties had run back to the village, and as it was known that I was staying at the bungalow, a man had immediately been dispatched to inform me.

The wife of the man I was speaking to had been of the party, and she now pointed out the tree, on the shoulder of the hill, under which the girl had been taken. None of the party had looked back to see if the tiger was carrying away its victim and, if so, in which direction it had gone.

Instructing the crowd not to make a noise, and to remain in the village until I returned, I set off in the direction of the tree. The ground here was quite open and it was difficult to conceive how an animal the size of a tiger could have approached twelve people unseen, and its presence not detected, until attention had been attracted by the choking sound made by the girl.

The spot where the girl had been killed was marked by a pool of blood and near it, in vivid contrast to the crimson pool, was a broken necklace of brightly coloured blue beads which the girl had been wearing. From this spot the track led up and round the shoulder of the hill.

The track of the tigress was clearly visible. On one side of it were great splashes of blood where the girl's head had hung down, and on the other side the trail of her feet. Half a mile up the hill I found the girl's sari, and on the brow of the hill her skirt. Once again the tigress was carrying a naked woman, but mercifully on this occasion her burden was dead.

On the brow of the hill the track led through a thicket of blackthorn, on the thorns of which long strands of the girl's raven-black hair had caught. Beyond this was a bed of nettles through which the tigress had gone, and I was looking for a way round this obstruction when I heard footsteps behind me. Turning round I saw a man armed with a rifle coming towards me. I asked him why he had followed me when I had left instructions at the village that no one was to leave it. He said the Tahsildar had instructed him to accompany me, and that he was afraid to disobey orders. As he appeared determined to carry out his orders, and to argue the point would have meant the loss of valuable time, I told him to remove the heavy pair of boots he was wearing and, when he had hidden them under a bush, I advised him to keep close to me, and to keep a sharp look-out behind.

I was wearing a very thin pair of stockings, shorts, and a pair of rubber-soled shoes, and as there appeared to be no way round the nettles I followed the tigress through them—much to my discomfort.

Beyond the nettles the blood trail turned sharply to the left, and went straight down the very steep hill, which was densely clothed with bracken and ringals. A hundred yards down, the blood trail led into a narrow and very steep watercourse, down which the tigress had gone with some difficulty, as could be seen from the dislodged stones and earth. I followed this watercourse for five or six hundred yards, my companion getting more and more agitated the further we went. A dozen times he caught my arm and whispered—in a voice full of tears—that he could hear the tiger, either on one side or the other, or behind us. Halfway down the hill we came on a great pinnacle of rock some thirty feet high, and as the man had by now had all the man-eater hunting he could stand, I told him to climb the rock and remain on it until I returned. Very gladly he went up, and when he straddled the top and signalled to me that he was all right I continued on down the watercourse, which, after skirting round the rock, went straight down for a hundred yards to where it met a deep ravine coming down from the left. At the junction was a small pool, and as I approached it I saw patches of blood on my side of the water.

The tigress had carried the girl straight down on this spot, and my approach had disturbed her at her meal. Splinters of bone were scattered round the deep pug marks into which discoloured water was slowly seeping, and at the edge of the pool was an object which had puzzled me as I came down the watercourse, and which I now found was part of a human leg. In all the subsequent years I have hunted man-eaters, I have not seen anything as pitiful as that young comely leg—bitten off a little below the knee as clean as though severed by the stroke of an axe—out of which the warm blood was trickling.

While looking at the leg I had forgotten all about the tigress until I suddenly felt that I was in a great danger. Hurriedly grounding the butt of the rifle I put two fingers on the triggers, raising my head as I did so, and saw a little earth from the fifteen-foot bank in front of me, come rolling down the steep side and plop into the pool. I was new to this game of man-eater hunting or I should not have exposed myself to an attack in the way I had done. My prompt action in pointing the rifle upwards had possibly saved my life, and in stopping her spring, or in turning to get away, the tigress had dislodged the earth from the top of the bank.

The bank was too steep for scrambling, and the only way of getting up was to take it at a run. Going up the watercourse a short distance I sprinted down, took the pool in my stride, and got far enough up the other side to grasp a bush and pull myself on to the bank. A bed of Strobilanthes, the bent stalks of which were slowly regaining their upright position, showed where, and how recently, the tigress had passed, and a little further on under an overhanging rock I found where she had left her kill when she came to have a look at me.

Her tracks now—as she carried away the girl—led into a wilderness of rocks, some acres in extent, where the going was both difficult and dangerous. The cracks and chasms between the rocks were masked with ferns and blackberry vines, and a false step, which might easily have resulted in a broken limb, would have been fatal. Progress under these conditions was of necessity slow, and the tigress was taking advantage of it to continue her meal. A dozen times I found where she had rested and after each of these rests the blood trail became more distinct.

This was her 436th human kill and she was quite accustomed to being disturbed at her meals by rescue parties, but this, I think, was the first time she had been followed up so persistently and she now began to show her resentment by growling. To appreciate a tiger's growl to the full it is necessary to be situated as I then was—rocks all round with dense vegetation between, and the imperative necessity of testing each footstep to avoid falling headlong into unseen chasms and caves.

I cannot expect you who read this at your fireside to appreciate my feelings at the time. The sound of the growling and the expectation of an attack terrified me at the same time as it gave me hope. If the tigress lost her temper sufficiently to launch an attack, it would not only give me an opportunity of accomplishing the object for which I had come, but it would enable me to get even with her for all the pain and suffering she had caused.

The growling, however, was only a gesture, and when she found that instead of shooing me off it was bringing me faster on her heels, she abandoned it.

I had now been on her track for over four hours. Though I had repeatedly seen the undergrowth moving I had not seen so much as a hair of her hide, and a glance at the shadows climbing up the opposite hillside warned me it was time to retrace my steps if I was to reach the village before dark.

The late owner of the severed leg was a Hindu, and some portion of her would be needed for the cremation, so as I passed the pool I dug a hole in the bank and buried the leg where it would be safe from the tigress, and could be found when wanted.

My companion on the rock was very relieved to see me. My long absence, and the growling he had heard, had convinced him that the tigress had secured another kill and his difficulty, as he quite frankly admitted, was how he was going to get back to the village alone.

I thought when we were climbing down the watercourse that I knew of no more dangerous proceeding than walking in front of the nervous man carrying a loaded gun, but I changed my opinion when on walking behind him he slipped and fell, and I saw where the muzzle of his gun—a converted ·450 without a safety catch—was pointing. Since that day—except when accompanied by Ibbotson [My friend Sir William Ibbotson, lately Adviser to the Governor of the United Provinces and who had very recently been posted to Garhwal as Deputy Commissioner]—I have made it a hard and fast rule to go alone when hunting man-eaters, for if one's companion is unarmed it is difficult to protect him, and if he is armed, it is even more difficult to protect oneself.

Arrived at the crest of the hill, where the man had hidden his boots, I sat down to have a smoke and think out my plans for the morrow.

The tigress would finish what was left of the kill during the night, and would certainly lie among the rocks the next day.

On the ground she was on there was very little hope of my being able to stalk her, and if I disturbed her without getting a shot, she would probably leave the locality and I should lose touch with her. A beat therefore was the only thing to do, provided I could raise sufficient men.

I was sitting on the south edge of the great amphitheatre of hills, without a habitation of any kind in sight. A stream entering from the west had fretted its way down, cutting a deep valley right across the amphitheatre. To the east the stream had struck solid rock, and turning north had left the amphitheatre by a narrow gorge.

The hill in front of me, rising to a height of some 2,000 feet, was clothed in short grass with a pine tree dotted here and there, and the hill to the east was too precipitous for anything but a ghooral to negotiate. If I could collect sufficient men to man the entire length of the ridge from the stream to the precipitous hill, and get them to stir up the tigress, her most natural line of retreat would be through the narrow gorge.

Admittedly a very difficult beat, for the steep hillside facing north, on which I had left the tigress, was densely wooded and roughly three-quarters of a mile long and half-a-mile wide; however, if I could get the beaters to carry out instructions, there was a reasonable chance of my getting a shot.

The Tahsildar was waiting for me at the village. I explained the position to him, and asked him to take immediate steps to collect as many men as he could, and to meet me at the tree where the girl had been killed at ten o'clock the following morning. Promising to do his best, he left for Champawat, while I climbed the hill to the bungalow.

I was up at crack of dawn next morning, and after a substantial meal told my men to pack up and wait for me at Champawat, and went down to have another look at the ground I intended beating. I could find nothing wrong with the plans I had made, and an hour before my time I was at the spot where I had asked the Tahsildar to meet me.

That he would have a hard time in collecting the men I had no doubt, for the fear of the man-eater had sunk deep into the countryside and more than mild persuasion would be needed to make the men leave the shelter of their homes. At ten o'clock the Tahsildar and one man turned up, and thereafter the men came in twos, and threes and tens, until by midday 298 had collected.

The Tahsildar had let it be known that he would turn a blind eye towards all unlicensed firearms, and further that he would provide ammunition where required; and the weapons that were produced that day would have stocked a museum.

When the men were assembled and had received the ammunition they needed, I took them to the brow of the hill where the girl's skirt was lying, and pointing to a pine tree on the opposite hill that had been struck by lightning and stripped of bark, I told them to line themselves up along the ridge and, when they saw me wave a handkerchief from under the pine, those of them who were armed were to fire off their pieces, while the others beat drums, shouted, and rolled down rocks, and that no one was on any account to leave the ridge until I returned and personally collected him. When I was assured that all present had heard and understood my instructions, I set off with the Tahsildar, who said he would be safer with me than with the beaters whose guns would probably burst and cause many casualties.

Making a wide detour I crossed the upper end of the valley, gained the opposite hill, and made my way down to the blasted pine. From here the hill went steeply down and the Tahsildar, who had on a thin pair of patent leather shoes, said it was impossible for him to go any further. While he was removing his inadequate footgear to ease his blisters, the men on the ridge, thinking I had forgotten to give the pre-arranged signal, fired off their guns and set up a great shout. I was still 150 yards from the gorge, and that I did not break my neck a dozen times in covering this distance was due to my having been brought up on the hills, and being in consequence as sure-footed as a goat.

As I ran down the hill I noticed that there was a patch of green grass near the mouth of the gorge, and as there was no time to look round for a better place, I sat down in the grass, with my back to the hill down which I had just come. The grass was about two feet high and hid half my body, and if I kept perfectly still there was a good chance of my not being seen. Facing me was the hill that was being beaten, and the gorge that I hoped the tigress would make for was behind my left shoulder.

Pandemonium had broken loose on the ridge. Added to the fusillade of guns was the wild beating of drums and the shouting of hundreds of men, and when the din was at its worst, I caught sight of the tigress bounding down a grassy slope between two ravines to my right front, and about 300 yards away. She had only gone a short distance when the Tahsildar from his position under the pine let off both barrels of his shotgun. On hearing the shots the tigress whipped round and went straight back the way she had come and as she disappeared into thick cover I threw up my rifle and sent a despairing bullet after her.

The men on the ridge, hearing the three shots, not unnaturally concluded that the tigress had been killed. They emptied all their guns and gave a final yell, and I was holding my breath and listening for the screams that would herald the tigress's arrival on the ridge, when she suddenly broke cover to my left front and, taking the stream at a bound, came straight for the gorge. The ·500 modified cordite rifle, sighted at sea level, shot high at this altitude, and when the tigress stopped dead I thought the bullet had gone over her back, and that she had pulled up on finding her retreat cut off; as a matter of fact I had hit her all right, but a little far back. Lowering her head, she half turned towards me, giving me a beautiful shot at the point of her shoulder at a range of less than thirty yards. She flinched at this second shot but continued, with her ears laid flat and bared teeth, to stand her ground, while I sat with rifle to shoulder trying to think what it would be best for me to do when she charged, for the rifle was empty and I had no more cartridges. Three cartridges were all that I had brought with me, for I never thought I should get a chance of firing more than two shots, and the third cartridge was for an emergency.

Fortunately the wounded animal most unaccountably decided against a charge. Very slowly she turned, crossed the stream to her right, climbed over some fallen rocks, and found a narrow ledge that went diagonally up and across the face of the precipitous hill to where there was a great flat projecting rock. Where this rock joined the cliff a small bush had found roothold, and going up to it the tigress started to strip its branches. Throwing caution to the winds I shouted to the Tahsildar to bring me his gun. A long reply was shouted back, the only word of which I caught was 'feet'. Laying down my rifle I took the hill at a run, grabbed the gun out of the Tahsildar's hands and raced back.

As I approached the stream the tigress left the bush and came out on the protecting rock towards me. When I was within twenty feet of her I raised the gun and found to my horror that there was a gap of about three-eighths of an inch between the barrels and the breech-block. The gun had not burst when both barrels had been fired, and would probably not burst now, but there was danger of being blinded by a blow back. However, the risk would have to be taken, and, aligning the great blob of a bead that did duty as a sight on the tigress's open mouth, I fired. Maybe I bobbed, or maybe the gun was not capable of throwing the cylindrical bullet accurately for twenty feet; anyway, the missile missed the tigress's mouth and struck her on the right paw, from where I removed it later with my finger-nails. Fortunately she was at her last gasp, and the tap on the foot was sufficient to make her lurch forward. She came to rest with her head projecting over the side of the rock.

From the moment the tigress had broken cover in her attempt to get through the gorge I had forgotten the beaters, until I was suddenly reminded of their existence by hearing a shout, from a short distance up the hill, of 'There it is on the rock! Pull it down and let us hack it to bits.' I could not believe my ears when I heard 'hack it to bits', and yet I had heard aright, for others now had caught sight of the tigress and from all over the hillside the shout was being repeated.

The ledge by which the wounded animal had gained the projecting rock was fortunately on the opposite side from the beaters, and was just wide enough to permit my shuffling along it sideways. As I reached the rock and stepped over the tigress—hoping devoutly she was dead for I had not had time to carry out the usual test of pelting her with stones—the men emerged from the forest and came running across the open, brandishing guns, axes, rusty swords, and spears.

At the rock, which was twelve to fourteen feet in height, their advance was checked, for the outer face had been worn smooth by the stream when in spate and afforded no foothold even for their bare toes. The rage of the crowd on seeing their dread enemy was quite understandable, for there was not a man among them who had not suffered at her hands. One man, who appeared demented and was acting as ringleader, was shouting over and over again as he ran to and fro brandishing a sword, 'This is the shaitan that killed my wife and my two sons.' As happens with crowds, the excitement died down as suddenly as it had flared up, and to the credit of the man who had lost his wife and sons be it said that he was the first to lay down his weapon. He came near to the rock and said, 'We were mad, Sahib, when we saw our enemy, but the madness has now passed, and we ask you and the Tahsildar Sahib to forgive us.' Extracting the unspent cartridge, I laid the gun across the tigress and hung down by my hands and was assisted to the ground. When I showed the men how I had gained the rock the dead animal was very gently lowered and carried to an open spot, where all could crowd round and look at her.

When the tigress had stood on the rock looking down at me I had noticed that there was something wrong with her mouth, and on examining her now I found that the upper and lower canine teeth on the right side of her mouth were broken, the upper one in half, and the lower one right down to the bone. This permanent injury to her teeth—the result of a gunshot wound—had prevented her from killing her natural prey, and had been the cause of her becoming a man-eater.

The men begged me not to skin the tigress there, and asked me to let them have her until nightfall to carry through their villages, saying that if their womenfolk and children did not see her with their own eyes, they would not believe that their dread enemy was dead.

Two saplings were now cut and laid one on either side of the tigress, and with pugrees, waistbands and loincloths she was carefully and very securely lashed to them. When all was ready the saplings were manned and we moved to the foot of the precipitous hill; the men preferred to take the tigress up this hill, on the far side of which their villages lay, to going up the densely wooded hill which they had just beaten. Two human ropes were made by the simple expedient of the man behind taking a firm grip of the waistband, or other portion of clothing, of the man in front of him. When it was considered that the ropes were long and strong enough to stand the strain, they attached themselves to the saplings, and with men on either side to hold the feet of the bearers and give them foothold, the procession moved up the hill, looking for all the world like an army of ants carrying a beetle up the face of a wall. Behind the main army was a second and a smaller one—the Tahsildar being carried up. Had the ropes broken at any stage of that thousand-foot climb, the casualties would have been appalling, but the rope did not break. The men gained the crest of the hill and set off eastwards, singing on their triumphal march, while the Tahsildar and I turned west and made for Champawat.

Our way lay along the ridge and once again I stood among the blackthorn bushes on the thorns of which long tresses of the girl's hair had caught, and for the last time looked down into the amphitheatre which had been the scene of our recent exploit.

On the way down the hill the beaters had found the head of the unfortunate girl, and a thin column of smoke rising straight up into the still air from the mouth of the gorge showed where the relations were performing the last rites of the Champawat man-eater's last victim, on the very spot on which the man-eater had been shot.

After dinner, while I was standing in the courtyard of the Tahsil, I saw a long procession of pine torches winding its way down the opposite hillside, and presently the chanting of a hill song by a great concourse of men was borne up on the still night air. An hour later, the tigress was laid down at my feet.

It was difficult to skin the animal with so many people crowding round, and to curtail the job I cut the head and paws from the trunk and left them adhering to the skin, to be dealt with later. A police guard was then mounted over the carcass, and next day, when all the people of the countryside were assembled, the trunk, legs, and tail of the tigress were cut up into small pieces and distributed. These pieces of flesh and bone were required for the lockets which hill children wear around their necks, and the addition of a piece of tiger to the other potent charms is credited with giving the wearer courage, as well as immunity from the attacks of wild animals. The fingers of the girl which the tigress had swallowed whole were sent to me in spirits by the Tahsildar, and were buried by me in the Naini Tal lake close to the Nandadevi temples.

While I had been skinning the tigress the Tahsildar and his staff, assisted by the Headmen and greybeards of the surrounding villages and merchants of the Champawat bazaar, had been busy drawing up a programme for a great feast and dance for the morrow, at which I was to preside. Round about midnight, when the last of the great throng of men had left with shouts of delight at being able to use roads and village paths that the man-eater had closed for four years, I had a final smoke with the Tahsildar, and telling him that I could not stay any longer and that he would have to take my place at the festivities, my men and I set off on our seventy-five-mile journey, with two days in hand to do it in.

At sunrise I left my men and, with the tigress's skin strapped to the saddle of my horse, rode on ahead to put in a few hours in cleaning the skin at Dabidhura, where I intended spending the night. When passing the hut on the hill at Pali it occurred to me that it would be some little satisfaction to the dumb woman to know that her sister had been avenged, so leaving the horse to browse—he had been bred near the snowline and could eat anything from oak trees to nettles—I climbed the hill to the hut, and spread out the skin with the head supported on a stone facing the door. The children of the house had been round-eyed spectators of these proceedings and, hearing me talking to them, their mother, who was inside cooking, came to the door.

I am not going to hazard any theories about shock, and counter-shock, for I know nothing of these matters. All I know is that this woman, who was alleged to have been dumb a twelvemonth and who four days previously had made no attempt to answer any questions, was now running backwards and forwards from the hut to the road calling to her husband and the people in the village to come quickly and see what the sahib had brought. This sudden return of speech appeared greatly to mystify the children, who could not take their eyes off their mother's face.

I rested in the village while a dish of tea was being prepared for me and told the people who thronged round how the man-eater had been killed. An hour later I continued my journey and for half a mile along my way I could hear the shouts of goodwill of the men of Pali.

I had a very thrilling encounter with a leopard the following morning, which I only mention because it delayed my start from Dabidhura and put an extra strain on my small mount and myself. Fortunately the little pony was as strong on his legs as he was tough inside, and by holding his tail on the up-grades, riding him on the flat, and running behind him on the down-grades, we covered the forty-five miles to Naini Tal between 9 a.m. and 6 p.m.

At a durbar held in Naini Tal a few months later Sir John Hewett, Lieutenant-Governor of the United Provinces, presented the Tahsildar of Champawat with a gun, and the man who accompanied me when I was looking for the girl with a beautiful hunting-knife, for the help they had given me. Both weapons were suitably engraved and will be handed down as heirlooms in the respective families.

The Leopard of Panar

While I was hunting the Champawat man-eater in 1907, I heard of a man-eating leopard that was terrorizing the inhabitants of villages on the eastern border of Almora district. This leopard, about which questions were asked in the House of Commons, was known under several names and was credited with having killed 400 human beings. I knew the animal under the name of the Panar man-eater, and I shall therefore use this name for the purpose of my story.

No mention is made in government records of man-eaters prior to the year 1905 and it would appear that until the advent of the Champawat tiger and the Panar leopard, man-eaters were unknown in Kumaon. When therefore these two animals—who between them killed 836 human beings—made their appearance, the Government was faced with a difficult situation for it had no machinery to put in action against them and had to rely on personal appeals to sportsmen. Unfortunately there were very few sportsmen in Kumaon at that time who had any inclination for this new form of sport which, rightly or wrongly was considered as hazardous as Wilson's solo attempt—made a few years later—to conquer Everest. I myself was as ignorant of man-eaters as Wilson was of Everest and that I succeeded in my attempt, where he apparently failed in his, was due entirely to luck.

When I returned to my home in Naini Tal after killing the Champawat tiger I was asked by the Government to undertake the shooting of the Panar leopard. I was working hard for a living at the time and several weeks elapsed before I was able to spare the time to undertake this task, and then just as I was ready to start for the outlying area of Almora district in which the leopard was operating, I received an urgent request from Berthoud, the Deputy Commissioner of Naini Tal, to go to the help of the people of Muktesar where a man-eating tiger had established a reign of terror. After hunting down the tiger, an account of which I have given, I went in pursuit of the Panar leopard.

As I had not previously visited the vast area over which this leopard was operating, I went via Almora to learn all I could about the leopard from Stiffe, the Deputy Commissioner of Almora. He kindly invited me to lunch, provided me with maps, and then gave me a bit of a jolt when wishing me goodbye by asking me if I had considered all the risks and prepared for them by making my will.

My maps showed that there were two approaches to the affected area, one via Panwanaula on the Pithoragarh road, and the other via Lamgara on the Dabidhura road. I selected the latter route and after lunch set out in good heart—despite the reference to a will—accompanied by one servant and four men carrying my luggage. My men and I had already done a stiff march of fourteen miles from Khairna, but being young and fit we were prepared to do another long march before calling it a day.

As the full moon was rising we arrived at a small isolated building which, from the scribbling on the walls and the torn bits of paper lying about, we assumed was used as a school. I had no tent with me and as the door of the building was locked I decided to spend the night in the courtyard with my men, a perfectly safe proceeding for we were still many miles from the man-eater's hunting grounds. This courtyard, which was about twenty feet square, abutted on the public road and was surrounded on three sides by a two-foot-high wall. On the fourth side it was bounded by the school building.

There was plenty of fuel in the jungle behind the school and my men soon had a fire burning in a corner of the courtyard for my servant to cook my dinner. I was sitting with my back to the locked door, smoking, and my servant had just laid a leg of mutton on the low wall nearest the road and turned to attend to the fire, when I saw the head of a leopard appear over the wall close to the leg of mutton. Fascinated, I sat motionless and watched—for the leopard was facing me—and when the man had moved away a few feet the leopard grabbed the meat and bounded across the road into the jungle beyond. The meat had been put down on a big sheet of paper, which had stuck to it, and when my servant heard the rustle of paper and saw what he thought was a dog running away with it he dashed forward shouting, but on realizing that he was dealing with a leopard and not with a mere dog he changed direction and dashed towards me with even greater speed. All white people in the East are credited with being a little mad—for other reasons than walking about in the midday sun—and I am afraid my good servant thought I was a little more mad than most of my kind when he found I was laughing, for he said in a very aggrieved voice, 'It was your dinner that the leopard carried away and I have nothing else for you to eat.' However, he duly produced a meal that did him credit, and to which I did as much justice as I am sure the hungry leopard did to his leg of prime mutton.

Making an early start next morning, we halted at Lamgara for a meal, and by evening reached the Dol Dak Bungalow on the border of the man-eater's domain. Leaving my men at the bungalow I set out the following morning to try to get news of the man-eater. Going from village to village, and examining the connecting footpaths for leopard pug marks, I arrived in the late evening at an isolated homestead consisting of a single stone-built slate-roofed house, situated in a few acres of cultivated land and surrounded by scrub jungle. On the footpath leading to this homestead I found the pug marks of a big male leopard.

As I approached the house a man appeared on the narrow balcony and, climbing down a few wooden steps, came across the courtyard to meet me. He was a young man, possibly twenty-two years of age, and in great distress. It appeared that the previous night while he and his wife were sleeping on the floor of the single room that comprised the house, with the door open for it was April and very hot, the man-eater climbed on to the balcony and getting a grip of his wife's throat started to pull her head-foremost out of the room. With a strangled scream the woman flung an arm round her husband who, realizing in a flash what was happening, seized her arm with one hand and placing the other against the lintel of the door, for leverage, jerked her away from the leopard and closed the door. For the rest of the night the man and his wife cowered in a corner of the room, while the leopard tried to tear down the door. In the hot unventilated room the woman's wounds started to turn septic and by morning her suffering and fear had rendered her unconscious.

Throughout the day the man remained with his wife, too frightened to leave her for fear the leopard should return and carry her away, and too frightened to face the mile of scrub jungle that lay between him and his nearest neighbour. As day was closing down and the unfortunate man was facing another night of terror he saw me coming towards the house, and when I had heard his story I was no longer surprised that he had run towards me and thrown himself sobbing at my feet.

A difficult situation faced me. I had not up to that time approached Government to provide people living in areas in which a man-eater was operating with first-aid sets, so there was no medical or any other kind of aid nearer than Almora, and Almora was twenty-five miles away. To get help for the woman I would have to go for it myself and that would mean condemning the man to lunacy, for he had already stood as much as any man could stand and another night in that room, with the prospect of the leopard returning and trying to gain entrance, would of a certainty have landed him in a mad-house.

The man's wife, a girl of about eighteen, was lying on her back when the leopard clamped its teeth into her throat, and when the man got a grip of her arm and started to pull her back, the leopard—to get a better purchase—drove the claws of one paw into her breast. In the final struggle the claws ripped through the flesh, making four deep cuts. In the heat of the small room, which had only one door and no windows and in which a swarm of flies were buzzing, all the wounds in the girl's throat and on her breast had turned septic, and whether medical aid could be procured or not, the chances of her surviving were very slight; so, instead of going for help, I decided to stay the night with the man. I very sincerely hope that no one who reads this story will ever be condemned to seeing and hearing the sufferings of a human being, or of an animal, that has had the misfortune of being caught by the throat by either a leopard or a tiger and not having the means—other than a bullet—of alleviating or of ending the suffering.

The balcony which ran the length of the house, and which was boarded up at both ends, was about fifteen feet long and four feet wide, accessible by steps hewn in a pine sapling. Opposite these steps was the one door of the house, and under the balcony was an open recess four feet wide and four feet high, used for storing firewood.

The man begged me to stay in the room with him and his wife but it was not possible for me to do this, for, though I am not squeamish, the smell in the room was overpowering and more than I could stand. So between us we moved the firewood from one end of the recess under the balcony, clearing a small space where I could sit with my back to the wall. Night was now closing in, so after a wash and a drink at a nearby spring I settled down in my corner and told the man to go up to his wife and keep the door of the room open. As he climbed the steps the man said, 'The leopard will surely kill you, Sahib, and then what will I do?' 'Close the door,' I answered, 'and wait for morning.'

The moon was two nights off the full and there would be a short period of darkness. It was this period of darkness that was worrying me. If the leopard had remained scratching at the door until daylight, as the man said it had, it would not have gone far and even now it might be lurking in the bushes watching me. I had been in position for half an hour, straining my eyes into the darkening night and praying for the moon to top the hills to the east, when a jackal gave its alarm call. This call, which is given with the full force of the animal's lungs, can be heard for a very long distance and can be described as 'pheaon, pheaon', repeated over and over again as long as the danger that has alarmed the jackal is in sight. Leopards when hunting or when approaching a kill move very slowly, and it would be many minutes before this one—assuming it was the man-eater—covered the half mile between us, and even if in the meantime the moon had not risen it would be giving sufficient light to shoot by, so I was able to relax and breathe more freely.

Minutes dragged by. The jackal stopped calling. The moon rose over the hills, flooding the ground in front of me with brilliant light. No movement to be seen anywhere, and the only sound to be heard in all the world was the agonized fight for breath of the unfortunate girl above me. Minutes gave way to hours. The moon climbed the heavens and then started to go down in the west, casting the shadow of the house on the ground I was watching. Another period of danger, for if the leopard had seen me he would, with a leopard's patience, be waiting for these lengthening shadows to mask his movements. Nothing happened, and one of the longest nights I have ever watched through came to an end when the light from the sun lit up the sky where, twelve hours earlier, the moon had risen.

The man, after his vigil of the previous night, had slept soundly and as I left my corner and eased my aching bones—only those who have sat motionless on hard ground for hours know how bones can ache—he came down the steps. Except for a few wild raspberries I had eaten nothing for twenty-four hours, and as no useful purpose would have been served by my remaining any longer, I bade the man goodbye and set off to rejoin my men at the Dol Dak Bungalow, eight miles away, and summon aid for the girl. I had only gone a few miles when I met my men. Alarmed at my long absence they had packed up my belongings, paid my dues at the Dak Bungalow, and then set out to look for me. While I was talking to them the Road Overseer, whom I have mentioned in my story of the Temple tiger ['The Fortunate Tiger'], came along. He was well mounted on a sturdy Bhootia pony, and as he was on his way to Almora he gladly undertook to carry a letter from me to Stiffe. Immediately on receipt of my letter Stiffe dispatched medical aid for the girl, but her sufferings were over when it arrived.

It was this Road Overseer who informed me about the human kill that took me to Dabidhura, where I met with one of the most interesting and the most exciting shikar experiences I have ever had. After that experience I asked the old priest of the Dabidhura temple if the man-eater had as effective protection from his temple as the tiger I had failed to shoot, and he answered, 'No, no, Sahib. This Shaitan (devil) has killed many people who worshipped at my temple and when you come back to shoot him, as you say you will, I shall offer prayers for your success morning and evening.'

~

My first attempt to shoot the Panar leopard was made in April 1910, and it was not until September of the same year that I was able to spare the time to make a second attempt. I have no idea how many human beings were killed by the leopard between April and September, for no bulletins were issued by Government and beyond a reference to questions asked in the House of Commons no mention of the leopard—as far as I am aware—was made in the Indian press. The Panar leopard was credited with having killed 400 human beings, against 125 killed by the Rudraprayag leopard, and the fact that the former received such scant publicity while the latter was headline news throughout India was due entirely to the fact that the Panar leopard operated in a remote area far from the beaten track, whereas the Rudraprayag leopard operated in an area visited each year by 60,000 pilgrims ranging from the humblest in the land to the highest, all of whom had to run the gauntlet of the man-eater. It was these pilgrims, and the daily bulletins issued by the Government, that made the Rudraprayag leopard so famous, though it caused far less human suffering than the Panar leopard.

Accompanied by a servant and four men carrying my camp kit and provisions, I set out from Naini Tal on 10 September on my second attempt to shoot the Panar leopard. The sky was overcast when we left home at 4 a.m. and we had only gone a few miles when a deluge of rain came on. Throughout the day it rained and we arrived at Almora, after a twenty-eight-mile march, wet to the bone. I was to have spent the night with Stiffe, but not having a stitch of dry clothing to put on I excused myself and spent the night at the Dak Bungalow. There were no other travellers there and the man in charge very kindly put two rooms at my disposal, with a big wood fire in each, and by morning my kit was dry enough for me to continue my journey.

It had been my intention to follow the same route from Almora that I had followed in April, and start my hunt for the leopard from the house in which the girl had died of her wounds. While I was having breakfast a mason by the name of Panwa, who did odd jobs for us in Naini Tal, presented himself. Panwa's home was in the Panar valley, and on learning from my men that I was on my way to try to shoot the man-eater he asked for permission to join our party, for he wanted to visit his home and was frightened to undertake the journey alone. Panwa knew the country and on his advice I altered my plans and instead of taking the road to Dabidhura via the school where the leopard had eaten my dinner, I took the road leading to Pithoragarh. Spending the night at the Panwa Naula Dak Bungalow, we made an early start next morning and after proceeding a few miles left the Pithoragarh road for a track leading off to the right. We were now in the man-eater's territory where there were no roads, and where the only communication was along footpaths running from village to village.

Progress was slow, for the villages were widely scattered over many hundreds of square miles of country, and as the exact whereabouts of the man-eater were not known it was necessary to visit each village to make inquiries. Going through Salan and Rangot pattis (a group of villages), I arrived late on the evening of the fourth day at Chakati, where I was informed by the headman that a human being had been killed a few days previously at a village called Sanouli on the far side of the Panar river. Owing to the recent heavy rain the Panar was in flood and the headman advised me to spend the night in his village, promising to give me a guide next morning to show me the only safe ford over the river, for the Panar was not bridged.

The headman and I had carried on our conversation at one end of a long row of double-storeyed buildings and when, on his advice, I elected to stay the night in the village, he said he would have two rooms vacated in the upper storey for myself and my men. I had noticed while talking to him that the end room on the ground floor was untenanted, so I told him I would stay in it and that he need only have one room vacated in the upper storey for my men. The room I had elected to spend the night in had no door, but this did not matter for I had been told that the last kill had taken place on the far side of the river and I knew the man-eater would not attempt to cross the river while it was in flood.

The room had no furniture of any kind, and after my men had swept all the straw and bits of rags out of it, complaining as they did so that the last tenant must have been a very dirty person, they spread my groundsheet on the mud floor and made up my bed. I ate my dinner—which my servant cooked on an open fire in the courtyard—sitting on my bed, and as I had done a lot of walking during the twelve hours I had been on my feet, it did not take me long to get to sleep. The sun was just rising next morning, flooding the room with light, when on hearing a slight sound in the room I opened my eyes and saw a man sitting on the floor near my bed. He was about fifty years of age, and in the last stage of leprosy. On seeing that I was awake this unfortunate living death said he hoped I had spent a comfortable night in his room. He went on to say that he had been on a two-days' visit to friends in an adjoining village, and finding me asleep in his room on his return had sat near my bed and waited for me to awake.

Leprosy, the most terrible and the most contagious of all diseases in the East, is very prevalent throughout Kumaon, and especially bad in Almora district. Being fatalists the people look upon the disease as a visitation from God, and neither segregate the afflicted nor take any precautions against infection. So quite evidently, the headman did not think it necessary to warn me that the room I had selected to stay in had for years been the home of a leper. It did not take me long to dress that morning, and as soon as our guide was ready we left the village.

Moving about as I have done in Kumaon I have always gone in dread of leprosy, and I have never felt as unclean as I did after my night in that poor unfortunate's room. At the first stream we came to I called a halt, for my servant to get breakfast ready for me and for my men to have their food. Then, telling my men to wash my groundsheet and lay my bedding out in the sun, I took a bar of carbolic soap and went down the stream to where there was a little pool surrounded by great slabs of rock. Taking off every stitch of clothing I had worn in that room, I washed it all in the pool and, after laying it out on the slabs of rock, I used the remainder of the soap to scrub myself as I had never scrubbed myself before. Two hours later, in garments that had shrunk a little from the rough treatment they had received, I returned to my men feeling clean once again, and with a hunter's appetite for breakfast.

Our guide was a man about four feet six inches tall with a big head crowned with a mop of long hair; a great barrel of a body, short legs, and few words. When I asked him if we had any stiff climbing to do, he stretched out his open hand, and answered, 'Flat as that.' Having said this he led us down a very steep hill into a deep valley. Here I expected him to turn and follow the valley down to its junction with the river. But no. Without saying a word or even turning his head he crossed the open ground and went straight up the hill on the far side. This hill, in addition to being very steep and overgrown with thorn bushes, had loose gravel on it which made the going difficult, and as the sun was now overhead and very hot, we reached the top in a bath of sweat. Our guide, whose legs appeared to have been made for climbing hills, had not turned a hair.

There was an extensive view from the top of the hill, and when our guide informed us that we still had the two high hills in the foreground to climb before reaching the Panar river, Panwa, the mason, who was carrying a bundle containing presents for his family and a great coat made of heavy dark material, handed the coat to the guide and said that as he was making us climb all the hills in Kumaon he could carry the coat for the rest of the way. Unwinding a length of goat-hair cord from round his body the guide folded up the coat and strapped it securely to his back. Down and up we went, and down and up again, and then away down in a deep valley we saw the river. So far we had been going over trackless ground, without a village in sight, but we now came on a narrow path running straight down to the river. The nearer we got to the river the less I liked the look of it. The path leading to the water and up the far side showed that there was a ford here, but the river was in flood and the crossing appeared to me to be a very hazardous one. The guide assured us, however, that it was perfectly safe to cross, so removing my shoes and stockings I linked arms with Panwa and stepped into the water. The river was about forty yards wide and from its broken surface I judged it was running over a very rough bed. In this I was right, and after stubbing my toes a few times and narrowly avoiding being washed off our feet, we struggled out on the far bank.

Our guide had followed us into the river and on looking back, I saw that the little man was in difficulties. The water which for us had been thigh deep was for him waist deep and on reaching the main stream, instead of bracing his back against it and walking crab fashion, he very foolishly faced up-stream with the result that he was swept over backwards and submerged under the fast-running current. I was barefoot and helpless on the sharp stones, but Panwa—to whom sharp stones were no obstacle—threw down the bundle he was carrying and without a moment's hesitation sprinted along the bank to where fifty yards farther down, a big slab of rock jutted into the river at the head of a terrifying rapid. Running out on to this wet and slippery rock Panwa lay down, and as the drowning man was swept past, grabbed him by his long hair and after a desperate struggle drew him on to the rock. When the two men rejoined me—the guide looking like a drowned rat—I complimented Panwa on his noble and brave act in having saved the little man's life, at great risk to his own. After looking at me in some surprise Panwa said, 'Oh, it was not his life that I wanted to save, but my new coat that was strapped to his back.' Anyway, whatever the motive, a tragedy had been averted, and after my men had linked arms and crossed safely I decided to call it a day and spend the night on the river bank. Panwa, whose village was five miles farther up the river, now left me, taking with him the guide, who was frightened to attempt a second crossing of the river.

~

Next morning we set out to find Sanouli, where the last human kill had taken place. Late in the evening of that day we found ourselves in a wide open valley, and as there were no human habitations in sight, we decided to spend the night on the open ground. We were now in the heart of the man-eater's country and after a very unrestful night, spent on cold wet ground, arrived about midday at Sanouli. The inhabitants of this small village were overjoyed to see us and they very gladly put a room at the disposal of my men, and gave me the use of an open platform with a thatched roof.

The village was built on the side of a hill overlooking a valley in which there were terraced fields, from which a paddy crop had recently been harvested. The hill on the far side of the valley sloped up gradually, and a hundred yards from the cultivated land there was a dense patch of brushwood, some twenty acres in extent. On the brow of the hill, above this patch of brushwood, there was a village, and on the shoulder of the hill to the right another village. To the left of the terraced fields the valley was closed in by a steep grassy hill. So, in effect, the patch of brushwood was surrounded on three sides by cultivated land, and on the fourth by open grass land.

While breakfast was being got ready, the men of the village sat round me and talked. During the second half of March and the first half of April, four human beings had been killed in this area by the man-eater. The first kill had taken place in the village on the shoulder of the hill, the second and third in the village on the brow of the hill, and the fourth in Sanouli.

All four victims had been killed at night and carried some 500 yards into the patch of brushwood, where the leopard had eaten them at his leisure, for—having no firearms—the inhabitants of the three villages were too frightened to make any attempt to recover the bodies. The last kill had taken place six days before, and my informants were convinced that the leopard was still in the patch of brushwood.

I had purchased two young male goats in a village we passed through earlier that day, and towards evening I took the smaller one and tied it at the edge of the path of brushwood to test the villagers' assertion that the leopard was still in the cover. I did not sit over the goat, because there were no suitable trees nearby and also because clouds were banking up and it looked as though there might be rain during the night. The platform that had been placed at my disposal was open all round, so I tied the second goat near it in the hope that if the leopard visited the village during the night it would prefer a tender goat to a tough human being. Long into the night I listened to the two goats calling to each other. This convinced me that the leopard was not within hearing distance. However, there was no reason why he should not return to the locality, so I went to sleep hoping for the best.

There was a light shower during the night and when the sun rose in a cloudless sky every leaf and blade of grass was sparkling with raindrops and every bird that had a song to sing was singing a joyful welcome to the day. The goat near my platform was contentedly browsing off a bush and bleating occasionally, while the one across the valley was silent. Telling my servant to keep my breakfast warm, I crossed the valley and went to the spot where I had tied up the smaller goat. Here I found that, some time before the rain came on, a leopard had killed the goat, broken the rope, and carried away the kill. The rain had washed out the drag-mark, but this did not matter for there was only one place to which the leopard could have taken his kill, and that was into the dense patch of brushwood.

Stalking a leopard, or a tiger, on its kill is one of the most interesting forms of sport I know of, but it can only be indulged in with any hope of success when the conditions are favourable. Here the conditions were not favourable, for the brushwood was too dense to permit of a noiseless approach. Returning to the village, I had breakfast and then called the villagers together, as I wanted to consult them about the surrounding country. It was necessary to visit the kill to see if the leopard had left sufficient for me to sit over and, while doing so, I would not be able to avoid disturbing the leopard. What I wanted to learn from the villagers was whether there was any other heavy cover, within a reasonable distance, to which the leopard could retire on being disturbed by me. I was told that there was no such cover nearer than two miles, and that to get to it the leopard would have to cross a wide stretch of cultivated land.

At midday I returned to the patch of brushwood and, a hundred yards from where he had killed it, I found all that the leopard had left of the goat—its hooves, horns, and part of its stomach. As there was no fear of the leopard leaving the cover at that time of day for the jungle two miles away, I tried for several hours to stalk it, helped by bulbuls, drongos, thrushes, and scimitar-babblers, all of whom kept me informed of the leopard's every movement. In case any should question why I did not collect the men of the three villages and get them to drive the leopard out on to the open ground, where I could have shot it, it is necessary to say that this could not have been attempted without grave danger to the beaters. As soon as the leopard found he was being driven towards open ground, he would have broken back and attacked anyone who got in his way.

On my return to the village after my unsuccessful attempt to get a shot at the leopard, I went down with a bad attack of malaria and for the next twenty-four hours I lay on the platform in a stupor. By the evening of the following day the fever had left me and I was able to continue the hunt. On their own initiative the previous night my men had tied out the second goat where the first had been killed, but the leopard had not touched it. This was all to the good, for the leopard would now be hungry, and I set out on that third evening full of hope.

On the near side of the patch of brushwood, and about a hundred yards from where the goat had been killed two nights previously there was an old oak tree. This tree was growing out of a six-foot-high bank between two terraced fields and was leaning away from the hill at an angle that made it possible for me to walk up the trunk in my rubber soled shoes. On the underside of the trunk and about fifteen feet from the ground there was a branch jutting out over the lower field. This branch, which was about a foot thick, offered a very uncomfortable and a very unsafe seat for it was hollow and rotten. However, as it was the only branch on the tree, and as there were no other trees within a radius of several hundred yards, I decided to risk the branch.

As I had every reason to believe—from the similarity of the pug marks I had found in the brushwood to those I had seen in April on the path leading to the homestead where the girl was killed—that the leopard I was dealing with was the Panar man-eater, I made my men cut a number of long blackthorn shoots. After I had taken my seat with my back to the tree and my legs stretched out along the branch, I made the men tie the shoots into bundles and lay them on the trunk of the tree and lash them to it securely with strong rope. To the efficient carrying out of these small details I am convinced I owe my life.

Several of the blackthorn shoots, which were from ten to twenty feet long, projected on either side of the tree; and as I had nothing to hold on to, to maintain my balance, I gathered the shoots on either side of me and held them firmly pressed between my arms and my body. By five o'clock my preparations were complete. I was firmly seated on the branch with my coat collar pulled up well in front to protect my throat, and my soft hat pulled down well behind to protect the back of my neck. The goat was tied to a stake driven into the field thirty yards in front of me, and my men were sitting out in the field smoking and talking loudly.

Up to this point all had been quiet in the patch of brushwood, but now, a scimitar-babbler gave its piercing alarm call followed a minute or two later by the chattering of several white-throated laughing thrushes. These two species of birds are the most reliable informants in the hills, and on hearing them I signalled to my men to return to the village. This they appeared to be very glad to do, and as they walked away, still talking loudly, the goat started bleating. Nothing happened for the next half-hour and then, as the sun was fading off the hill above the village, two drongos that had been sitting on the tree above me, flew off and started to bait some animal on the open ground between me and the patch of brushwood. The goat while calling had been facing in the direction of the village, and it now turned round, facing me, and stopped calling. By watching the goat I could follow the movements of the animal that the drongos were baiting and that the goat was interested in, and this animal could only be a leopard.

The moon was in her third quarter and there would be several hours of darkness. In anticipation of the leopard's coming when light conditions were not favourable, I had armed myself with a twelve-bore double-barrelled shot gun loaded with slugs, for there was a better chance of my hitting the leopard with eight slugs than with a single rifle bullet. Aids to night shooting, in the way of electric lights and torches, were not used in India at the time I am writing about, and all that one had to rely on for accuracy of aim was a strip of white cloth tied round the muzzle of the weapon.

Again nothing happened for many minutes, and then I felt a gentle pull on the blackthorn shoots I was holding and blessed my forethought in having had the shoots tied to the leaning tree, for I could not turn round to defend myself and at best the collar of my coat and my hat were poor protection. No question now that I was dealing with a man-eater, and a very determined man-eater at that. Finding that he could not climb over the thorns, the leopard, after his initial pull, had now got the butt ends of the shoots between his teeth and was jerking them violently, pulling me hard against the trunk of the tree. And now the last of the daylight faded out of the sky and the leopard, who did all his human killing in the dark, was in his element and I was out of mine, for in the dark a human being is the most helpless of all animals and—speaking for myself—his courage is at its lowest ebb. Having killed 400 human beings at night, the leopard was quite unafraid of me, as was evident from the fact that while tugging at the shoots, he was growling loud enough to be heard by the men anxiously listening in the village. While this growling terrified the men, as they told me later, it had the opposite effect on me, for it let me know where the leopard was and what he was doing. It was when he was silent that I was most terrified, for I did not know what his next move would be. Several times he had nearly unseated me by pulling on the shoots vigorously and then suddenly letting them go, and now that it was dark and I had nothing stable to hold on to, I felt sure that if he sprang up he would only need to touch me to send me crashing to the ground.

After one of these nerve-racking periods of silence the leopard jumped down off the high bank and dashed towards the goat. In the hope that the leopard would come while there was still sufficient light to shoot by, I had tied the goat thirty yards from the tree to give me time to kill the leopard before it got to the goat. But now, in the dark, I could not save the goat—which, being white, I could only just see as an indistinct blur—so I waited until it had stopped struggling and then aimed where I thought the leopard would be and pressed the trigger. My shot was greeted with an angry grunt and I saw a white flash as the leopard went over backwards, and disappeared down another high bank into the field beyond.

For ten or fifteen minutes I listened anxiously for further sounds from the leopard, and then my men called out and asked if they should come to me. It was now quite safe for them to do so, provided they kept to the high ground. So I told them to light pine torches, and thereafter carry out my instructions. These torches, made of twelve to eighteen inches long splinters of resin-impregnated pine-wood cut from a living tree, give a brilliant light and provide the remote villages in Kumaon with the only illumination they have ever known.

After a lot of shooting and running about, some twenty men each carrying a torch left the village and, following my instructions, circled round above the terraced fields and approached my tree from behind. The knots in the ropes securing the blackthorn shoots to the tree had been pulled so tight by the leopard that they had to be cut. After the thorns had been removed men climbed the tree and helped me down, for the uncomfortable seat had given me cramps in my legs.

The combined light from the torches lit up the field on which the dead goat was lying, but the terraced field beyond was in shadow. When cigarettes had been handed round I told the men I had wounded the leopard but did not know how badly, and that we would return to the village now and I would look for the wounded animal in the morning. At this, great disappointment was expressed. 'If you have wounded the leopard it must surely be dead by now. There are many of us, and you have a gun, so there is no danger.' 'At least let us go as far as the edge of the field and see if the leopard has left a blood trail.' After all arguments for and against going to look for the leopard immediately had been exhausted, I consented against my better judgement to go as far as the edge of the field, from where we could look down on the terraced field below.

Having acceded to their request, I made the men promise

that they would walk in line behind me, hold their torches high, and not run away and leave me in the dark if the leopard charged. This promise they very willingly gave, and after the torches had been replenished and were burning brightly we set off, I walking in front and the men following five yards behind.

Thirty yards to the goat, and another twenty yards to the edge of the field. Very slowly, and in silence, we moved forward. When we reached the goat—no time now to look for a blood trail—the farther end of the lower field came into view. The nearer we approached the edge, the more of this field became visible, and then, when only a narrow strip remained in shadow from the torches, the leopard, with a succession of angry grunts, sprang up the bank and into full view.

There is something very terrifying in the angry grunt of a charging leopard, and I have seen a line of elephants that were staunch to tiger turn and stampede from a charging leopard; so I was not surprised when my companions, all of whom were unarmed, turned as one man and bolted. Fortunately for me, in their anxiety to get away they collided with each other and some of the burning splinters of pine—held loosely in their hands—fell to the ground and continued to flicker, giving me sufficient light to put a charge of slugs into the leopard's chest.

On hearing my shot the men stopped running, and then I heard one of them say, '*Oh, no*. He won't be angry with us, for he knows that this devil has turned our courage to water.' Yes, I knew, from my recent experience on the tree, that fear of a man-eater robs a man of courage. As for running away, had I been one of the torchbearers I would have run with the best. So there was nothing for me to be angry about. Presently, while I was making believe to examine the leopard, to ease their embarrassment, the men returned in twos and threes. When they were assembled, I asked, without looking up, 'Did you bring a bamboo pole and rope to carry the leopard back to the village?' 'Yes,' they answered eagerly, 'we left them at the foot of the tree.' 'Go and fetch them,' I said, 'for I want to get back to the village for a cup of hot tea.' The cold night-wind blowing down from the north had brought on another attack of malaria, and now that all the excitement was over I was finding it difficult to remain on my feet.

That night, for the first time in years, the people of Sanouli slept, and have since continued to sleep, free from fear.

The Man-eating Tigress of Chowgarh

The map of Eastern Kumaon that hangs on the wall before me is marked with a number of crosses, and below each cross is a date. These crosses indicate the locality, and the date, of the officially recorded human victims of the man-eating tiger of Chowgarh. There are sixty-four crosses on the map. I do not claim this as being a correct tally, for the map was posted up by me for two years and during this period all kills were not reported to me; further, victims who were only mauled, and who died subsequently, have not been awarded a cross and a date.

HUMAN BEINGS KILLED BY THE CHOWGARH MAN-EATER

Village	Number
Thali	1
Debgura	1
Barhon	2
Chamoli	6
Kahor	1
Am	2
Dalkania	7
Lohar	8
Aghaura	2

Village	Number
Paharpani	1
Padampuri	2
Tanda	1
Nesoriya	1
Jhangaon	1
Kabragaon	1
Kala Agar	8
Rikhakot	1
Matela	3
Kundal	3
Babyar	1
Khansiun	1
Gargari	1
Hairakhan	2
Ukhaldhunga	1
Pakhari	1
Dungari	2
Galni	3
Total	**64**

Annual	Totals
1926	15 Killed
1927	9 Killed
1928	14 Killed
1929	17 Killed
1930	9 Killed
Total	**64**

The first cross is dated 15 December 1925, and the last, 21 March 1930. The distance between the extreme crosses, north to south, is fifty miles, and east to west, thirty miles, an area of 1,500 square miles of mountain and vale where the snow lies deep during winter, and the valleys are scorching hot in summer. Over this area the Chowgarh tiger had established a reign of terror. Villages of varying size, some with a population of hundred or more, and others with only a small family or two, are scattered throughout the area. Footpaths, beaten hard by bare feet, connect the villages. Some of these paths pass through thick forests, and when a man-eater renders their passage dangerous, inter-village communication is carried on by shouting. Standing on a commanding point, maybe a big rock or the roof of a house, a man cooees to attract the attention of the people in a neighbouring village, and when the cooee is answered, the message is shouted across in a high-pitched voice. From village to village the message is tossed, and is broadcast throughout large areas in an incredibly short space of time.

It was at a District Conference in February 1929 that I found myself committed to have a try for this tiger. There were at that time three man-eaters in the Kumaon Division, and as the Chowgarh tiger had done most damage I promised to go in pursuit of it first.

The map with the crosses and date, furnished to me by the Government, showed that the man-eater was most active in the villages on the north and east face of the Kala Agar ridge. This ridge, some forty miles in length, rises to a height of 8,500 feet and is thickly wooded along the crest. A forest road runs along the north face of the ridge, in some places passing for miles through dense forests of oak and rhododendron, and in others forming a boundary between the forest and cultivated land. In one place the road forms a loop, and in this loop is situated the Kala Agar Forest Bungalow. This bungalow was my objective, and after a four days' march, culminating in a stiff climb of

4,000 feet, I arrived at it one evening in April 1929. The last human victim in this area was a young man of twenty-two, who had been killed while out grazing cattle, and while I was having breakfast, the morning after my arrival, the grandmother of the young man came to see me.

She informed me that the man-eater had, without any provocation, killed the only relative she had in the world. After giving me her grandson's history from the day he was born, and extolling his virtues, she pressed me to accept her three milch buffaloes to use as a bait for the tiger, saying that if I killed the tiger with the help of her buffaloes, she would have the satisfaction of feeling that she had assisted in avenging her grandson. These full-grown animals were of no use to me, but knowing that refusal to accept them would give offence, I thanked the old lady and assured her I would draw on her for bait as soon as I had used up the four young male buffaloes I had brought with me from Naini Tal. The Headmen of the nearby villages had now assembled, and from them I learned that the tiger had last been seen ten days previously in a village twenty miles away, on the eastern slope of the ridge, where it had killed and eaten a man and his wife.

A trail ten days old was not worth following up, and after a long discussion with the Headmen, I decided to make for Dalkania village on the eastern side of the ridge. Dalkania is ten miles from Kala Agar, and about the same distance from the village where the man and his wife had been killed.

From the number of crosses Dalkania and the villages adjoining it had earned, it appeared that the tiger had its headquarters in the vicinity of these villages.

After breakfast next morning I left Kala Agar and followed the forest road, which I was informed would take me to the end of the ridge, where I should have to leave the road and take a path two miles downhill to Dalkania. This road, running right to the end of the ridge through dense forest was very little used, and, examining it for tracks as I went along, I arrived at the point where the path took off at about 2 p.m. Here I met a number of men from Dalkania. They had heard—via the cooee method of communication—of my intention of camping at their village and had come up to the ridge to inform me that the tiger had that morning attacked a party of women, while they had been cutting their crops in a village ten miles to the north of Dalkania.

The men carrying my camp equipment had done eight miles and were quite willing to carry on, but on learning from the villagers that the path of this village, ten miles away, was very rough and ran through dense forest, I decided to send my men with the villagers to Dalkania, and visit the scene of tiger's attack alone. My servant immediately set about preparing a substantial meal for me, and at 3 p.m., having fortified myself, I set out on my ten-mile walk. Ten miles under favourable conditions is a comfortable two-and-a-half hours' walk, but here the conditions were anything but favourable. The track running along the east face of the hill wound in and out through deep ravines and was bordered alternately by rocks, dense undergrowth, and trees; and when every obstruction capable of concealing sudden death, in the form of a hungry man-eater, had to be approached with caution, progress was of necessity slow. I was still several miles from my objective when the declining day warned me it was time to call a halt.

In any other area, sleeping under the stars on a bed of dry leaves would have ensured a restful night, but here, to sleep on the ground would have been to court death in a very unpleasant form. Long practice in selecting a suitable tree, and the ability to dispose myself comfortably in it, has made sleeping up aloft a simple matter. On this occasion I selected an oak tree, and, with the rifle tied securely to a branch, had been asleep for some hours when I was awakened by the rustling of several animals under the tree. The sound moved on, and presently I heard the scraping of claws on bark and realized that a family of bears were climbing some karphal* trees I had noticed growing a little way down the hill side. Bears are very quarrelsome when feeding, and sleep was impossible until they had eaten their fill and moved on.

The sun had been up a couple of hours when I arrived at the village, which consisted of two huts and a cattle shed, in a clearing of five acres surrounded by forest. The small community was in a state of terror and was overjoyed to see me. The wheatfield, a few yards from the huts, where the tiger, with belly to ground, had been detected only just in time, stalking the three women cutting the crop, was eagerly pointed out to me. The man who had seen the tiger, and given the alarm, told me that the tiger had retreated into the jungle, where it had been joined by a second tiger, and that the two animals had gone down the hill side into the valley below. The occupants of the two huts had had no sleep, for the tigers, baulked of their prey, had called at short intervals throughout the night, and had only ceased calling a little before my arrival. This statement, that there were two tigers, confirmed the reports I had already received that the man-eater was accompanied by a full-grown cub.

Our hill folk are very hospitable, and when the villagers learned that I had spent the night in the jungle, and that my camp was at Dalkania, they offered to prepare a meal for me. This I knew would strain the resources of the small community, so I asked for a dish of tea, but as there was no tea in the village I was given a drink of fresh milk sweetened to excess with jaggery, a very satisfying and not unpleasant drink—when one gets used to it. At the request of my hosts I mounted guard while the remaining portion of the wheat crop was cut; and at

---

* Karphal is found on our hills at an elevation of 6,000 feet. The tree grows to a height of about forty feet and produces a small red and very sweet berry, which is greatly fancied by both human beings and bears.

midday, taking the good wishes of the people with me, I went down into the valley in the direction in which the tigers had been heard calling.

The valley, starting from the watershed of the three rivers Ladhya, Nandhour and Eastern Goula, runs south-west for twenty miles and is densely wooded. Tracking was impossible, and my only hope of seeing the tigers was to attract them to myself, or helped by the jungle folk to stalk them.

To those of you who may be inclined to indulge in the sport of man-eater hunting on foot, it will be of interest to know that the birds and animals of the jungle, and the four winds of heaven, play a very important part in this form of sport. This is not the place to give the names of the jungle folk on whose alarm calls the sportsman depends, to a great extent, for his safety and knowledge of his quarry's movements; for in a country in which a walk up or downhill of three or four miles might mean a difference in altitude of as much as a thousand feet, the variation in fauna, in a well-stocked area, is considerable. The wind, however, at all altitudes, remains a constant factor, and a few words relevant to its importance in connexion with man-eater hunting on foot will not be out of place.

Tigers do not know that human beings have no sense of smell, and when a tiger becomes a man-eater it treats human beings exactly as it treats wild animals, that is, it approaches its victims up-wind, or lies up in wait for them down-wind.

The significance of this will be apparent when it is realized that, while the sportsman is trying to spot the tiger, the tiger in all probability is trying to stalk the sportsman, or is lying up in wait for him. The contest, owing to the tiger's height, colouring, and ability to move without making a sound, would be very unequal were it not for the wind-factor operating in favour of the sportsman.

In all cases where killing is done by stalking or stealth, the victim is approached from behind. This being so, it would be suicidal for the sportsman to enter the dense jungle in which he had every reason to believe a man-eater was lurking, unless he was capable of making full use of the currents of air. For example, assuming that the sportsman has to proceed, owing to the nature of the ground, in the direction from which the wind is blowing, the danger would lie behind him, where he would be least able to deal with it, but by frequently tacking across the wind he could keep the danger alternately to right and left of him. In print this scheme may not appear very attractive, but in practice it works; and, short of walking backwards, I do not know of a better or safer method of going up-wind through dense cover in which a hungry man-eater is lurking.

By evening I had reached the upper end of the valley, without having seen the tigers and without having received any indication from bird or animal of their presence in the jungle. The only habitation then in sight was a cattle shed, high up on the north side of the valley.

I was careful in the selection of a tree on this second night, and was rewarded by an undisturbed night's rest. Not long after dark the tigers called, and a few minutes later two shots from a muzzle-loader came echoing down the valley, followed by a lot of shouting from the graziers at the cattle station. Thereafter the night was silent.

By the afternoon of the following day I had explored every bit of the valley, and I was making my way up a grassy slope intent on rejoining my men at Dalkania when I heard a long-drawn-out cooee from the direction of the cattle shed. The cooee was repeated once and again, and on my sending back an answering call I saw a man climb on a projecting rock, and from this vantage point he shouted across the valley to ask if I was the sahib who had come from Naini Tal to shoot the man-eater. On my telling him I was that sahib, he informed me that his cattle had stampeded out of a ravine on my side of the valley at about midday, and that when he counted them on arrival at the cattle station he found that one—a white cow—was missing.

He suspected that the cow had been killed by the tigers he had heard calling the previous night, half a mile to the west of where I was standing. Thanking him for his information, I set off to investigate the ravine. I had gone but a short distance along the edge of the ravine when I came on the tracks of the stampeding cattle, and following these tracks back I had no difficulty in finding the spot where the cow had been killed. After killing the cow the tigers had taken it down the steep hillside into the ravine. An approach along the drag was not advisable, so going down into the valley I made a wide detour, and approached the spot where I expected the kill to be from the other side of the ravine. This side of the ravine was less steep than the side down which the kill had been taken, and was deep in young bracken—ideal ground for stalking over. Step by step, and as silently as a shadow, I made my way through the bracken, which reached above my waist, and when I was some thirty yards from the bed of the ravine a movement in front of me caught my eye. A white leg was suddenly thrust up into the air and violently agitated, and the next moment there was a deep-throated growl—the tigers were on the kill and were having a difference of opinion over some toothful morsel.

For several minutes I stood perfectly still; the leg continued to be agitated, but the growl was not repeated. A nearer approach was not advisable, for even if I succeeded in covering the thirty yards without being seen, and managed to kill one of the tigers, the other, as likely as not, would blunder into me, and the ground I was on would give me no chance of defending myself. Twenty yards to my left front, and about the same distance from the tigers, there was an outcrop of rock, some ten to fifteen feet high. If I could reach this rock without being seen, I should in all probability get an easy shot at the tigers. Dropping on hands and knees, and pushing the rifle before me, I crawled through the bracken to the shelter of the rocks, paused a minute to regain my breath and make quite sure the rifle was loaded, and then climbed the rock. When my eyes were level with the top, I looked over, and saw the two tigers.

One was eating at the hind quarters of the cow, while the other was lying nearby licking its paws. Both tigers appeared to be about the same size, but the one that was licking its paws was several shades lighter than the other; and concluding that her light colouring was due to age and that she was the old man-eater, I aligned the sights very carefully on her, and fired. At my shot she reared up and fell backwards, while the other bounded down the ravine and was out of sight before I could press the second trigger. The tiger I had shot did not move again, and after pelting it with stones to make sure it was dead, I approached and met with a great disappointment; for a glance at close quarters showed me I had make a mistake and shot the cub—a mistake that during the ensuing twelve months cost the district fifteen lives and incidentally nearly cost me my own life.

Disappointment was to a certain extent mitigated by the thought that this young tigress, even if she had not actually killed any human beings herself, had probably assisted her old mother to kill (this assumption I later found to be correct), and in any case, having been nurtured on human flesh, she could— to salve my feelings—be classified as a potential man-eater.

Skinning a tiger with assistance on open ground and with the requisite appliances is an easy job, but here the job was anything but easy, for I was alone, surrounded by thick cover, and my only appliance was a penknife; and though there was no actual danger to be apprehended from the man-eater, for tigers never kill in excess of their requirements, there was the uneasy feeling in the back of my mind that the tiger had returned and was watching my every movement.

The sun was near setting before the arduous task was completed, and as I should have to spend yet another night in the jungles I decided to remain where I was. The tigress was a very old animal, as I could see from her pug marks, and having lived all her life in a district in which there are nearly as many fire-arms as men to use them, had nothing to learn about men and their ways. Even so, there was just a chance that she might return to the kill some time during the night, and remain in the vicinity until light came in the morning.

My selection of a tree was of necessity limited, and the one I spent that night in proved, by morning, to be the most uncomfortable tree I have ever spent twelve hours in. The tigress called at intervals throughout the night, and as morning drew near the calling became fainter and fainter, and eventually died away on the ridge above me.

Cramped, and stiff, and hungry—I had been without food for sixty-four hours—and with my clothes clinging to me—it had rained for an hour during the night—I descended from the tree when objects were clearly visible, and, after tying the tiger's skin up in a coat, set off for Dalkania.

I have never weighed a tiger's skin when green, and if the skin, plus the head and paws, which I carried for fifteen miles that day weighed forty pounds at the start, I would have taken my oath it weighed 200 pounds before I reached my destination.

In a courtyard, flagged with great slabs of blue slate, and common to a dozen houses, I found my men in conference with a hundred or more villagers. My approach, along a yard-wide lane between two houses, had not been observed, and the welcome I received when, bedraggled and covered with blood, I staggered into the circle of squatting men will live in my memory as long as memory lasts.

My 40-lb. tent had been pitched in a field of stubble a hundred yards from the village, and I had hardly reached it before tea was laid out for me on a table improvised out of a couple of suitcases and planks borrowed from the village. I was told later by the villagers that my men, who had been with me for years and had accompanied me on several similar expeditions, refusing to believe that the man-eater had claimed me as a victim, had kept a kettle on the boil night and day in anticipation of my return, and, further, had stoutly opposed the Headmen of Dalkania and the adjoining villages sending a report to Almora and Naini Tal that I was missing.

A hot bath, taken of necessity in the open and in full view of the village—I was too dirty and too tired to care who saw me—was followed by an ample dinner, and I was thinking of turning in for the night when a flash of lightning succeeded by a loud peal of thunder heralded the approach of a storm. Tent-pegs are of little use in a field, so long stakes were hurriedly procured and securely driven into the ground, and to these stakes the tent-ropes were tied. For further safety all the available ropes in camp were criss-crossed over the tent and lashed to the stakes. The storm of wind and rain lasted an hour and was one of the worst the little tent had ever weathered. Several of the guy-ropes were torn from the canvas, but the stakes and criss-cross ropes held. Most of my things were soaked through, and a little stream several inches deep was running from end to end of the tent; my bed, however, was comparatively dry, and by 10 o'clock my men were safely lodged behind locked doors in the house the villagers had placed at their disposal, while I, with a loaded rifle for company, settled down to a sleep which lasted for twelve hours.

The following day was occupied in drying my kit and in cleaning and pegging out the tiger's skin. While these operations were in progress the villagers, who had taken a holiday from their field work, crowded round to hear my experiences and to tell me theirs. Every man present had lost one or more relatives, and several bore tooth and claw marks, inflicted by the man-eater, which they will carry to their graves. My regret at having lost an opportunity of killing the man-eater was not endorsed by the assembled men. True, there had originally been only one man-eater; but, of recent months, rescue parties who had gone out to recover the remains of human victims had found two tigers on the kills, and only a fortnight previously a man and his wife had been killed simultaneously, which was proof sufficient for them that both tigers were established man-eaters.

My tent was on a spur of the hill, and commanded an extensive view. Immediately below me was the valley of the Nandhour river, with a hill, devoid of any cultivation, rising to a height of 9,000 feet on the far side. As I sat on the edge of the terraced fields that evening with a pair of good binoculars in my hand and the Government map spread out beside me, the villagers pointed out the exact positions where twenty human beings had been killed during the past three years. These kills were more or less evenly distributed over an area of forty square miles.

The forests in this area were open to grazing, and on the cattle-paths leading to them I decided to tie up my four young buffaloes.

During the following ten days no news was received of the tigress, and I spent the time in visiting the buffaloes in the morning, searching the forests in the day, and tying out the buffaloes in the evening. On the eleventh day my hopes were raised by the report that a cow had been killed on a ravine on the hill above my tent. A visit to the kill, however, satisfied me the cow had been killed by an old leopard, whose pug marks I had repeatedly seen. The villagers complained that the leopard had for several years been taking heavy toll of their cattle and goats, so I decided to sit up for him. A shallow cave close to the dead cow gave me the cover I needed. I had not been long in the cave when I caught sight of the leopard coming down the opposite side of the ravine, and I was raising my rifle for a shot when I heard a very agitated voice from the direction of the village calling to me.

There could be but one reason for this urgent call, and grabbing up my hat I dashed out of the cave, much to the consternation of the leopard, who first flattened himself out on the ground, and then with an angry woof went bounding back the way he had come, while I scrambled up my side of the ravine; and, arriving at the top, shouted to the man that I was coming, and set off at top speed to join him.

The man had run all the way uphill from the village, and when he regained his breath he informed me that a woman had just been killed by the man-eater, about half a mile on the far side of the village. As we ran down the hillside I saw a crowd of people collected in the courtyard already alluded to. Once again my approach through the narrow lane was not observed, and looking over the heads of the assembled men, I saw a girl sitting on the ground.

The upper part of her clothing had been torn off her young body, and with head thrown back and hands resting on the ground behind to support her, she sat without sound or movement, other than the heaving up and down of her breast, in the hollow of which the blood, that was flowing down her face and neck, was collecting in a sticky congealed mass.

My presence was soon detected and a way made for me to approach the girl. While I was examining her wounds, a score of people, all talking at the same time, informed me that the attack on the girl had been made on comparatively open ground in full view of a number of people including the girl's husband; that alarmed at their combined shouts the tiger had left the girl and gone off in the direction of the forest; that leaving the girl for dead where she had fallen her companions had run back to the village to inform me; that subsequently the girl had regained consciousness and returned to the village; that she would without doubt die of her injuries in a few minutes; and that they would then carry her back to the scene of the attack, and I could sit up over the corpse and shoot the tiger.

While this information was being imparted to me the girl's eyes never left my face and followed my every movement with the liquid pleading gaze of a wounded and frightened animal. Room to move unhampered, quiet to collect my wits, and clean air for the girl to breathe were necessary, and I am afraid the methods I employed to gain them were not as gentle as they might have been. When the last of the men had left in a hurry, I set the women, who up to now had remained in the background, to warming water and to tearing my shirt, which was comparatively clean and dry, into bandages, while one girl, who appeared to be on the point of getting hysterics, was bundled off to scour the village for a pair of scissors. The water and bandages were ready before the girl I had sent for the scissors returned with the only pair, she said, the village could produce. They had been found in the house of a tailor, long since dead, and had been used by the widow for digging up potatoes. The rusty blades, some eight inches long, could not be made to meet at any point, and after a vain attempt I decided to leave the thick coils of blood-caked hair alone.

The major wounds consisted of two claw cuts, one starting between the eyes and extending right over the head and down to the nape of the neck, leaving the scalp hanging in two halves, and the other, starting near the first, running across the forehead up to the right ear. In addition to these ugly gaping wounds there were a number of deep scratches on the right breast, right shoulder and neck, and one deep cut on the back of the right hand, evidently inflicted when the girl had put up her hand in a vain attempt to shield her head.

A doctor friend whom I had once taken out tiger-shooting on foot had, on our return after an exciting morning, presented me with a two-ounce bottle of yellow fluid which he advised me to carry whenever I went out shooting. I had carried the bottle in the inner pocket of my shooting jacket for over a year and a portion of the fluid had evaporated; but the bottle was still three-parts full, and after I had washed the girl's head and body I knocked the neck off the bottle and poured the contents, to the last drop, into the wounds. This done I bandaged the head, to try to keep the scalp in position, and then picked up the girl and carried her to her home—a single room combining living quarters, a kitchen and a nursery—with the women following behind.

Dependent from a rafter near the door was an open basket, the occupant of which was now clamouring to be fed. This was a complication with which I could not deal, so I left the solution of it to the assembled women. Ten days later, when on the eve of my departure I visited the girl for the last time, I found her sitting on the doorstep of her home with the baby asleep in her lap.

Her wounds, except for a sore at the nape of her neck where the tiger's claws had sunk deepest into the flesh, were all healed, and when parting her great wealth of raven-black hair to show me where the scalp had made a perfect join, she said, with a smile, that she was very glad her young sister had—quite by mistake—borrowed the wrong pair of scissors from the tailor's widow (for a shorn head here is the sign of widowhood). If these lines should ever be read by my friend, the doctor, I should like him to know that the little bottle of yellow fluid he so thoughtfully provided for me, saved the life of a very brave young mother.

While I had been attending to the girl my men had procured a goat. Following back the blood trail made by the girl I found the spot where the attack had taken place, and tying the goat to a bush I climbed into a stunted oak, the only tree in the vicinity, and prepared for an all-night vigil. Sleep, even in snatches, was not possible, for my seat was only a few feet from the ground, and the tigress was still without her dinner. However, I neither saw nor heard anything throughout the night.

On examining the ground in the morning—I had not had time to do this the previous evening—I found that the tigress, after attacking the girl, had gone up the valley for half a mile to where a cattle track crossed the Nandhour river. This track it had followed for two miles, to its junction with the forest road on the ridge above Dalkania. Here on the hard ground I lost the tracks.

For two days the people in all the surrounding villages kept as close to their habitations as the want of sanitary conveniences permitted, and then on the third day news was brought to me by four runners that the man-eater had claimed a victim at Lohali, a village five miles to the south of Dalkania. The runners stated that the distance by the forest road was ten miles, but only five by a short cut by which they proposed taking me back. My preparations were soon made, and a little after midday I set off with my four guides.

A very stiff climb of two miles brought us to the crest of the long ridge south of Dalkania and in view of the valley three miles below, where the 'kill' was reported to have taken place. My guides could give me no particulars. They lived in a small village a mile on the near side of Lohali, and at 10 a.m. a message had come to them—in the manner already described—that a woman of Lohali had been killed by the man-eater, and they were instructed to convey this information to me at Dalkania.

The top of the hill on which we were standing was bare of trees, and, while I regained my breath and had a smoke, my companions pointed out the landmarks. Close to where we were resting, and under the shelter of a great rock, there was a small ruined hut, with a circular thorn enclosure nearby. Questioned about this hut, the men told me the following story. Four years previously a Bhutia (a man from across the border), who had all the winter been sending packages of gur, salt, and other commodities from the bazaars at the foothills into the interior of the district, had built the hut with the object of resting and fattening his flock of goats through the summer and rains, and getting them fit for the next winter's work. After a few weeks the goats wandered down the hill and damaged my informants' crops, and when they came up to lodge a protest, they found the hut empty, and the fierce sheep-dog these men invariably keep with them, to guard their camps at night, chained to an iron stake and dead. Foul play was suspected, and next day men were collected from adjoining villages and a search organized. Pointing to an oak tree scored by lightning and distant some 400 yards, my informants said that under it the remains of the man—his skull and a few splinters of bone—and his clothes had been found. This was the Chowgarh man-eater's first human victim.

There was no way of descending the precipitous hill from where we were sitting, and the men informed me we should have to proceed half a mile along the ridge to where we should find a very steep and rough track which would take us straight down, past their village, to Lohali, which we could see in the valley below. We had covered about half the distance we had to go along the ridge, when all at once, and without being able to ascribe any reason for it, I felt we were being followed. Arguing with myself against this feeling was of no avail; there was only one man-eater in all this area and she had procured a kill three miles away which she was not likely to leave. However, the uneasy feeling persisted, and as we were now at the widest part of the grassy ridge I made the men sit down, instructing them not to move until I returned, and myself set out on a tour of investigation. Retracing my steps to where we had first come out on the ridge I entered the jungle, and carefully worked round the open ground and back to where the men were sitting. No alarm call of animal or bird indicated that a tiger was anywhere in the vicinity, but from there on I made the four men walk in front of me, while I brought up the rear, with thumb on safety-catch and a constant look-out behind.

When we arrived at the little village my companions had started from, they asked for permission to leave me. I was very glad of this request, for I had a mile of dense scrub jungle to go through, and though the feeling that I was being followed had long since left me, I felt safer and more comfortable with only my own life to guard. A little below the outlying terraced fields, and where the dense scrub started, there was a crystal-clear spring of water, from which the village drew its water-supply. Here in the soft wet ground I found the fresh pug marks of the man-eater.

These pug marks, coming from the direction of the village I was making for, coupled with the uneasy feeling I had experienced on the ridge above, convinced me that something had gone wrong with the 'kill' and that my quest would be fruitless. As I emerged from the scrub jungle I came in view of Lohali, which consisted of five or six small houses. Near the door of one of these houses a group of people were collected.

My approach over the steep open ground and narrow terraced fields was observed, and a few men detached themselves from the group near the door and advanced to meet me. One of the number, on old man, bent down to touch my feet, and with tears streaming down his cheeks implored me to save the life of his daughter. His story was as short as it was tragic. His daughter, who was a widow and the only relative he had in the world, had gone out at about ten o'clock to collect dry sticks with which to cook their midday meal. A small stream flows through the valley, and on the far side of the stream from the village the hill goes steeply up. On the lower slope of this hill there are a few terraced fields. At the edge of the lowest field, and distant about 150 yards from the home, the woman had started to collect sticks. A little later, some women who were washing their clothes in the stream heard a scream, and on looking up saw the woman and a tiger disappearing together into the dense thorn bushes, which extended from the edge of the field right down to the stream. Dashing back to the village, the women raised an alarm. The frightened villagers made no attempt at a rescue, and a message for help was shouted to a village higher up the valley, from where it was tossed back to the village from which the four men had set out to find me. Half an hour after the message had been sent, the wounded woman crawled home. Her story was that she had seen the tiger just as it was about to spring on her, and as there was no time to run, she had jumped down the almost perpendicular hillside and while she was in the air the tiger had caught her and they had gone down the hill together. She remembered nothing further until she regained consciousness and found herself near the stream; and being unable to call for help, she had crawled back to the village on her hands and knees.

We had reached the door of the house while this tale was being told. Making the people stand back from the door—the only opening in the four walls of the room—I drew the bloodstained sheet off the woman, whose pitiful condition I am not going to attempt to describe. Had I been a qualified doctor, armed with modern appliances, instead of just a mere man with a little permanganate of potash in his pocket, I do not think it would have been possible to have saved the woman's life; for the deep tooth and claw wounds in her face, neck, and other parts of her body had, in that hot unventilated room, already turned septic. Mercifully she was only semi-conscious. The old father had followed me into the room, and, more for his satisfaction than for any good I thought it would do, I washed the caked blood from the woman's head and body, and cleaned out the wounds as best I could with my handkerchief and a strong solution of permanganate.

It was now too late to think of returning to my camp, and a place would have to be found in which to pass the night. A little way up the stream, and not far from where the women had been washing their clothes, there was a giant pipal tree, with a foot-high masonry platform round it used by the villagers for religious ceremonies.

I undressed on the platform and bathed in the stream; and when the wind had carried out the functions of a towel, dressed again, put my back to the tree and, laying the loaded rifle by my side, prepared to see the night out. Admittedly it was an unsuitable place in which to spend the night, but any place was preferable to the village, and that dark room, with its hot fetid atmosphere and swarm of buzzing flies, where a woman in torment fought desperately for breath.

During the night the wailing of women announced that the sufferer's troubles were over, and when I passed through the village at day break preparations for the funeral were well advanced.

From the experience of this unfortunate woman, and that of the girl at Dalkania, it was now evident that the old tigress had depended, to a very great extent, on her cub to kill the human beings she attacked. Usually only one out of every 100 people attacked by man-eating tigers escapes, but in the case of this man-eater it was apparent that more people would be mauled than killed outright, and as the nearest hospital was fifty miles away, when I returned to Naini Tal I appealed to Government to send a supply of disinfectants and dressings to all the Headmen of villages in the area in which the man-eater was operating. On my subsequent visit I was glad to learn that the request had been complied with, and that the disinfectants had saved the lives of a number of people.

I stayed at Dalkania for another week and announced on a Saturday that I would leave for home the following Monday. I had now been in the man-eater's domain for close on a month, and the constant strain of sleeping in an open tent, and of walking endless miles during the day with the prospect of every step being the last, was beginning to tell on my nerves. The villagers received my announcement with consternation, and only desisted from trying to make me change my decision when I promised them I would return at the first opportunity.

After breakfast on Sunday morning the Headman of Dalkania paid me a visit and requested me to shoot them some game before I left. The request was gladly acceded to, and half an hour later, accompanied by four villagers and one of my own men, and armed with a ·275 rifle and a clip of cartridges, I set off for the hill on the far side of the Nandhour river, on the upper slopes of which I had, from my camp, frequently seen ghooral feeding.

One of the villagers accompanying me was a tall gaunt man with a terribly disfigured face. He had been a constant visitor to my camp, and finding in me a good listener had told and retold his encounter with the man-eater so often that I could, without effort, repeat the whole story in my sleep. The encounter had taken place four years previously and is best told in his own words.

'Do you see that pine tree, Sahib, at the bottom of the grassy slope on the shoulder of the hill? Yes, the pine tree with a big white rock to the east of it. Well, it was at the upper edge of the grassy slope that the man-eater attacked me. The grassy slope is as perpendicular as the wall of a house, and none but a hillman could find foothold on it. My son, who was eight years of age at the time, and I had cut grass on that slope on the day of my misfortune, carrying the grass up in armfuls to the belt of trees where the ground is level.

'I was stooping down at the very edge of the slope, tying the grass into a big bundle, when the tiger sprang at me and buried its teeth, one under my right eye, one in my chin and the other two here at the back of my neck. The tiger's mouth struck me with a threat blow and I fell over on my back, while the tiger lay on top of me chest to chest, with its stomach between my legs. When falling backwards I had flung out my arms and my right hand had come in contact with an oak sapling. As my fingers grasped the sapling, an idea came to me. My legs were free, and if I could draw them up and insert my feet under and against the tiger's belly, I might be able to push the tiger off, and run away. The pain, as the tiger crushed all the bones on the right side of my face, was terrible; but I did not lose consciousness, for you see, Sahib, at that time I was a young man, and in all the hills there was no one to compare with me in strength. Very slowly, so as not to anger the tiger I drew my legs up on either side of it, and gently inserted my bare feet against its belly. Then placing my left hand against its chest and pushing and kicking upwards with all my might, I lifted the tiger right off the ground and, we being on the very edge of the perpendicular hillside, the tiger went crashing down and belike would have taken me with him, had my hold on the sapling not been a good one.

'My son had been too frightened to run away, and when the tiger had gone, I took his loincloth from him and wrapped it round my head, and holding his hand I walked back to the village. Arrived at my home I told my wife to call all my friends together, for I wished to see their faces before I died. When my friends were assembled and saw my condition, they wanted to put me on a charpoy and carry me fifty miles to the Almora hospital, but this I would not consent to; for my suffering was great, and being assured that my time had come, I wanted to die where I had been born, and where I had lived all my life. Water was brought, for I was thirsty and my head was on fire, but when it was poured into my mouth, it all flowed out through the holes in my neck. Thereafter, for a period beyond measure, there was great confusion in my mind, and much pain in my head and in my neck, and while I waited and longed for death to end my sufferings, my wounds healed of themselves, and I became well.

'And now, Sahib, I am as you see me, old and thin, and with white hair, and a face that no man can look on without repulsion. My enemy lives and continues to claim victims but do not be deceived into thinking it is a tiger, for it is no tiger but an evil spirit, who, when it craves for human flesh and blood, takes on for a little while the semblance of a tiger. But they say you are a sadhu, Sahib, and the spirits that guard sadhus are more powerful than this evil spirit, as is proved by the fact that you spent three days and three nights alone in the jungle, and came out—as your men said you would—alive and unhurt.'

Looking at the great frame of the man, it was easy to picture him as having been a veritable giant. And a giant in strength he must have been, for no man, unless he had been endowed with strength far above the average, could have lifted the tigress into the air, torn its hold from the side of his head, carrying away, as it did, half his face with it, and hurled it down the precipitous hill.

My gaunt friend constituted himself our guide, and with a beautifully polished axe, with a long tapering handle, over his shoulder, led us by devious steep paths to the valley below. Fording the Nandhour river, we crossed several wide terraced fields, now out of cultivation for fear of the man-eater, and on reaching the foot of the hill started what proved to be a very stiff climb, through forest, to the grass slopes above. Gaunt my friend may have been, but he lacked nothing in wind, and tough as I was it was only by calling frequent halts—to admire the view—that I was able to keep up with him.

Emerging from the tree forest, we went diagonally across the grassy slope, in the direction of a rock cliff that extended upwards for a thousand feet or more. It was on this cliff, sprinkled over with tufts of short grass, that I had seen ghooral feeding from my tent. We had covered a few hundred yards when one of these small mountain-goats started up out of a ravine, and at my shot crumpled up and slipped back out of sight. Alarmed by the report of the rifle, another ghooral, that had evidently been lying asleep at the foot of the cliff, sprang to his feet and went up the rock face, as only he or his big brother the tahr could have done. As he climbed upwards, I lay down and, putting the sight to 200 yards, waited for him to stop. This he presently did, coming out on a projecting rock to look down on us. At my shot he staggered, regained his footing, and very slowly continued his climb. At the second shot he fell, hung for a second or two on a narrow ledge, and then fell through space to the grassy slope from whence he had started. Striking the ground he rolled over and over, passing within a hundred yards of us, and eventually came to rest on a cattle track a hundred and fifty yards below.

I have only once, in all the three years I have been shooting, witnessed a similar sight to the one we saw during the next few minutes, and on that occasion the marauder was a leopard.

The ghooral had hardly come to rest when a big Himalayan bear came lumbering out of a ravine on the side of the grassy slope and, with never a pause or backward look, came at a fast trot along the cattle track. On reaching the dead goat he sat down and took it into his lap, and as he started nosing the goat, I fired. Maybe I hurried over my shot, or allowed too much for refraction; anyway the bullet went low and struck the bear in the stomach instead of in the chest. To the six of us who were intently watching, it appeared that the bear took the smack of the bullet as an assault from the ghooral, for, rearing up, he flung the animal from him and came galloping along the track, emitting angry grunts. As he passed a hundred yards below us I fired my fifth and last cartridge, the bullet, as I found later, going through the fleshy part of his hind quarters.

While the men retrieved the two ghooral, I descended to examine the blood trail. The blood on the track showed the bear to be hard hit, but even so there was danger in following it up with an empty rifle, for bears are bad-tempered at the best of times, and are very ugly customers to deal with when wounded.

When the men rejoined me a short council of war was held. Camp was three and a half miles away, and as it was now 2 p.m. it would not be possible to fetch more ammunition, track down and kill the bear, and get back home by dark; so it was unanimously decided that we should follow up the wounded animal and try to finish it off with stones and the axe.

The hill was steep and fairly free of undergrowth, and by keeping above the bear there was a sporting chance of our being able to accomplish our task without serious mishap. We accordingly set off, I leading the way, followed by three men, the rear being brought up by two men each with a ghooral strapped to his back. Arrived at the spot where I had fired my last shot, additional blood on the track greatly encouraged us. Two hundred yards further on, the blood trail led down into a deep ravine. Here we divided up our force, two men crossing to the far side, the owner of the axe and I remaining on the near side, with the men carrying the ghooral following in our rear. On the word being given we started to advance down the hill. In the bed of the ravine, and fifty feet below us, was a dense patch of stunted bamboo, and when a stone was thrown into this thicket, the bear got up with a scream of rage; and six men, putting their best foot foremost, went straight up the hill. I was not trained to this form of exercise, and on looking back to see if the bear was gaining on us, I saw, much to my relief, that he was going as hard downhill as we were going uphill. A shout to my companions, a rapid change of direction, and we were off in a full cry and rapidly gaining on our quarry. A few well-aimed shots had been registered, followed by delighted shouts from the marksmen, and angry grunts from the bear, when at a sharp bend in the ravine, which necessitated a cautious advance, we lost touch with the bear. To have followed the blood trail would have been easy, but here the ravine was full of big rocks, behind any of which the bear might have been lurking, so while the encumbered men sat down for a rest, a cast was made on either side of the ravine. While my companion went forward to look down into the ravine, I went to the right to prospect a rocky cliff that went sheer down for some 200 feet. Holding on to a tree for support, I leaned over and saw the bear lying on a narrow ledge forty feet immediately below me. I picked up a stone, about thirty pounds in weight, and, again advancing to the edge and in imminent danger of going over myself, I raised the stone above my head with both hands and hurled it.

The stone struck the ledge a few inches from the bear's head, and scrambling to his feet he disappeared from sight, to reappear a minute later on the side of the hill. Once again the hunt was on. The ground was here more open and less encumbered with rocks, and the four of us who were running light had no difficulty in keeping up with him. For a mile or more we ran him at top speed, until we eventually cleared the forest and emerged on to the terraced fields. Rainwater had cut several deep and narrow channels across the fields, and in one of these channels the bear took cover.

The man with the distorted face was the only armed member of the party and he was unanimously elected executioner. Nothing loth, he cautiously approached the bear and, swinging his beautifully polished axe aloft, brought the square head down on the bear's skull. The result was as alarming as it was unexpected. The axe-head rebounded off the bear's skull as though it had been struck on a block of rubber, and with a scream of rage the animal reared up on his hind legs. Fortunately he did not follow up his advantage, for we were bunched together, and in trying to run got in each other's way.

The bear did not appear to like this open ground, and after going a short way down the channel again took cover. It was now my turn with the axe. The bear, however, having once been struck resented my approach, and it was only after a great deal of manoeuvring that I eventually got within striking distance. It has been my ambition when a boy to be a lumber-man in Canada, and I had attained sufficient proficiency with an axe to split a match-stick. I had no fear, therefore, as the owner had, of the axe glancing off and getting damaged on the stones, and the moment I got within reach I buried the entire blade in the bear's skull.

Himalayan bearskins are very greatly prized by our hill folk, and the owner of the axe was a very proud and envied man when I told him he could have the skin in addition to a double share of the ghooral meat. Leaving the men, whose numbers were being rapidly augmented by new arrivals from the village, to skin and divide up the bag, I climbed up to the village and paid, as already related, a last visit to the injured girl. The day had been a strenuous one, and if the man-eater had paid me a visit that night she would have 'caught me napping'.

On the road I had taken when coming to Dalkania there was several long stiff climbs up treeless hills, and when I mentioned the discomforts of this road to the villagers they had suggested that I should go back via Haira Khan. This route would necessitate only one climb to the ridge above the village, from where it was downhill all the way to Ranibagh, whence I could complete the journey to Naini Tal by car.

I had warned my men overnight to prepare for an early start, and a little before sunrise, leaving them to pack up and follow me, I said good-bye to my friends at Dalkania, and started on the two-mile climb to the forest road on the ridge above. The footpath I took was not the one by which my men, and later I, had arrived at Dalkania, but was one the villagers used when going to, and returning from, the bazaars in the foothills.

The path wound in and out of deep ravines, through thick oak and pine forests and dense undergrowth. There had been no news of the tigress for a week. This absence of news made me all the more careful, and an hour after leaving camp I arrived without mishap at an open glade near the top of the hill, within a hundred yards of the forest road.

The glade was pear-shaped, roughly a hundred yards long and fifty yards wide, with a stagnant pool of rainwater in the centre of it. Sambhar and other game used this pool as a drinking place and wallow and, curious to see the tracks round it, I left the path, which skirted the left-hand side of the glade and passed close under a cliff of rock which extended up to the road. As I approached the pool I saw the pug marks of the tigress in the soft earth at the edge of the water. She had approached the pool from the same direction as I had, and, evidently disturbed by me, had crossed the water and gone into the dense tree and scrub jungle on the right-hand side of the glade. A great chance lost, for had I kept as careful a look-out in front as I had behind I should have seen her before she saw me. However, though I had missed a chance, the advantages were now all on my side and distinctly in my favour.

The tigress had seen me, or she would not have crossed the pool and hurried for shelter, as her tracks showed she had done. Having seen me she had also seen that I was alone, and watching me from cover as she undoubtedly was, she would assume I was going to the pool to drink as she had done. My movements up to this point had been quite natural, and if I could continue to make her think I was unaware of her presence, she would possibly give me a second chance. Stooping down and keeping a very sharp look-out from under my hat, I coughed several times, splashed the water about, and then, moving very slowly and gathering dry sticks on the way, I went to the foot of the steep rock. Here I built a small fire, and putting my back to the rock, lit a cigarette. By the time the cigarette had been smoked the fire had burnt out. I then lay down, and pillowing my head on my left arm placed the rifle on the ground with my finger on the trigger.

The rock above me was too steep for any animal to find foothold on. I had therefore only my front to guard, and as the heavy cover nowhere approached to within less than twenty yards of my position I was quite safe. I had all this time neither seen nor heard anything; nevertheless, I was convinced that the tigress was watching me. The rim of my hat, while effectually shading my eyes, did not obstruct my vision and inch by inch I scanned every bit of the jungle within my range of view. There was not a breath of wind blowing, and not a leaf or a blade of grass stirred. My men, whom I had instructed to keep close together and sing from the time they left camp until they joined me on the forest road, were not due for an hour and a half, and during this time it was more than likely that the tigress would break cover and try to stalk, or rush, me.

There are occasions when time draws, and others when it files. My left arm, on which my head was pillowed, had lone since ceased to prick and had gone dead, but even so the singing of the men in the valley below reached me all too soon. The voices grew louder, and presently I caught sight of the men as they rounded a sharp bend. It was possibly at this bend that the tigress had seen me as she turned round to retrace her steps after having her drink. Another failure, and the last chance on this trip gone.

After my men had rested we climbed up to the road, and set off on what proved to be a very long twenty-mile march to the forest Rest House at Haira Khan. After going a couple of hundred yards over open ground, the road entered very thick forest, and here I made the men walk in front while I brought up the rear. We had gone about two miles in this order, when on turning a corner I saw a man sitting on the road, herding buffaloes. It was now time to call a halt for breakfast, so I asked the man where we could get the water. He pointed down the hill straight in front of him, and said there was a spring down there from which his village, which was just round the shoulder of the hill, drew its water-supply. There was, however, no necessity for us to go down the hill for water, for if we continued a little further we should find a good spring on the road.

His village was at the upper end of the valley in which the woman of Lohali had been killed the previous week, and he told me that nothing had been heard of the man-eater since, and added that the animal was possibly now at the other end of the district. I disabused his mind on this point by telling him about the fresh pug marks I had seen at the pool, and advised him very strongly to collect his buffaloes and return to the village. His buffaloes, some ten in number, were straggling up towards the road and he said he would leave as soon they had grazed up to where he was sitting. Handing him a cigarette, I left him with a final warning. What occurred after I left was related to me by the men of the village, when I paid the district a second visit some months later.

When the man eventually got home that day he told the assembled villagers of our meeting, and my warning, and said that after he had watched me go round a bend in the road a hundred yards away he started to light the cigarette I had given him. A wind was blowing, and to protect the flame of the match he bend forward, and while in this position he was seized from behind by the right shoulder and pulled backwards. His first thought was of the party who had just left him, but unfortunately, his cry for help was not heard by them. Help, however, was near at hand, for as soon as the buffaloes heard his cry, mingled with the growl of the tigress, they charged on to the road and drove the tigress off. His shoulder and arm were broken, and with great difficulty he managed to climb on the back of one of his brave rescuers, and, followed by the rest of the herd, reached his home. The villagers tied up his wounds as best they could and carried him thirty miles, non-stop to the Haldwani hospital, where he died shortly after admission.

When Atropos who snips the threads of life misses one thread she cuts another, and we who do not know why one thread is missed and another cut, call it Fate, Kismet, or what we will.

For a month I had lived in an open tent, a hundred yards from the nearest human being, and from dawn to dusk had wandered through the jungles, and on several occasions had disguised myself as a woman and cut grass in places where no local inhabitant dared to go. During this period the man-eater had, quite possibly, missed many opportunities of adding me to her bag and now, when making a final effort, she had quite by chance encountered this unfortunate man and claimed him as a victim.

~

The following February I returned to Dalkania. A number of human beings had been killed, and many more wounded, over a wide area since my departure from the district the previous summer, and as the whereabouts of the tigress was not known and the chances in one place were as good as in another, I decided to return and camp on the ground with which I was now familiar.

On my arrival at Dalkania I was told that a cow had been killed the previous evening, on the hill on which the bear hunt had taken place. The men who had been herding the cattle at the time were positive that the animal they had seen killing the cow was a tiger. The kill was lying near some bushes at the edge of a deserted field, and was clearly visible from the spot where my tent was being put up. Vultures were circling over the kill, and looking through my field-glasses I saw several of these birds perched on a tree, to the left of the kill. From the fact that the kill was lying out in the open, and the vultures had not descended on it, I concluded (a) that the cow had been killed by a leopard, and (b) that the leopard was lying up close to the kill.

The ground below the field on which the cow was lying was very steep and overgrown with dense brushwood. The man-eater was still at large, and an approach over this ground was therefore inadvisable.

To the right was a grassy slope, but the ground here was too open to admit of my approaching the kill without being seen. A deep heavily wooded ravine, starting from near the crest of the hill, ran right down to the Nandhour river, passing within a short distance of the kill. The tree on which the vultures were perched was growing on the edge of this ravine. I decided on this ravine as my line of approach. While I had been planning out the stalk with the assistance of the villagers, who knew every foot of the ground, my men had prepared tea for me. The day was now on the decline but by going hard I should just have time to visit the kill and return to camp before nightfall.

Before setting off I instructed my men to be on the look-out. If, after hearing a shot, they saw me on the open ground near the kill, three or four of them were immediately to leave camp, and, keeping to the open ground, to join me. On the other hand if I did not fire, and failed to return by morning, a search party was to be organized.

The ravine was overgrown with raspberry bushes and strewn with great rocks, and as the wind was blowing downhill, my progress was slow. After a stiff climb I eventually reached the tree on which the vultures were perched, only to find that the kill was not visible from this spot. The deserted field, which through my field-glasses had appeared to be quite straight, I found to be crescent-shaped, ten yards across at its widest part and tapering to a point at both ends. The outer edge was bordered with dense undergrowth, and the hill fell steeply away from the inner edge. Only two-thirds of the field was visible from where I was standing, and in order to see the remaining one-third, on which the kill was lying, it would be necessary either to make a wide detour and approach from the far side or climb the tree on which the vultures were perched.

I decided on the latter course. The cow, as far as I could judge, was about twenty yards from the tree, and it was quite possible that the animal that had killed her was even less than that distance from me. To climb the tree without disturbing the killer would have been an impossible feat, and would not have been attempted had it not been for the vultures. There were by now some twenty of these birds on the tree and their number was being added to by new arrivals, and as the accommodation on the upper branches was limited there was much flapping of wings and quarrelling. The tree was leaning outwards away from the hill, and about ten feet from the ground a great limb projected out over the steep hillside. Hampered with the rifle I had great difficulty in reaching this limb. Waiting until a fresh quarrel had broken out among the vultures, I stepped out along the branch—a difficult balancing feat where a slip or false step would have resulted in a fall of a hundred or more feet on to the rocks below—reached a fork, and sat down.

The kill, from which only a few pounds of flesh had been eaten, was now in full view. I had been in position about ten minutes, and was finding my perch none too comfortable, when two vultures, who had been circling round and were uncertain of their reception on the tree, alighted on the field a short distance from the cow. They had hardly come to rest when they were on the wing again, and at the same moment the bushes on my side of the kill were gently agitated and out into the open stepped a fine male leopard.

Those who have never seen a leopard under favourable conditions in his natural surroundings can have no conception of the grace of movement, and beauty of colouring, of this the most graceful and the most beautiful of all animals in our Indian jungles. Nor are his attractions limited to outward appearances, for, pound for pound, his strength is second to none, and in courage he lacks nothing. To class such an animal as VERMIN, as is done in some parts of India, is a crime which only those could perpetrate whose knowledge of the leopard is limited to the miserable, underfed, and mangy specimens seen in captivity.

But beautiful as the specimen was that stood before me, his life was forfeit, for he had taken to cattle killing, and I had promised the people of Dalkania and other villages on my last visit that I would rid them of this their minor enemy, if opportunity offered. The opportunity had now come, and I do not think the leopard heard the shot that killed him.

Of the many incomprehensible things one meets with in

life, the hardest to assign any reason for is the way in which misfortune dogs an individual, or a family. Take as an example the case of the owner of the cow over which I had shot the leopard. He was a boy, eight years of age, and an only child. Two years previously his mother, while out cutting grass for the cow, had been killed and eaten by the man-eater, and twelve months later his father had suffered a like fate. The few pots and pans the family possessed had been sold to pay off the small debt left by the father, and the son started life as the owner of one cow; and this particular cow the leopard had selected, out of a herd of two or three hundred head of village cattle, and killed. (I am afraid my attempt to repair a heartbreak was not very successful in this case, for though the new cow, a red one, was an animal of parts, it did not make up to the boy for the loss of his lifelong white companion.)

My young buffaloes had been well cared for by the man in whose charge I had left them, and the day after my arrival I started tying them out, though I had little hope of the tigress accepting them as bait.

Five miles down the Nandhour valley nestles a little village at the foot of a great cliff of rock, some thousand or more feet high. The man-eater had, during the past few months, killed four people on the outskirts of this village. Shortly after I shot the leopard, a deputation came from this village to request me to move my camp from Dalkania to a site that had been selected for me near their village. I was told that the tiger had frequently been seen on the cliff above the village and that it appeared to have its home in one of the many caves in the cliff face. That very morning, I was informed, some women out cutting grass had seen the tiger, and the villagers were now in a state of terror, and too frightened to leave their homes. Promising the deputation I would do all I could to help them, I made a very early start next morning, climbed the hill opposite the village, and scanned the cliff for an hour or more through my field-glasses. I then crossed the valley, and by way of a very deep ravine climbed the cliff above the village. Here the going was very difficult and not at all to my liking, for added to the danger of a fall, which would have resulted in a broken neck, was the danger of an attack on ground on which it would be impossible to defend oneself.

By 2 p.m. I had seen as much of the rock cliff as I shall ever want to see again, and was making my way up the valley towards my camp and breakfast, when on looking back before starting the stiff climb to Dalkania I saw two men running towards me from the direction in which I had just come. On joining me the men informed me that a tiger had just killed a bullock in the deep ravine up which I had gone earlier in the day. Telling one of the men to go on up to my camp and instruct my servant to send tea and some food, I turned round and, accompanied by the other man, retraced my steps down the valley.

The ravine where the bullock had been killed was about 200 feet deep and 100 feet wide. As we approached it I saw a number of vultures rising, and when we arrived at the kill I found the vultures had cleaned it out, leaving only the skin and bones. The spot where the remains of the bullock were lying was only a hundred yards from the village but there was no way up the steep bank, so my guide took me a quarter of a mile down the ravine, to where a cattle track crossed it. This track, after gaining the high ground, wound in and out through dense scrub jungle before it finally fetched up at the village. On arrival at the village I told the Headman that the vultures had ruined the kill, and asked him to provide me with a young buffalo and a short length of stout rope; while these were being procured, two of my men arrived from Dalkania with the food I had sent for.

The sun was near setting when I re-entered the ravine, followed by several men leading a vigorous young male buffalo which the Headman had purchased for me from an adjoining village. Fifty yards from where the bullock had been killed, one end of a pine tree washed down from the hill above had been buried deep in the bed of the ravine. After tying the buffalo very securely to the exposed end of the pine, the men returned to the village. There were no trees in the vicinity, and the only possible place for a sit-up was a narrow ledge on the village side of the ravine. With great difficulty I climbed to this ledge, which was about two feet wide by five feet long, and twenty feet above the bed of the ravine. From a little below the ledge the rock shelved inwards, forming a deep recess that was not visible from the ledge. The ledge canted downwards at an uncomfortable angle, and when I had taken my seat on it, I had my back towards the direction from which I expected the tiger to come, while the tethered buffalo was to my left front, and distant about thirty yards from me.

The sun had set when the buffalo, who had been lying down, scrambled to his feet and faced up the ravine, and a moment later a stone came rolling down. It would not have been possible for me to have fired in the direction from which the sound had come, so to avoid detection I sat perfectly still. After some time the buffalo gradually turned to the left until he was facing in my direction. This showed that whatever he was frightened of— and I could see he was frightened—was in the recess below me. Presently the head of a tiger appeared directly under me. A head-shot at a tiger is only justified in an emergency, and any movement on my part might have betrayed my presence. For a long minute or two the head remained perfectly still, and then, with a quick dash forward, and one great bound, the tiger was on the buffalo. The buffalo, as I have stated, was facing the tiger, and to avoid a frontal attack with the possibility of injury from the buffalo's horns, the tiger's dash carried him to the left of the buffalo, and he made his attack at right angles. There was no fumbling for tooth-hold, no struggle, and no sound beyond the impact of the two heavy bodies, after which the buffalo lay quite still with the tiger lying partly over it and holding it by the throat. It is generally believed that tigers kill by delivering a smashing blow on the neck. This is incorrect. Tigers kill with their teeth.

The right side of the tiger was towards me and, taking careful aim with the ·275 I had armed myself with when leaving camp that morning, I fired. Relinquishing its hold on the buffalo, the tiger, without making a sound, turned and bounded off up the ravine and out of sight. Clearly a miss, for which I was unable to assign any reason. If the tiger had not seen me or the flash of the rifle there was a possibility that it would return; so recharging the rifle I sat on.

The buffalo, after the tiger left him, lay without movement, and the conviction grew on me that I had shot him instead of the tiger. Ten, fifteen minutes had dragged by, when the tiger's head for a second time appeared from the recess below me. Again there was a long pause, and then, very slowly, the tiger emerged, walked up to the buffalo and stood looking down at it. With the whole length of the back as a target I was going to make no mistake the second time. Very carefully the sights were aligned, and the trigger slowly pressed; but instead of the tiger falling dead as I expected it to, it sprang to the left and went tearing up a little ravine, dislodging stones as it went up the steep hillside.

Two shots fired in comparatively good light at a range of thirty yards, and heard by anxious villagers for miles round; and all I should have to show for them would be, certainly one, and quite possibly two, bullet holes in a dead buffalo. Clearly my eyesight was failing, or in climbing the rock I had knocked the foresight out of alignment. But on focusing my eyes on small objects I found there was nothing wrong with my eyesight, and a glance along the barrel showed that the sights were all right, so the only reason I could assign for having missed the tiger twice was bad shooting.

There was no chance of the tiger returning a third time; and even if it did return, there was nothing to be gained by risking the possibility of only wounding it in bad light when I had not been able to kill it while the light had been comparatively good. Under these circumstances there was no object in my remaining any longer on the ledge.

My clothes were still damp from my exertions earlier in the day, a cold wind was blowing and promised to get colder, my shorts were of thin khaki and the rock was hard and cold, and a hot cup of tea awaited me in the village. Good as these reasons were, there was a better and a more convincing reason for my remaining where I was—the man-eater. It was now quite dark. A quarter-of-mile walk, along a boulder-strewn ravine and a winding path through dense undergrowth, lay between me and the village. Beyond the suspicions of the villagers that the tiger they had seen the previous day—and that I had quite evidently just fired at—was the man-eater, I had no definite knowledge of the man-eater's whereabouts; and though at that moment she might have been fifty miles away, she might also have been watching me from a distance of fifty yards, so, uncomfortable as my perch was, prudence dictated that I should remain where I was. As the long hours dragged by, the conviction grew on me that man-eater shooting, by night, was not a pastime that appealed to me, and that if this animal could not be shot during daylight hours she would have to be left to die of old age. This conviction was strengthened, when, cold and stiff, I started to climb down as soon as there was sufficient light to shoot by, and slipping on the dew-drenched rock completed the descent with my feet in the air. Fortunately I landed on a bed of sand, without doing myself or the rifle any injury.

Early as it was I found the village astir, and I was quickly in the middle of a small crowd. In reply to the eager questions from all sides, I was only able to say that I had been firing at an imaginary tiger with blank ammunition.

A pot of tea drunk while sitting near a roaring fire did much to restore warmth to my inner and outer man, and then, accompanied by most of the men and all the boys of the village, I went to where a rock jutted out over the ravine and directly above my overnight exploit. To the assembled throng I explained how the tiger had appeared from the recess under me and had bounded on to the buffalo, and how after I fired it had dashed off in *that* direction; and as I pointed up the ravine there was an excited shout of 'Look, Sahib, there's the tiger lying dead!' My eyes were strained with an all-night vigil, but even after looking away and back again there was no denying the fact the tiger was lying there, dead. To the very natural question of why I had fired a second shot after a period of twenty or thirty minutes, I said that the tiger had appeared a second time from exactly the same place, and that I had fired at it while it was standing near the buffalo and that it had gone up *that* side ravine—and there were renewed shouts, in which the women and girls who had now come up joined, of 'Look, Sahib, there is another tiger lying dead!' Both tigers appeared to be about the same size and both were lying sixty yards from where I had fired.

Questioned on the subject of this second tiger, the villagers said that when the four human beings had been killed, and also on the previous day when the bullock had been killed, only one tiger had been seen. The mating season for tigers is an elastic one extending from November to April, and the man-eater—if either of two tigers lying within view was the man-eater—had evidently provided herself with a mate.

A way into the ravine, down the steep rock face, was found some 200 yards below where I had sat up, and, followed by the entire population of the village, I went past the dead buffalo to where the first tiger was lying. As I approached it hopes rose high, for she was an old tigress. Handing the rifle to the nearest man I got down on my knees to examine her feet. On that day when the tigress had tried to stalk the women cutting wheat she had left some beautiful pug marks on the edge of the field. They were the first pug marks I had seen of the man-eater, and

I had examined them very carefully. They showed the tigress to be a very old animal, whose feet had splayed out with age. The pads of the forefeet were heavily rutted, one deep rut running right across the pad of the right forefoot, and the toes were elongated to a length I had never before seen in a tiger. With these distinctive feet it would have been easy to pick the man-eater out of a hundred dead tigers. The animal before me was, I found to my great regret, not the man-eater. When I conveyed this information to the assembled throng of people there was a murmur of strong dissent from all sides. It was asserted that I myself, on my previous visit, had declared the man-eater to be an old tigress, and such an animal I had now shot a few yards from where, only a short time previously, four of their number had been killed. Against this convincing evidence, of what value was the evidence of the feet, for the feet of all tigers were alike!

The second tiger could, under the circumstances, only be a male, and while I made preparations to skin the tigress, I sent a party of men to fetch him. The side ravine was steep and narrow, and after a great deal of shouting and laughter the second tiger—a fine male—was laid down alongside the tigress.

The skinning of those two tigers that had been dead fourteen hours, with the sun beating down on my back and an ever-growing crowd pressing round, was one of the most unpleasant tasks I have ever undertaken. By early afternoon the job was completed, and with the skins neatly tied up for my men to carry I was ready to start on my five-mile walk back to camp.

During the morning Headmen and others had come in from adjoining villages, and before leaving I assured them that the Chowgarh man-eater was not dead and warned them that the slackening of precautions would give the tigress the opportunity she was waiting for. Had my warning been heeded, the man-eater would not have claimed as many victims as she did during the succeeding months.

There was no further news of the man-eater, and after a stay of a few weeks at Dalkania, I left to keep an appointment with the district officials in the terai.

~

In March 1950, Vivian, our District Commissioner, was touring through the man-eater's domain, and on the 22nd of the month I received an urgent request from him to go to Kala Agar, where he said he would await my arrival. It is roughly fifty miles from Naini Tal to Kala Agar, and two days after receipt of Vivian's letter I arrived in time for breakfast at the Kala Agar Forest Bungalow, where he and Mrs Vivian were staying.

Over breakfast the Vivians told me they had arrived at the bungalow on the afternoon of 21st, and while they were having tea on the verandah, one of six women who were cutting grass in the compound of the bungalow had been killed and carried off by the man-eater. Rifles were hurriedly seized and, accompanied by some of his staff, Vivian followed up the 'drag' and found the dead woman tucked away under a bush at the foot of an oak tree. On examining the ground later, I found that on the approach of Vivian's party the tigress had gone off down the hill, and throughout the subsequent proceedings had remained in a thicket of raspberry bushes, fifty yards from the kill. A machan was put up in the oak tree for Vivian, and two others in trees near the forest road which passed thirty yards above the kill, for members of his staff. The machans were occupied as soon as they were ready and the party sat up the whole night, without, however, seeing anything of the tigress.

Next morning the body of the woman was removed for cremation, and a young buffalo was tied up on the forest road about half a mile from the bungalow, and killed by the tigress the same night. The following evening the Vivians sat up over the buffalo. There was no moon, and just as daylight was fading out and nearby objects becoming indistinct, they first heard, and then saw an animal coming up to the kill, which in the uncertain light they mistook for a bear; but for this unfortunate mistake their very sporting effort would have resulted in their bagging the man-eater, for both the Vivians are good rifle shots.

On the 25th the Vivians left Kala Agar, and during the course of the day my four buffaloes arrived from Dalkania. As the tigress now appeared to be inclined to accept this form of bait I tied them up at intervals of a few hundred yards along the forest road. For three nights in succession the tigress passed within a few feet of the buffaloes without touching them, but on the fourth night the buffalo nearest the bungalow was killed. On examining the kill in the morning I was disappointed to find that the buffalo had been killed by a pair of leopards I had heard calling the previous night above the bungalow. I did not like the idea of firing in this locality, for fear of driving away the tigress, but it was quite evident that if I did not shoot the leopards they would kill my three remaining buffaloes, so I stalked them while they were sunning themselves on some big rocks above the kill, and shot both of them.

The forest road from the Kala Agar Bungalow runs for several miles due west through very beautiful forests of pine, oak, and rhododendron, and in these forests there is, compared with the rest of Kumaon, quite a lot of game in the way of sambhar, kakar, and pig, in addition to a great wealth of bird life. On two occasions I suspected the tigress of having killed sambhar in this forest, and though on both occasions I found the blood-stained spot where the animal had been killed, I failed to find either of the kills.

For the next fourteen days I spent all the daylight hours either on the forest road, on which no one but myself ever set foot, or in the jungle, and only twice during that period did I get near the tigress. On the first occasion I had been down to visit an isolated village, on the south face of Kala Agar ridge, that had been abandoned the previous year owing to the depredations of the man-eater, and on the way back had taken a cattle track that went over the ridge and down the far side to the forest road, when, approaching a pile of rocks, I suddenly felt there was danger ahead. The distance from the ridge to the forest road was roughly 300 yards. The track, after leaving the ridge, went steeply down for a few yards and then turned to the right and ran diagonally across the hill for a hundred yards; the pile of rocks was about midway on the right-hand side of this length of the track. Beyond the rocks a hairpin bend carried the track to the left, and a hundred yards further on, another sharp bend took it down to its junction with the forest road.

I had been along this track many times, and this was the first occasion on which I hesitated to pass the rocks. To avoid them I should either have had to go several hundred yards through dense undergrowth, or make a wide detour round and above them; the former would have subjected me to very great danger, and there was no time for the latter, for the sun was near setting and I had still two miles to go. So, whether I liked it or not, there was nothing for it but to face the rocks. The wind was blowing up the hills so I was able to ignore the thick cover on the left of the track, and concentrate all my attention on the rocks to my right. A hundred feet would see me clear of the danger zone, and this distance I covered foot by foot, walking sideways with my face to the rocks and the rifle to my shoulder; a strange mode of progression, had there been any to see it.

Thirty yards beyond the rocks was an open glade, starting from the right-hand side of the track and extending up the hill for fifty or sixty yards, and screened from the rocks by a fringe of bushes. In this glade a kakar was grazing. I saw her before she saw me, and watched her out of the corner of my eye. On catching sight of me she threw up her head, and as I was not looking in her direction and was moving slowly on she stood stock still, as these animals have a habit of doing when they are under the impression that they have not been seen. On arrival at the hairpin bend I looked over my shoulder and saw that the kakar had lowered her head, and was once more cropping the grass.

I had walked a short distance along the track after passing the bend when the kakar went dashing up the hill, barking hysterically. In a few quick strides I was back at the bend, and was just in time to see a movement in the bushes on the lower side of the track. That the kakar had seen the tigress was quite evident, and the only place where she could have seen her was on the track. The movement I had seen might have been caused by the passage of a bird, on the other hand it might have been caused by the tigress; anyway, a little investigation was necessary before proceeding further on my way.

A trickle of water seeping out from under the rocks had damped the red clay of which the track was composed, making an ideal surface for the impression of tracks. In this damp clay I had left footprints, and over these footprints I now found the splayed-out pug marks of the tigress where she had jumped down from the rocks and followed me, until the kakar had seen her and given its alarm call, whereupon the tigress had left the track and entered the bushes where I had seen the movement. The tigress was undoubtedly familiar with every foot of the ground, and not having had an opportunity of killing me at the rocks—and her chance of bagging me at the first hairpin bend having been spoilt by the kakar—she was probably now making her way through the dense undergrowth to try to intercept me at the second bend.

Further progress along the track was now not advisable, so I followed the kakar up the glade, and turning to the left worked my way down, over open ground, to the forest road below. Had there been sufficient daylight I believe I could, that evening, have turned the tables on the tigress, for the conditions, after she left the shelter of the rocks, were all in my favour. I knew the ground as well as she did, and while she had no reason to suspect my intention towards her, I had the advantage of knowing, very clearly, her intentions towards me. However, though the conditions were in my favour, I was unable to take advantage of them owing to the lateness of the evening.

    I have made mention elsewhere of the sense that warns us of impending danger, and will not labour the subject further beyond stating that this sense is a very real one and that I do not know, and therefore cannot explain, what brings it into operation. On this occasion I had neither heard nor seen the tigress, nor had I received any indication from bird or beast of her presence, and yet I knew, without any shadow of doubt, that she was lying up for me among the rocks. I had been out for many hours that day and had covered many miles of jungle with unflagging caution, but without one moment's unease, and then, on cresting the ridge, and coming in sight of the rocks, I knew they held danger for me, and this knowledge was confirmed a few minutes later by the kakar's warning call to the jungle folk, and by my finding the man-eater's pug marks superimposed on my footprints.

~

To those of my readers who have had the patience to accompany me so far in my narrative, I should like to give a clear and a detailed account of my first—and last—meeting with the tigress.

    The meeting took place in the early afternoon of the 11th of April 1930, nineteen days after my arrival at Kala Agar.

    I had gone out that day at 2 p.m. with the intention of tying up my three buffaloes at selected places along the forest road, when at a point a mile from the bungalow, where the road crosses a ridge and goes from the north to the west face of the Kala Agar range, I came on a large party of men who had been out collecting firewood. In the party was an old man who, pointing down the hill to a thicket of young oak trees some 500 yards from where we were standing, said it was in that thicket where the man-eater, a month previously, had killed his only son, a lad eighteen years of age. I had not heard the father's version of the killing of his son, so, while we sat on the edge of the road smoking, he told his story, pointing out the spot where the lad had been killed, and where all that was left of him had been found the following day. The old man blamed the twenty-five men who had been out collecting firewood on that day for the death of his son, saying, very bitterly, that they had run away and left him to be killed by the tiger. Some of the men sitting near me had been in that party of twenty-five and they hotly repudiated responsibility for the lad's death, accusing him of having been responsible for the stampede by screaming out that he had heard the tiger growling and telling everyone to run for their lives. This did not satisfy the old man. He shook his head and said, 'You are grown men and he was only a boy, and you ran away and left him to be killed.' I was sorry for having asked the questions that had led to this heated discussion, and more to placate the old man than for any good it would do, I said I would tie up one of my buffaloes near the spot where he said his son had been killed. So, handing two of the buffaloes over to the party to take back to the bungalow, I set off followed by two of my men leading the remaining buffalo.

A footpath, taking off close to where we had been sitting, went down the hill to the valley below and zigzagged up the opposite pine-clad slope to join the forest road two miles further on. The path passed close to an open patch of ground which bordered the oak thicket in which the lad had been killed. On this patch of ground, which was about thirty yards square, there was a solitary pine sapling. This I cut down. I tied the buffalo to the stump, set one man to cutting a supply of grass for it, and sent the other man, Madho Singh, who served in the Garhwalis during the Great War and is now serving in the United Provinces Civil Pioneer Force, up an oak tree with instructions to strike a dry branch with the head of his axe and call at the top of his voice as hill people do when cutting leaves for their cattle. I then took up a position on a rock, about four feet high, on the lower edge of the open ground. Beyond the rock the hill fell steeply away to the valley below and was densely clothed with tree and scrub jungle.

The man on the ground had made several trips with the grass he had cut, and Madho Singh on the tree was alternately shouting and singing lustily, while I stood on the rock smoking, with the rifle in the hollow of my left arm, when, all at once, I became aware that the man-eater had arrived. Beckoning urgently to the man on the ground to come to me, I whistled to attract Madho Singh's attention and signalled to him to remain quiet. The ground on three sides was comparatively open. Madho Singh on the tree was to my left front, the man cutting grass had been in front of me, while the buffalo—now showing signs of uneasiness—was to my right front. In this area the tigress could not have approached without my seeing her; and as she *had* approached, there was only one place where she could now be, and that was behind and immediately below me.

When taking up my position I had noticed that the further side of the rock was steep and smooth, that it extended down the hill for eight or ten feet, and that the lower portion of it was masked by thick undergrowth and young pine saplings. It would have been a little difficult, but quite possible, for the tigress to have climbed the rock, and I relied for my safety on hearing her in the undergrowth should she make the attempt.

I have no doubt that the tigress, attracted, as I had intended she should be, by the noise Madho Singh was making, had come to the rock, and that it was while she was looking up at me and planning her next move that I had become aware of her presence. My change of front, coupled with the silence of the men, may have made her suspicious; anyway, after a lapse of a few minutes, I heard a dry twig snap a little way down the hill;

thereafter the feeling of unease left me, and the tension relaxed. An opportunity lost; but there was still a very good chance of my getting a shot, for she would undoubtedly return before long, and when she found us gone would probably content herself with killing the buffalo. There were still four or five hours of daylight, and by crossing the valley and going up the opposite slope I should be able to overlook the whole of the hillside on which the buffalo was tethered. The shot, if I did get one, would be a long one of from two to three hundred yards, but the ·275 rifle I was carrying was accurate, and even if I only wounded the tigress I should have a blood trail to follow, which would be better than feeling about for her in hundreds of square miles of jungle, as I had been doing these many months.

The men were a difficulty. To have sent them back to the bungalow alone would have been nothing short of murder, so of necessity I kept them with me.

Tying the buffalo to the stump in such a manner as to make it impossible for the tigress to carry it away, I left the open ground and rejoined the path to carry out the plan I have outlined, of trying to get a shot from the opposite hill.

About a hundred yards along the path I came to a ravine. On the far side of this the path entered very heavy undergrowth, and as it was inadvisable to go into thick cover with two men following me, I decided to take to the ravine, follow it down to its junction with the valley, work up the valley and pick up the path on the far side of the undergrowth.

The ravine was about ten yards wide and four or five feet deep, and as I stepped down into it a nightjar fluttered off a rock on which I had put my hand. On looking at the spot from which the bird had risen, I saw two eggs. These eggs, straw-coloured, with rich brown markings, were of a most unusual shape, one being long and very pointed, while the other was as round as a marble; and as my collection lacked nightjar eggs I decided to add this odd clutch to it. I had no receptacle of any kind in which to carry the eggs, so cupping my left hand I placed the eggs in it and packed them round with a little moss.

As I went down the ravine the banks became higher, and sixty yards from where I had entered it I came on a deep drop of some twelve to fourteen feet. The water that rushes down all these hill ravines in the rains had worn the rock as smooth as glass, and as it was too steep to offer a foothold I handed the rifle to the men and, sitting on the edge, proceeded to slide down. My feet had hardly touched the sandy bottom when the two men, with a flying leap, landed one on either side of me, and thrusting the rifle into my hand asked in a very agitated manner if I had heard the tiger. As a matter of fact I had heard nothing, possibly due to the scraping of my clothes on the rocks, and when questioned, the men said that what they had heard was a deep-throated growl from somewhere close at hand, but exactly from which direction the sound had come, they were unable to say. Tigers do not betray their presence by growling when looking for their dinner and the only, and very unsatisfactory, explanation I can offer is that the tigress followed us after we left the open ground, and on seeing that we were going down the ravine had gone ahead and taken up a position where the ravine narrowed to half its width; and that when she was on the point of springing out on me, I had disappeared out of sight down the slide and she had involuntarily given vent to her disappointment with a low growl. Not a satisfactory reason, unless one assumes—without any reason—that she had selected me for her dinner, and therefore had no interest in the two men.

Where the three of us now stood in a bunch we had the smooth steep rock behind us, to our right a wall of rock slightly leaning over the ravine and fifteen feet high, and to our left a tumbled bank of big rocks thirty or forty feet high. The sandy bed of the ravine, on which we were standing, was roughly forty feet long and ten feet wide. At the lower end of this sandy bed a great pine tree had fallen across, damming the ravine, and the collection of the sand was due to this dam. The wall of overhanging rock came to an end twelve or fifteen feet from the fallen tree, and as I approached the end of the rock, my feet making no sound on the sand, I very fortunately noticed that the sandy bed continued round to the back of the rock.

This rock about which I have said so much I can best describe as a giant school slate, two feet thick as its lower end, and standing up—not quite perpendicularly—on one of its long sides.

As I stepped clear of the giant slate, I looked behind me over my right shoulder and—looked straight into the tigress's face.

I would like you to have a clear picture of the situation.

The sandy bed behind the rock was quite flat. To the right of it was the smooth slate fifteen feet high and leaning slightly outwards, to the left of it was a scoured-out steep bank also some fifteen feet high overhung by a dense tangle of thorn bushes, while at the far end was a slide similar to, but a little higher than, the one I had glissaded down. The sandy bed, enclosed by the these three natural walls, was about twenty feet long and half as wide, and lying on it, with her fore-paws stretched out and her hind legs well tucked under her, was the tigress. Her head, which was raised a few inches off her paws, was eight feet (measured later) from me, and on her face was a smile, similar to that one sees on the face of a dog welcoming his master home after a long absence.

Two thoughts flashed through my mind, one, that it was up to me to make the first move, and the other, that the move would have to be made in such a manner as not to alarm the tigress or make her nervous.

The rifle was in my right hand held diagonally across my chest, with the safety-catch off, and in order to get it to bear on the tigress the muzzle would have to be swung round three-quarters of a circle.

The movement of swinging round the rifle, with one hand, was begun very slowly, and hardly perceptibly, and when a quarter of a circle had been made, the stock came in contact with my right side. It was now necessary to extend my arm, and as the stock cleared my side, the swing was very slowly continued. My arm was now at full stretch and the weight of the rifle was beginning to tell. Only a little further now for the muzzle to go, and the tigress—who had not once taken her eyes off mine—was still looking up at me, with the pleased expression still on her face.

How long it took the rifle to make the three-quarter circle, I am not in a position to say. To me, looking into the tigress's eyes and unable therefore to follow the movement of the barrel, it appeared that my arm was paralysed, and that the swing would never be completed. However, the movement was completed at last, and as soon as the rifle was pointing at the tigress's body, I pressed the trigger.

I heard the report, exaggerated in that restricted space, and felt the jar of the recoil, and but for these tangible proofs that the rifle had gone off, I might, for all the immediate result the shot produced, have been in the grip of one of those awful nightmares in which triggers are vainly pulled of rifles that refused to be discharged at the critical moment.

For a perceptible fraction of time the tigress remained perfectly still, and then, very slowly, her head sank on to her outstretched paws, while at the same time a jet of blood issued from the bullet-hole. The bullet had injured her spine and shattered the upper portion of her heart.

The two men who were following a few yards behind me, and who were separated from the tigress by the thickness of the rock, came to a halt when they saw me stop and turn my head. They knew instinctively that I had seen the tigress and judged from my behaviour that she was close at hand, and Madho Singh said afterwards that he wanted to call out and tell me to drop the eggs and get both hands on the rifle. When I had fired my shot and lowered the point of the rifle on to my toes,

Madho Singh, at a sign, came forward to relieve me of it, for very suddenly my legs appeared to be unable to support me, so I made for the fallen tree and sat down. Even before looking at the pads of her feet I knew it was the Chowgarh tigress I had sent to the Happy Hunting Grounds, and that the shears that had assisted her to cut the threads of sixty-four human lives—the people of the district put the number at twice that figure—had, while the game was in her hands, turned, and cut the thread of her own life.

Three things, each of which would appear to you to have been to my disadvantage, were actually in my favour. These were (a) the eggs in my left hand, (b) the light rifle I was carrying, and (c) the tiger being a man-eater. If I had not had the eggs in my hand I should have had both hands on the rifle, and when I looked back and saw the tiger at such close quarters I should instinctively have tried to swing round to face her, and the spring that was arrested by my lack of movement would inevitably have been launched. Again, if the rifle had not been a light one it would not have been possible for me to have moved it in the way it was imperative I should move it, and then discharge it at the full extent of my arm. And lastly, if the tiger had been just an ordinary tiger, and not a man-eater, it would, on finding itself cornered, have made for the opening and wiped me out of the way; and to be wiped out of the way by a tiger usually has fatal results.

While the men made a detour and went up the hill to free the buffalo and secure the rope, which was needed for another and more pleasant purpose, I climbed over the rocks and went up the ravine to restore the eggs to their rightful owner. I plead guilty of being as superstitious as my brother sportsmen. For three long periods, extending over a whole year, I had tried—and tried hard—to get a shot at the tigress, and had failed; and now within a few minutes of having picked up the eggs my luck had changed.

The eggs, which all this time had remain safely in the hollow of my left hand, were still warm when I replaced them in the little depression in the rock that did duty as a nest, when I again passed that way half an hour later, they had vanished under the brooding mother whose colouring so exactly matched the mottled rock that it was difficult for me, who knew the exact spot where the nest was situated, to distinguish her from her surroundings.

The buffalo, who after months of care was now so tame that it followed like a dog, came scrambling down the hill in the wake of the men, nosed the tigress and lay down on the sand to chew the cud of contentment, while we lashed the tigress to the stout pole the men had cut.

I had tried to get Madho Singh to return to the bungalow for help, but this he would not hear of doing. With no one would he and his companion share the honour of carrying in the man-eater, and if I would lend a hand the task, he said, with frequent halts for rest, would not be too difficult. We were three hefty men—two accustomed from childhood to carrying heavy loads—and all three hardened by a life of exposure; but even so, the task we set ourselves was a herculean one.

The path down which we had come was too narrow and too winding for the long pole to which the tigress was lashed, so, with frequent halts to regain breath and readjust pads to prevent the pole biting too deep into shoulder muscles, we went straight up the hill through a tangle of raspberry and briar bushes, on the thorns of which we left a portion of our clothing and an amount of skin which made bathing for many days a painful operation.

The sun was still shining on the surrounding hills when three dishevelled and very happy men, followed by a buffalo, carried the tigress to the Kala Agar Forest Bungalow, and from that evening to this day no human being has been killed—or wounded—over the hundreds of square miles of mountain and vale over which the Chowgarh tigress, for a period of five years, held sway.

I have added one more cross and date to the map of Eastern Kumaon that hangs on the wall before me—the cross and the date the man-eater earned. The cross is two miles west of Kala Agar, and the date under it is 11 April 1930.

The tigress's claws were broken, and bushed out, and one of her canine teeth was broken, and her front teeth were worn down to the bone. It was these defects that had made her a man-eater and were the cause of her not being able to kill outright—and by her own efforts—a large proportion of the human beings she had attacked since the day she had been deprived of the assistance of the cub I had, on my first visit, shot by mistake.

The Chuka Man-eater

Chuka—which gave its name to the man-eating tiger of the Ladhya valley—is a small village of some ten ploughs on the right bank of the Sarda river near its junction with the Ladhya. From the north-west corner of the village a path runs for a quarter of a mile along a fire track before it divides, one arm going straight up a ridge to Thak village and the other diagonally up and across the hills to Kotekindri, a village owned by the people of Chuka.

Along this latter path a man was driving two bullocks in the winter of 1936, and as he approached Chuka, a tiger suddenly appeared on the fire track. With very commendable courage the man interposed himself between the tiger and his bullocks and, brandishing his stick and shouting, attempted to drive the tiger away. Taking advantage of the diversion created in their favour the bullocks promptly bolted to the village and the tiger, baulked of his prey, turned his attention to the man. Alarmed at the threatening attitude of the tiger the man turned to run and, as he did so, the tiger sprang on him. Across his shoulders the man had a heavy wooden plough, and on his back he was carrying a bag containing the provisions he needed for his stay at Chuka. While the tiger was expending its teeth and claws on the plough and bag, the man, relieved of his burdens, sprinted towards the village shouting for help as he ran. His relatives and friends, hearing his shouts, rallied to his assistance and he reached the village without further incident. One claw of the tiger had ripped his right arm from shoulder to wrist, inflicting a deep wound.

Some weeks later two men returning from the market at Tanakpur were climbing the steep path to Kotekindri, when a tiger crossed the path fifty yards ahead of them. Waiting for a few minutes to give the tiger time to move away from the vicinity of the path, the men proceeded on their way, shouting as they went. The tiger had not moved away, however, and as the leading man came abreast of it, it sprang on him. This man was carrying a sack of gur (unrefined sugar), half of which was on his head and the other half on his back. The tiger's teeth caught in the sack and he carried it away down the hillside, without doing the man any injury. There is no record of what the tiger thought of the captures he had made so far—a plough and a sack of gur—but it can be assumed he was not satisfied with his bag, for, from now on, he selected human beings who were not burdened with either ploughs or sacks.

Thak, which is about 3,000 feet above Chuka, has quite a large population for a hill village. The Chand Rajas who ruled Kumaon before the advent of the Gurkhas, gave the lands of Thak to the forefathers of the present holders for their maintenance, and appointed them hereditary custodians of the Purnagiri temples. Rich lands and a considerable income from the temples have enabled the people of Thak to build themselves good substantial houses, and to acquire large herds of cattle.

On a day early in June 1937, seven men and two boys were

herding the village cattle, 200 yards to the west of Thak. At 10 a.m. it was noticed that some of the cattle were beginning to stray off the open ground towards the jungle and one of the boys, aged fourteen, was sent to turn them back. Six hours later the men, who had been sleeping through the heat of the day, were aroused by the barking of a kakar in the jungle bordering the open ground, into which all the cattle had by now strayed, and the second boy who was also about fourteen was sent to drive them out. Shortly after he entered the jungle the cattle stampeded and as they were crossing an open ravine on their way to the village a tiger sprang on one of the cows, and killed it in full view of the seven men. The bellowing of the cattle and the shouts of the men attracted the attention of the people in the village, and a crowd soon collected on the high ground overlooking the ravine. The mother—a widow—of the second boy was among these people and, on hearing the men calling to her son, she ran towards them to inquire what had happened. On learning that her son had entered the jungle to drive out the cattle and had not returned, she set off to look for him. At this moment the parents of the first boy arrived on the scene and it was only when they asked where their son was that the seven men remembered they had not seen him since 10 a.m.

Followed by the large crowd of men who had now collected in the ravine near the dead cow, the distraught mother went into the jungle and found her son where the tiger had killed and left him, and under a nearby bush the parents of the first boy found their son dead and partly eaten. Close to this boy was a dead calf. From the accounts the villagers subsequently gave me of the tragic happenings of that day, I believe that the tiger was lying up in the jungle overlooking the ground on which the cattle were grazing, and when the calf, unseen by the men, entered the jungle the tiger killed it, and before it was able to carry it away, the boy either inadvertently or through curiosity approached the calf, was killed, dragged under the bush, and partly eaten. After this the tiger apparently lay up near his two kills until 4 p.m. when a kakar on its way to drink at the small pool on the edge of the clearing either saw or smelt it and started barking. This aroused the men to the fact that the cattle had strayed into the jungle, and the second boy who was sent to drive them out had the ill luck to go straight to the spot where the tiger was guarding his kills.

The killing of the second boy was evidently witnessed by the cattle, who rallied to his rescue—I have seen this happen with both cows and buffaloes—and after driving the tiger from the boy they stampeded. Enraged at being driven off his kills, and at the rough treatment he had quite possibly received in the process, the tiger followed the stampeding cattle and wreaked his vengeance on the first one he was able to get hold of. Had the herd not run right on into the village he would probably not have been satisfied with killing only one of his attackers. In a similar case of attempted rescue I once saw an entire herd of five buffaloes wiped out in a titanic fight with an enraged tiger. The tiger killed one of their number and the other four big-hearted animals attacked him and fought on until the last of them had been killed. The tiger evidently suffered severely in the fight, for when he left the battle-ground he left a trail of blood.

The seemingly wanton slaughter of two human beings and two animals on the same day—resulting I am convinced from the tiger's having been disturbed on his first kill—caused a great outcry in the districts of Naini Tal and Almora, and every effort was made to kill the tiger. On several occasions district officials sat up all night on machans over kills, and though the tiger had been wounded on two occasions—unfortunately only with buckshot—he continued to prey on human beings, and claimed yet another victim from the ill-fated village of Thak.

Two hundred yards above Thak there is a wheat field. The crop had been cut from this field and two boys were grazing a few cattle on the stubble. For safety's sake the boys, who were brothers and orphans ten and twelve years of age, were sitting in the middle of the field. On the far side of the field, from the village, there was a light fringe of bushes. From these the hill went steeply up for a thousand feet, and from anywhere on the hill the two boys sitting in the open would have been visible. Towards the afternoon a cow strayed towards the bushes and the boys, keeping close together, set off to drive it back on to the field. The elder boy was leading and as he passed a bush the tiger, who was lying in wait, pounced on him and carried him away. The younger boy fled back to the village and dashing up to a group of men fell sobbing at their feet. When the boy was able to speak coherently he told the men that a big red animal—it was the first tiger he had ever seen—had carried away his brother. A search party was hastily organized and with very commendable bravery the blood trail was followed for about a mile into the densely wooded Suwar Gadh ravine to the east of the village. Night was now closing in, so the party returned to Thak. The following day, assisted by men from adjoining villages, a daylong search was made but all that was found of the boy was his red cap and his torn and bloodstained clothes. That was the Chuka man-eater's last human victim.

I do not think it is possible to appreciate courage until danger that brought it into being has been experienced. Those who have never lived in an area in which a man-eating tiger is operating may be inclined to think that there was nothing courageous in a mother going to look for her son, in two boys grazing cattle, or in a party of men going out to look for a missing boy. But to one who has lived in such an area the entry of the mother into a dense patch of jungle in which she knew there was an angry tiger; the two small boys sitting close together for protection; and the party of unarmed men following on the blood trail left by a man-eater were acts calling for a measure of courage that merits the greatest admiration.

~

The Chuka man-eater was now disorganizing life for everyone in the Ladhya valley, and shortly after Ibbotson had been appointed Deputy Commissioner-in-Charge of the three districts of Naini Tal, Almora, and Garhwal, we joined forces to try to rid his division of the menace.

It was early afternoon on a sweltering hot day in April 1937 that Ibby, his wife Jean, and I, alighted from our motor bus at the Boom above Baramdeo. We had left Naini Tal in the early hours of the morning and, travelling via Haldwani and Tanakpur, arrived at the Boom at the hottest time of the day, covered in dust from head to foot, and with many sore spots in unseen and tender places. A cup of tea drunk while sitting on yielding sand on the bank of the Sarda river helped restore our spirits, and taking the short cut along the river bank we set off on foot to Thuli Gadh where our tents, sent in advance, had been pitched.

Starting after breakfast next morning we went to Kaladhunga. The distance between Thuli Gadh and Kaladhunga via the Sarda gorge is eight miles, and via Purnagiri, fourteen miles. The Ibbotsons and I went through the gorge while our servants and the men carrying our kit went via Purnagiri. The gorge is four miles long and was at one time traversed by a tramway line blasted out of the rock cliff by J. V. Collier when extracting the million cubic feet of sal timber presented by the Nepal Durbear to the Government of India as a thank-offering after the First World War. The tramway line has long since been swept away by landslides and floods, and these four miles necessitate a great deal of rock climbing where a false step or the slipping of a hand-hold would inevitably precipitate one into the cold river. We negotiated the gorge without mishap, and at the upper end, where Collier's tramline entered the forest, we caught two fish in a run where a rock of the size of a house juts out into the river.

Word had been sent ahead for the patwaris and forest guards working in the area to meet us at Kaladhunga and give us the latest news of the man-eater. We found four men awaiting our arrival at the bungalow and the reports they gave us were encouraging. No human beings had been killed within the past few days, and the tiger was known to be in the vicinity of Thak village where three days previously it had killed a calf.

Kaladhunga is a gently rising cone-shaped peninsula roughly four miles long and a mile wide, surrounded on three sides by the Sarda river and backed on the fourth by a ridge of hills 5,000 feet high. The bungalow, a three-roomed house with a wide veranda, faces east and is situated at the northern or upper end of the peninsula. The view from the veranda as the morning sun rises over the distant hills and the mist is lifting is one of the most pleasing prospects it is possible to imagine. Straight in front, and across the Sarda, is a wide open valley running deep into Nepal. The hills on either side are densely wooded, and winding through the valley is a river fringed with emerald-green elephant grass. As far as the eye can see there are no human habitations and, judging from the tiger and other animal calls that can be heard from the bungalow, there appears to be an abundant stock of game in the valley. It was from this valley that Collier extracted the million cubic feet of timber.

We spent a day at Kaladhunga, and while our men went on to Chuka to pitch our tents and make camp we fished, or, to be correct, the Ibbotsons fished while I, who had been laid up with malaria the previous night, sat on the bank and watched. From the broken water below the bungalow to the point of the peninsula—a stretch of some 500 yards—the Ibbotsons, who are expert thread-line casters, combed the river with their one-inch spoons without moving a fish. The small river that flows down the Nepal valley joins the Sarda opposite the point of the peninsula. Here the Sarda widens out and shallows, and flows for 200 yards over rocks before entering a big pool. It was at the upper end of this run and well out in the river that Ibby hooked his first fish—an eight-pounder—which needed careful handling on the light tackle before it was eventually brought to the bank and landed.

All keen anglers delight in watching others of the craft indulging in this, one of the best of outdoor sports. As for myself, I would just as soon watch another fishing than fish myself, especially when fish are on the take, the foothold uncertain—as it always is in the Sarda—and the river fairly fast. Shortly after Ibby killed his fish, Jean—who was fishing in broken water thirty yards from the bank—hooked a fish. Her reel only held a hundred yards of thread line, and fearing that the fish would make for the pool and break her, she attempted to walk backwards while playing the fish, and in doing so lost her footing and for a long minute all that was visible of her was the toe of one foot and the point of her rod. You will naturally assume that I, forgetting my recent attack of malaria, dashed out to her rescue. As a matter of fact I did nothing of the kind and only sat on the bank and laughed, for to attempt to rescue either of the Ibbotsons from a watery grave would be as futile as trying to save an otter from drowning. After a long and a violent struggle Jean upended herself, and reaching the bank killed her fish, which weighed six pounds. Hardly had she done so when Ibby, in making a long cast, slipped off the rock on which he was standing and disappeared under water, rod and all.

From the bottom end of the pool below the run, the river turns to the right. On the Nepal side of this bend in the river there had stood a giant semul tree, in the upper branches of which a pair of ospreys had for many years built their nest. The tree had been an ideal home for the birds, for not only had it commanded an extensive view of the river, but the great branches growing out at right angles to the trunk had also provided tables on which to hold and devour their slippery prey. The monsoon floods of the previous year had cut into the bank and washed away the old tree and the ospreys had built themselves a new nest in a tall shisham tree standing at the edge of the forest, a hundred yards from the river.

The run was evidently the favourite fishing ground of ospreys, and while the female sat in the nest the male kept flying backwards and forwards over the Ibbotsons' heads. Eventually tiring of this unprofitable exercise it flew farther down the river to where a few partly submerged rocks broke the surface of the water, making a small run. Fish were evidently passing this spot, and a dozen times the osprey banked steeply, closed his wings, and dropped like a plummet and, checking himself with widespread wings and tail before reaching the water, rose flapping to regain height for his next cast. At last his patience was rewarded. An unwary fish had come to the surface directly below him, and without a moment's pause he went from flat flight into a lightning dive through a hundred feet of air and plunged deep into the broken water. His needle-sharp and steel-strong talons took hold, but the catch was evidently heavier than he anticipated. Time and time again with wildly threshing wings he attempted to launch himself into the air, only to sink down again on his breast feathers. I believe he would have had to relinquish his catch had not a gust of wind blowing up river come at this critical moment to help him. As the wind reached him he turned downstream and, making one last desperate effort, got the fish clear of the water. Home was in the opposite direction from that in which he was now heading but to turn was impossible, so, selecting a great slab of rock on the bank on which to land, he made straight for it.

I was not the only one who had been watching the osprey, for he had hardly landed on the rock when a woman who had been washing clothes on the Nepal side of the river called out excitedly, and a boy appeared on the high bank above her. Running down the steep track to where the woman was standing, he received his instructions and set off along the boulder-strewn bank at a pace that threatened his neck and limbs at every stride. The osprey made no attempt to carry off his prey, and as the boy reached the rock it took to the air, circling round his head as he held up the fish—which appeared to be about four pounds in weight—for the woman to see.

For some time thereafter I lost sight of the osprey, and we had finished our lunch before I again saw him quartering the air above the run in which he had caught the fish of which the boy had deprived him. Back and forth he flew for many minutes, always at the same height, and then he banked, dropped fifty feet, again banked and then plunged straight into the water. This time his catch was lighter—a kalabas about two pounds in weight—and without effort he lifted it clear of the water and, holding it like a torpedo to reduce wind pressure, made for his nest. His luck was out that day, however, for he had only covered half the distance he had to go, when a Pallas fish-eagle twice his weight and size came up from behind, rapidly overtaking him. The osprey saw him coming and altering his course a point to the right headed for the forest with the object of shaking off his pursuer among the branches of the trees. The eagle realizing the object of this manoeuvre emitted a scream of rage and increased his speed. Only twenty yards more to go to reach safety, but the risk was too great to take and, relinquishing his hold of the kalabas, the osprey—only just in time—hurled himself straight into the air. The fish had not fallen a yard before the eagle caught it and, turning in a graceful sweep, made off down river in the direction from which he had come. He was not to escape with his booty as easily as he expected, however, for he had only gone a short distance on his return journey when the pair of crows that fed on the osprey's leavings set off to bait him, and to shake them off he too was compelled to take to the forest. At the edge of the forest the crows turned back and the eagle had hardly disappeared from view when falling out of the sky came two Tawny eagles going at an incredible speed in the direct line the Pallas eagle had taken. I very greatly regret I did not see the end of the chase for, from the fact that while I watched neither of the birds rose out of the forest, I suspect that the Pallas eagle retained his hold on the fish too long. I have only once seen a more interesting chase. On that occasion I was taking a line of eighteen elephants through grass and the ten guns and five spectators who were sitting on the elephants, shooting black partridge, saw a bush chat pass—without once touching the ground—from a sparrow-hawk that killed it just in front of our line of elephants to a red-headed merlin, then to a honey buzzard, and finally to a peregrine falcon who swallowed the little bird whole. If any of the guns or spectators who were with me that February morning read this chapter, they will recall the occurrence as having taken place on the Rudrapur Maidan.

After an early breakfast next morning we moved from Kaladhunga to Chuka, an easy march of five miles. It was one of those gorgeous days that live long in the memory of a fisherman. The sun was pleasantly warm; a cool wind blowing down from the north; a run of chilwa (fingerlings) in progress; and the river full of big fish madly on the take. Fishing with light tackle we had many exciting battles, all of which we did not win. We ended the day, however, with enough fish to feed our camp of thirty men.

~

To assist us in our campaign against the man-eater, and to try to prevent further loss of human life, six young male buffaloes had been sent up from Tanakpur in advance of us, to be used as bait for the tiger. On our arrival at Chuka we were told that the buffaloes had been tied out for three nights, and that though a tiger's pug marks had been seen near several of them, none had been killed. During the next four days we visited the buffaloes in the early morning; tried to get in touch with the tiger during the day, and in the evening accompanied the men engaged in tying out the buffaloes. On the fifth morning we found that a buffalo we had tied up at Thak, at the edge of the jungle in which the two boys had lost their lives, had been killed and carried off by a tiger. Instead of taking its kill into the dense jungle as we had expected, the tiger had taken it across an open patch of ground, and up on to a rocky knoll. This it had evidently done to avoid passing near a machan from which it had been fired at—and quite possibly wounded—on two previous occasions. After the buffalo had been dragged for a short distance its horns got jammed between two rocks, and being unable to free it, the tiger had eaten a few pounds of flesh from the hindquarters of the kill and then left it. In casting round to see in which direction the tiger had gone, we found its pug marks in a buffalo wallow, between the kill and the jungle. These pug marks showed that the killer of the buffalo was a big male tiger.

It was generally believed by the District Officials—on what authority I do not know—that the man-eater was a tigress. On showing them the tracks in the buffalo wallow we were told by the villagers that they could not distinguish between the pug marks of different tigers and that they did not know whether the man-eater was male or female, but that they did know it had a broken tooth. In all the kills, human as well as animal, that had taken place near their village they had noticed that one of the tiger's teeth only bruised the skin and did not penetrate it. From this they concluded that one of the man-eater's canine teeth was broken.

Twenty yards from the kill there was a jamun tree. After we had dragged the kill out from between the rocks we sent a man up the tree to break a few twigs that were obstructing a view of the kill from the only branch of the tree in which it was possible to sit. This isolated tree on the top of the knoll was in full view of the surrounding jungle, and though the man climbed it and broke the twigs with the utmost care, I am inclined to think he was seen by the tiger.

It was now 11 a.m., so, sending our men back to the village

to have their midday meal, Ibby and I selected a bush under which to shelter from the sun and talked and dozed, and dozed and talked throughout the heat of the day. At 2.30 p.m., while we were having a picnic lunch, some kaleej pheasants started chattering agitatedly at the edge of the jungle where the buffalo had been killed, and on hearing them our men returned from the village. While Ibby and his big-hearted man, Sham Singh, went into the jungle where the pheasants were chattering—to attract the tiger's attention—I climbed silently into the jamun tree. Giving me a few minutes in which to settle down, Ibby and Sham Singh came out of the jungle and returned to our camp at Chuka, leaving my two men at Thak.

Shortly after Ibby had gone the pheasants started chattering again and a little later a kakar began barking. The tiger was evidently on the move, but there was little hope of his crossing the open ground and coming to the kill until the sun had set and the village had settled down for the night. The kakar barked for a quarter of an hour or more before it finally stopped, and from then until sunset, except for the natural calls of a multitude of birds, the jungle—as far as the tiger was concerned—was silent.

The red glow from the setting sun had faded from the Nepal hills on the far side of the Sarda river, and the village sounds had died down, when a kakar barked in the direction of the buffalo wallow; the tiger was returning to his kill along the line he had taken when leaving it. A convenient branch in front of me gave a perfect rest for my rifle, and the only movement it would be necessary to make when the tiger arrived would be to lower my head on to the rifle butt. Minute succeeded minute until a hundred had been added to my age and then, 200 yards up the hillside, a kakar barked in alarm and my hope of getting a shot, which I had put at ten to one, dropped to one in a thousand. It was now quite evident that the tiger had seen my man breaking the twigs off the tree, and that between sunset and the barking of this last kakar he had stalked the tree and seeing me on it had gone away. From then on kakar and sambhar called at intervals, each call a little farther away than the last. At midnight these alarm calls ceased altogether, and the jungle settled down to that nightly period of rest ordained by Nature, when strife ceases and the jungle fold can sleep in peace. Others who have spent nights in an Indian jungle will have noticed this period of rest, which varies a little according to the season of the year and the phases of the moon, and which as a rule extends from midnight to 4 a.m. Between these hours killers sleep. And those who go in fear of them are at peace. It may be natural for carnivores to sleep from midnight to 4 a.m., but I would prefer to think that Nature had set apart these few hours so that those who go in fear of their lives can relax and be at peace.

Day was a few minutes old when, cramped in every joint, I descended from the tree and, unearthing the thermos flask Ibby had very thoughtfully buried under a bush, indulged in a much needed cup of tea. Shortly after my two men arrived and while we were covering the kill with branches, to protect it from vultures, the tiger called three times on a hill half a mile away. As I passed through Thak on my way back to camp the greybeards of the village met me and begged me not to be discouraged by my night's failure, for, they said, they had consulted the stars and offered prayers and if the tiger did not die this day it would certainly die on the next or, may be, the day after.

A hot bath and a square meal refreshed me and at 1 p.m. I again climbed the steep hill to Thak and was told on my arrival that a sambhar had belled several times on the hill above the village. I had set out from camp with the intention of sitting up over a live buffalo; and, to ensure while doing so that the tiger did not feed in one place while I was waiting for him in another, I placed several sheets of newspaper near the kill I had sat over the previous night. There was a well-used cattle track through the jungle in which the villagers said the sambhar had called. In a tree on the side of this track I put up a rope seat, and to a root on the track I tied the buffalo. I climbed into the tree at three o'clock, and an hour later first a kakar and then a tiger called on the far side of the valley a thousand yards away. The buffalo had been provided with a big feed of green grass, and throughout the night it kept the bell I had tied round its neck ringing, but it failed to attract the tiger. At daylight my men came for me and they told me that sambhar and kakar had called during the night in the deep ravine in which the boy's red cap and torn clothes had been found, and at the lower end of which we had tied up a buffalo at the request of the villagers.

When I got back to Chuka I found that Ibby had left camp before dawn. News had been received late the previous evening that a tiger had killed a bullock eight miles up the Ladhya valley. He sat up over the kill all night without seeing anything of the tiger, and late the following evening he returned to camp.

~

Jean and I were having breakfast after my night in the tree over the live buffalo, when the men engaged in tying out our remaining five buffaloes came in to report that the one they had tied up at the lower end of the ravine in which my men had heard the sambhar and kakar calling the previous night was missing. While we were being given this news MacDonald, Divisional Forest Officer, who was moving camp that day from Kaladhunga to Chuka, arrived and told us he had seen the pug marks of a tiger at the lower end of a ravine where he presumed one of our buffaloes had been tied up. These pug marks, Mac said, were similar to those he had seen at Thak when on a previous visit he had tried to shoot the man-eater.

After breakfast, Jean and Mac went down the river to fish while I went off with Sham Singh to try to find out what had become of the missing buffalo. Beyond the broken rope and the tiger's pug marks there was nothing to show that the buffalo had been killed. However, on casting round I found where one of the buffalo's horns had come in contact with the ground and from here on there was a well-defined blood trail. Whether the tiger lost his bearings after killing the buffalo or whether he was trying to cover up his tracks I do not know, for after taking the kill over most difficult ground for several miles he brought it back to the ravine 200 yards from where he had started. At this point the ravine narrowed down to a bottle-neck some ten feet wide. The tiger was probably lying up with his kill on the far side of the narrow neck, and as I intended sitting up for him all night I decided to join the anglers and share their lunch before sitting up.

After fortifying the inner man, I returned with Sham Singh and three men borrowed from the fishing party, for if I found the kill and sat up over it it would not have been safe for Sham Singh to have gone back to camp alone. Walking well ahead of the four men I approached the bottle-neck for the second time, and as I did so the tiger started growling. The ravine here was steep and full of boulders and the tiger was growling from behind a dense screen of bushes, about twenty yards straight in front of me. An unseen tiger's growl at close range is the most terrifying sound in the jungle, and is a very definite warning to intruders not to approach any nearer. In that restricted space, and with the tiger holding a commanding position, it would have been foolish to have gone any farther. So, signalling to the men to retire, and giving them a few minutes to do so, I started to walk backwards very slowly—the only safe method of getting away from any animal with which one is anxious not to make contact. As soon as I was well clear of the bottle-neck I turned and, whistling to the men to stop, rejoined them a hundred yards farther down the ravine. I now knew exactly where the tiger was, and felt confident I would be able to deal with him; so, on rejoining the men, I told them to leave me and return to the fishing party. This, however, they were very naturally frightened to do. They believed, as I did, that the tiger they had just heard growling was a man-eater and they wanted to have the protection of my rifle. To have taken them back myself would have lost me two hours, and as we were in a sal forest and there was not a climbable tree in sight, I had of necessity to keep them with me.

Climbing the steep left bank we went straight away from the ravine for 200 yards. Here we turned to the left and after I had paced out 200 yards we again turned to the left and came back to the ravine a hundred yards above where we had heard the tiger growling. The tables were now turned and we held the advantage of position. I knew the tiger would not go down the ravine, for he had seen human beings in that direction, only a few minutes before; nor would he go up the ravine, for in order to do so he would have to pass us. The bank on our side was thirty feet high and devoid of undergrowth, so the only way the tiger could get out of the position we had manoeuvred him into would be to go up the opposite hillside. For ten minutes we sat on the edge of the ravine scanning every foot of ground in front of us. Then, moving back a few paces, we went thirty yards to the left and again sat down on the edge and, as we did so, the man sitting next to me whispered 'sher', and pointed across the ravine. I could see nothing, and on asking the man how much of the tiger he could see, and to describe its position, he said he had seen its ears move and that it was near some dry leaves. A tiger's ears are not conspicuous objects at fifty yards, and as the ground was carpeted with dead leaves his description did nothing to help me locate the tiger. From the breathing of the men behind me it was evident that excitement was rising to a high pitch. Presently one of the men stood up to get a better view, and the tiger, who had been lying down facing us, got up and started to go up the hill, and as his head appeared from behind a bush I fired. My bullet, I subsequently found, went through the ruff on his neck and striking a rock splintered back, making him spring straight up into the air, and on landing he got involved with a big creeper from which he found some difficulty in freeing himself. When we saw him struggling on the ground we thought he was down for good, but when he regained his feet and galloped off Sham Singh expressed the opinion, which I shared, that he was unwounded. Leaving the men I crossed the ravine and on examining the ground found the long hairs the bullet had clipped, the splintered rock, and the torn and bitten creeper, but I found no blood.

Blood does not always flow immediately after an animal has been hit, and my reconstruction of the shot may have been faulty; so it was necessary to find the kill, for it would tell me on the morrow whether or not the tiger was wounded. Here we had some difficulty, and it was not until we had gone over the ground twice that we eventually found the kill in a pool of water four feet deep, where the tiger had presumably put it to preserve it from hornets and blowflies. Sending the three men I had borrowed back to the fishing party—it was safe to do so now—Sham Singh and I remained hidden near the kill for an hour to listen for jungle sounds and then, hearing none, returned to camp. After an early breakfast next morning Mac and I returned to the ravine and found that the tiger had removed the kill from the pool, carried it a short distance, and eaten it out leaving only the head and hooves. This, together with the absence of blood on the ground on which he had been lying while eating, was proof that the tiger was not wounded and that he had recovered from his fright.

When we got back to camp we were informed that a cow had been killed in a wide open ravine on the far side of the Ladhya river, and that the men who had found it had covered it with branches. Ibby had not returned from his visit to the village eight miles up the Ladhya, and after lunch Mac and I went out to look at the cow. It had been covered up at midday and shortly afterwards the tiger had returned, dug it out from under the branches, and carried it away without leaving any mark of a drag. The forest here consisted of great big sal trees without any undergrowth, and it took us an hour to find the kill where the tiger had hidden it under a great pile of dead leaves. In a nearby tree Mac very gallantly put up a machan for me while I smoked and emptied his water-bottle—the shade temperature was about 110 degrees—and after seeing me into the tree he returned to camp. An hour later a small stone rolling down the steep hill on the far side of the ravine attracted my attention, and shortly after a tigress came into view, followed by two small cubs. This was quite evidently the first occasion on which the cubs had ever been taken to a kill, and it was very interesting to see the pains the mother took to impress on them the danger of the proceeding and the great caution it was necessary to exercise. The behaviour of the cubs was as interesting as their mother's. Step by step they followed in her tracks; never trying to pass each other, or her; avoiding every obstruction that she avoided no matter how small it was, and remaining perfectly rigid when she stopped to listen, which she did every few yards. The ground was carpeted with big sal leaves as dry as tinder over which it was impossible to move silently; however, every pad was put down carefully and as carefully lifted, and as little sound as possible was made.

Crossing the ravine, the tigress, closely followed by the cubs, came towards me and passing behind my tree lay down on a flat piece of ground overlooking the kill, and about thirty yards from it. Her lying down was apparently intended as a signal to the cubs to go forward in the direction in which her nose was pointing, and this they proceeded to do. By what means the mother conveyed the information to her cubs that there was food for them at this spot I do not know, but that she had conveyed this information to them there was no question. Passing their mother—after she had lain down—and exercising the same caution they had been made to exercise when following her, they set out with every appearance of being on a very definite quest. I have repeatedly asserted that tigers have no sense of smell, and the cubs were providing me with ample proof of that assertion. Though the kill had only been reported to us that morning the cow had actually been killed the previous day, and before hiding it under the pile of dead leaves the tigress had eaten the greater portion of it. The weather, as I have said, was intensely hot, and it was the smell that eventually enabled Mac and me to find the kill. And here, now, were two hungry cubs ranging up and down, back and forth, passing and repassing a dozen times within a yard of the kill and yet not being able to find it. It was the blowflies that disclosed its position and at length enabled them to find it. Dragging it out from under the leaves the cubs sat down together to have their meal. The tigress had watched her cubs as intently as I had and only once, when they were questing too far afield, had she spoken to them. As soon as the kill had been found the mother turned on to her back with her legs in the air and went to sleep.

As I watched the cubs feeding I was reminded of a scene I had witnessed some years previously at the foot of Trisul, I was lying on a ridge scanning with field glasses a rock cliff opposite me for tahr, the most sure-footed of all Himalayan goats. On a ledge half-way up the cliff a tahr and her kid were lying asleep. Presently the tahr got to her feet, stretched herself, and the kid immediately started to nuzzle her and feed. After a minute or so the mother freed herself, took a few steps along the ledge, poised for a moment, and then jumped down on to another and a narrower ledge some twelve to fifteen feet below her. As soon as it was left alone the kid started running backwards and forwards, stopping every now and then to peer down at its mother, but unable to summon the courage to jump down to her for, below the few-inches-wide ledge, was a sheer drop of a thousand feet. I was too far away to hear whether the mother was encouraging her young, but from the way her head was turned

I believe she was doing so. The kid was now getting more and more agitated and, possibly fearing that it would do something foolish, the mother went to what looked like a mere crack in the vertical rock face and, climbing it, rejoined her young. Immediately on doing so she lay down, presumably to prevent the kid from feeding. After a little while she again got to her feet, allowed the kid to drink for a minute, poised carefully on the brink, and jumped down, while the kid again ran backwards and forwards above her. *Seven* times in the course of the next half-hour this procedure was gone through, until finally the kid, abandoning itself to its fate, jumped, and landing safely beside its mother was rewarded by being allowed to drink its fill. The lesson, to teach her young that it was safe to follow where she led, was over for that day. Instinct helps, but it is the infinite patience of the mother and the unquestioning obedience of her offspring that enable the young of all animals in the wild to grow to maturity. I regret I lacked the means, when I had the opportunity, of making cinematographic records of the different species of animals I have watched training their young, for there is nothing more interesting to be seen in a jungle.

When the cubs finished their meal they returned to their mother and she proceeded to clean them, rolling them over and licking off the blood they had acquired while feeding. When this job was finished to her entire satisfaction she set off, with the cubs following close behind, in the direction of a shallow ford in the Ladhya, for nothing remained of the kill and there was no suitable cover for her cubs on this side of the river.

I did not know, and it would have made no difference if I had, that the tigress I watched with such interest that day would later, owing to gunshot wounds, become a man-eater and a terror to all who lived or worked in the Ladhya valley and the surrounding villages.

∼

The kill at Thak, over which I had sat the first night, had been uncovered to let the vultures eat it, and another buffalo had been tied up at the head of the valley to the west of the village and about 200 yards from the old kill. Four mornings later the headman of Thak sent word to us that this buffalo had been killed by a tiger and carried away.

Our preparations were soon made, and after a terribly hot climb Ibby and I reached the scene of the kill at about midday. The tiger, after killing the buffalo and breaking a very strong rope, had picked up the kill and gone straight down into the valley. Telling the two men we had brought to carry our lunch to keep close behind us, we set off to follow the drag. It soon became apparent that the tiger was making for some definite spot, for he led us for two miles through dense undergrowth, down steep banks, through beds of nettles and raspberry bushes, over and under fallen trees, and over great masses of rock until finally he deposited the kill in a small hollow under a box tree shaped like an umbrella. The buffalo had been killed the previous night and the fact that the tiger had left it without having a meal was disquieting. However, this was to a great extent offset by the pains he had taken in getting the kill to this spot, and if all went well there was every reason to hope that he would return to his kill, for, from the teeth-marks on the buffalo's neck, we knew he was the man-eater we were looking for and not just an ordinary tiger.

Our hot walk up to Thak and subsequent descent down the densely wooded hillside, over difficult ground, had left us in a bath of sweat, and while we rested in the hollow having lunch and drinking quantities of tea, I cast my eyes round for a convenient tree on which to sit and, if necessary in which to pass the night. Growing on the outer edge of the hollow and leaning away from the hill at an angle of forty-five degrees was a ficus tree. This, starting life in some decayed part of a giant of the forest, had killed the parent tree by weaving a trellis round it, and this trellis was now in course of coalescing to form a trunk for the parasite. Ten feet from the ground, and where the trellis had stopped and the parent tree had rotted and fallen away, there appeared to be a comfortable seat on which I decided to sit.

Lunch eaten and a cigarette smoked, Ibby took our two men sixty yards to the right and sent them up a tree to shake the branches and pretend they were putting up a machan, to distract the tiger's attention in case he was lying up close by and watching us, while I as silently as possible climbed into the ficus tree. The seat I had selected sloped forward and was cushioned with rotten wood and dead leaves and, fearing that if I brushed them off the sound and movement might be detected by the tiger, I left them as they were and sat down on them, hoping devoutly that there were no snakes in the hollow trunk below me or scorpions in the dead leaves. Placing my feet in an opening in the trellis, to keep from slipping forward, I made myself as comfortable as conditions permitted, and when I had done so Ibby called the men off the tree and went away talking to them in a loud voice.

The tree in which I had elected to sit was, as I have already said, leaning outwards at an angle of forty-five degrees, and ten feet immediately below me there was a flat bit of ground about ten feet wide and twenty feet long. From this flat piece of ground the hill fell steeply away and was overgrown with tall grass and dense patches of brushwood, beyond which I could hear a stream running; an ideal place for a tiger to lie up in.

Ibby and the two men had been gone about fifteen minutes when a red monkey on the far side of the valley started barking to warn the jungle folk of the presence of a tiger. From the fact that this monkey had not called when we were coming down the hill, following the drag, it was evident that the tiger had not moved off at our approach and that he was now coming to investigate—as tigers do—the sounds he had heard in the vicinity of his kill. Monkeys are blessed with exceptionally good eyesight, and though the one that was calling was a quarter of a mile away, it was quite possible that the tiger he was calling at was close to me.

I was sitting facing the hill with the kill to my left front, and the monkey had only called eight times when I heard a dry stick snap down the steep hillside behind me. Turning my head to the right and looking through the trellis, which on this side extended a little above my head, I saw the tiger standing and looking in the direction of my tree, from a distance of about forty yards. For several minutes he stood looking alternately in my direction and then in the direction of the tree the two men had climbed, until eventually, deciding to come in my direction, he started up the steep hillside. It would not have been possible for a human being to have got over that steep and difficult ground without using his hands and without making considerable noise, but the tiger accomplished the feat without making a sound. The nearer he came to the flat ground the more cautious he became and the closer he kept his belly to the ground. When he was near the top of the bank he very slowly raised his head, took a long look at the tree the men had climbed, and satisfied that it was not tenanted sprang up on to the flat ground and passed out of sight under me. I expected him to reappear on my left and go towards the kill, and while I was waiting for him to do so I heard the dry leaves under the tree being crushed as he lay down on them.

For the next quarter of an hour I sat perfectly still, and as no further sounds came to me from the tiger I turned my head to the right, and craning my neck looked through an opening in the trellis, and saw the tiger's head. If I had been able to squeeze a tear out of my eye and direct it through the opening it would, I believe, have landed plumb on his nose. His chin was resting on the ground and his eyes were closed. Presently he opened them, blinked a few times to drive away the flies, then closed them again and went to sleep. Regaining my position I now turned my head to the left. On this side there was no trellis nor were there any branches against which I could brace myself, and when I had craned my neck as far as I could without losing my balance I looked down and found I could see most of the tiger's tail, and a part of one hind leg.

The situation needed consideration. The bole of the tree against which I had my back was roughly three feet thick and afforded ideal cover, so there was no possibility of the tiger seeing me. That he would go to the kill if not disturbed was certain; the question was, when would he go? It was a hot afternoon, but the spot he had selected to lie on was in deep shade from my tree and, further, there was a cool breeze blowing up the valley. In these pleasant conditions he might sleep for hours and not approach the kill until day light had gone, taking with it my chance of getting a shot. The risk of waiting on the tiger's pleasure could not be taken, therefore, for apart from the reason given the time at our disposal was nearly up and this might be the last chance I would get of killing the tiger, while on that chance might depend the lives of many people. Waiting for a shot being inadvisable, then, there remained the possibility of dealing with the tiger where he lay. There were several openings in the trellis on my right through which I could have inserted the barrel of my rifle, but having done this it would not have been possible to depress the muzzle of the rifle sufficiently to get the sights to bear on the tiger's head. To have stood up, climbed the trellis, and fired over the top of it would not have been difficult. But this could not have been done without making a certain amount of noise, for the dry leaves I was sitting on would have crackled when relieved of my weight, and within ten feet of me was an animal with the keenest hearing of any in the jungle. A shot at the head end of the tiger not being feasible, there remained the tail end.

When I had both my hands on the rifle and craned my neck

to the left, I had been able to see most of the tiger's tail and a portion of one hind leg. By releasing my right hand from the rifle and getting a grip of the trellis I found I could lean out far enough to see one-third of the tiger. If I could maintain this position after releasing my hold, it would be possible to disable him. The thought of disabling an animal, and a sleeping one at that, simply because he occasionally liked a change of diet was hateful. Sentiment, however, where a man-eater was concerned was out of place. I had been trying for days to shoot this tiger to save farther loss of human life, and now that I had a chance of doing so the fact that I would have to break his back before killing him would not justify my throwing away that chance. So the killing would have to be done no matter how unpleasant the method might be, and the sooner it was done the better, for in bringing his kill to this spot the tiger had laid a two-mile-long scent trail, and a hungry bear finding that trail might at any moment take the decision out of my hands. Keeping my body perfectly rigid I gradually released my hold of the trellis, got both hands on the rifle, and fired a shot behind and under me which I have no desire ever to repeat. When I pressed the trigger of the 450/400 high-velocity rifle, the butt was pointing to heaven and I was looking under, not over, the sights. The recoil injured but did not break either my fingers or my wrist, as I had feared it would, and as the tiger threw the upper part of his body round and started to slide down the hill on his back, I swung round on my seat and fired the second barrel into his chest. I should have felt less a murderer if, at my first shot, the tiger had stormed and raved but—being the big-hearted animal that he was—he never opened his mouth, and died at my second shot without having made a sound.

 Ibby had left me with the intention of sitting up in the jamun tree over the buffalo which had been killed four days previously and which the vultures had, for some unknown reason, not eaten. He thought that if the tiger had seen me climbing into the ficus tree it might abandon the kill over which I was sitting and go back to its old kill at Thak and give him a shot. On hearing my two shots he came hurrying back to see if I needed his help, and I met him half a mile from the ficus tree. Together we returned to the scene of the killing to examine the tiger. He was a fine big male in the prime of life and in perfect condition, and would have measured—if we had had anything to measure him with—nine feet six inches between pegs, or nine feet ten over curves. And the right canine tooth in his lower jaw was broken. Later I found several pellets of buckshot embedded in different parts of his body.

The tiger was too heavy for the four of us to carry back to camp so we left him where he lay, after covering him up with grass, branches, and deadwood heaped over with big stones, to protect him from bears. Word travelled round that night that the man-eating tiger was dead and when we carried him to the foot of the ficus tree next morning to skin him, more than a hundred men and boys crowded round to see him. Among the latter was the ten-year-old brother of the Chuka man-eater's last human victim.

The Final Man-eater

Peace had reigned in the Ladhya valley for many months when in September 1938 a report was received in Naini Tal that a girl, twelve years of age, had been killed by a tiger at Kot Kindri village. The report which reached me through Donald Stewart of the Forest Department gave no details, and it was not until I visited the village some weeks later that I was able to get particulars of the tragedy. It appeared that, about noon one day, this girl was picking up windfalls from a mango tree close to and in full view of the village, when a tiger suddenly appeared. Before the men working nearby were able to render any assistance, it carried her off. No attempt was made to follow up the tiger, and as all signs of drag and blood trail had been obliterated and washed away long before I arrived on the scene, I was unable to find the place where the tiger had taken the body.

Kot Kindri is about four miles south-west of Chuka, and three miles due west of Thak. It was in the valley between Kot Kindri and Thak that the Chuka man-eater had been shot the previous April.

During the summer of 1938 the Forest Department had marked all the trees in this area for felling, and it was feared that if the man-eater was not accounted for before November—when the felling of the forest was due to start—the contractors would not be able to secure labour, and would repudiate their contracts. It was in this connexion that Donald Stewart had written to me shortly after the girl had been killed, and when in compliance with his request I promised to go to Kot Kindri, I must confess that it was more in the interests of the local inhabitants than in the interest of the contractors that I gave my promise.

My most direct route to Kot Kindri was to go by rail to Tanakpur, and from there by foot via Kaldhunga and Chuka. This route, however, though it would save me a hundred miles of walking, would necessitate my passing through the most deadly malaria belt in northern India, and to avoid it I decided to go through the hills to Mornaula, and from there along the abandoned Sherring road to its termination of the ridge above Kot Kindri.

While my preparations for this long trek were still under way a second report reached Naini Tal of a kill at Sem, a small village on the left bank of the Ladhya and distant about half a mile from Chuka.

The victim on this occasion was an elderly woman, the mother of the Headman of Sem. This unfortunate woman had been killed while cutting brushwood on a steep bank between two terraced fields. She had started work at the further end of the fifty-yard-long bank, and had cut the brushwood to within a yard of her hut when the tiger sprang on her from the field above. So sudden and unexpected was the attack that the woman only had time to scream once before the tiger killed her, and taking her up the twelve-foot-high bank crossed the upper field and disappeared with her into the dense jungle beyond. Her son, a lad some twenty years of age, was at the time working in a paddy field a few yards away and witnessed the whole occurrence, but was too frightened to try to render any assistance. In response to the lad's urgent summons the Patwari arrived at Sem two days later, accompanied by eighty men he had collected. Following up in the direction the tiger had gone, he found the woman's clothes and a few small bits of bone. This kill had taken place at 2 p.m. on a bright sunny day, and the tiger had eaten its victim only sixty yards from the hut where it had killed her.

On receipt of this second report Ibbotson, Deputy Commissioner of the three Districts of Almora, Naini Tal and Garhwal, and I held a council of war, the upshot of which was that Ibbotson, who was on the point of setting out to settle a land dispute at Askot on the border of Tibet, changed his tour programme and, instead of going via Bagashwar, decided to accompany me to Sem, and from there go on to Askot.

The route I had selected entailed a considerable amount of hill-climbing so we eventually decided to go up the Nandhour valley, cross the watershed between the Nandhour and Ladhya, and follow the latter river down to Sem. The Ibbotsons accordingly left Naini Tal on 12th October, and the following day I joined them at Chaurgallia.

Going up the Nandhour and fishing as we went—our best day's catch on light trout rods was 120 fish—we arrived on the fifth day at Durga Pepal. Here we left the river, and after a very stiff climb camped for the night on the watershed. Making an early start next morning we pitched our tents that night on the left bank of the Ladhya, twelve miles from Chalti.

The monsoon had given over early, which was very fortunate for us, for owing to the rock cliffs that run sheer down into the valley the river has to be crossed every quarter of a mile or so. At one of these fords my cook, who stands five feet in his boots, was washed away and only saved from a watery grave by the prompt assistance of the man who was carrying our lunch basket.

On the tenth day after leaving Chaurgallia we made camp on a deserted field at Sem, 200 yards from the hut where the woman had been killed, and a hundred yards from the junction of the Ladhya and Sarda rivers.

Gill Waddell, of the Police, whom we met on our way down the Ladhya, had camped for several days at Sem and had tied out a buffalo that MacDonald of the Forest Department had very kindly placed at our disposal, and though the tiger had visited Sem several times during Waddell's stay, it had not killed the buffalo.

The day following our arrival at Sem, while Ibbotson was interviewing Patwaris, Forest Guards, and Headmen of the surrounding villages, I went out to look for pug marks. Between our camp and the junction, and also on both banks of the Ladhya, there were long stretches of sand. On this sand I found the tracks of a tigress, and of a young male tiger—possibly one of the cubs I had seen in April. The tigress had crossed and recrossed the Ladhya a number of times during the last few days, and the previous night had walked along the strip of sand in front of our tents. It was this tigress the villagers suspected of being the man-eater, and as she had visited Sem repeatedly since the day the Headman's mother had been killed, they were probably correct.

An examination of the pug marks of the tigress showed her as being an average-sized animal, in the prime of life. Why she had become a man-eater would have to be determined later, but one of the reasons might have been that she had assisted to eat the victims of the Chuka tiger when they were together the previous mating season, and having acquired a taste for human flesh and no longer having a mate to provide her with it, had now turned a man-eater herself. This was only a surmise, and proved later to be incorrect.

Before leaving Naini Tal I had written to the Tahsildar of Tanakpur and asked him to purchase four young male buffaloes for me, and to send them to Sem. One of these buffaloes died on the road, the other three arrived on the 24th, and we tied them out the same evening together with the one MacDonald had given us. On going out to visit these animals next morning, I found the people of Chuka in a great state of excitement. The fields round the village had been recently ploughed, and the tigress the previous night had passed close to three families who were sleeping out on the fields with their cattle; fortunately in each case the cattle had seen the tigress and warned the sleepers of her approach. After leaving the cultivated land the tigress had gone up the track in the direction of Kot Kindri, and had passed close to two of our buffaloes without touching either of them.

The Patwari, Forest Guards, and villagers had told us on our arrival at Sem that it would be a waste of time tying out our young buffaloes, as they were convinced the man-eater would not kill them. The reason they gave was that this method of trying to shoot the man-eater had been tried by others without success, and that in any case if the tigress wanted to eat buffaloes there were many grazing in the jungles for her to choose from. In spite of this advice however we continued to tie out our buffaloes, and for the next two nights the tigress passed close to one or more of them, without touching them.

On the morning of the 27th, just as we were finishing breakfast, a party of men led by Tewari, the brother of the

Headman of Thak, arrived in camp and reported that a man of their village was missing. They stated that this man had left the village at about noon the previous day, telling his wife before leaving that he was going to see that his cattle did not stray beyond the village boundary, and as he had not returned they feared he had been killed by the man-eater.

Our preparations were soon made, and at ten o'clock the Ibbotsons and I set off for Thak, accompanied by Tewari and the men he had brought with him. The distance was only about two miles but the climb was considerable, and as we did not want to lose more time than we could possibly help we arrived at the outskirts of the village out of breath, and in a lather of sweat.

As we approached the village over the scrub-covered flat bit of ground which I have reason to refer to later, we heard a woman crying. The wailing of an Indian woman mourning her dead is unmistakable, and on emerging from the jungle we came on the mourner—the wife of the missing man—and some ten or fifteen men, who were waiting for us on the edge of the cultivated land. These people informed us that from their houses above they had seen some white object, which looked like part of the missing man's clothing, in a field overgrown with scrub thirty yards from where we were now standing. Ibbotson, Tewari and I set off to investigate the white object, while Mrs Ibbotson took the woman and the rest of the men up to the village.

The field, which had been out of cultivation for some years, was covered with a dense growth of scrub not unlike chrysanthemum, and it was not until we were standing right over the white object that Tewari recognized it as the loincloth of the missing man. Near it was the man's cap. A struggle had taken place at this spot, but there was no blood. The absence of blood where the attack had taken place and for some considerable distance along the drag could be accounted for by the tigress having retained her first hold, for no blood would flow in such a case until the hold had been changed.

Thirty yards on the hill above us there was a clump of bushes roofed over with creepers. This spot would have to be looked at before following up the drag, for it was not advisable to have the tigress behind us. In the soft earth under the bushes we found the pug marks of the tigress, and where she had lain before going forward to attack the man.

Returning to our starting point we agreed on the following plan of action. Our primary object was to try to stalk the tigress and shoot her on kill: to achieve this end I was to follow the trail and at the same time keep a look-out in front, with Tewari—who was unarmed—a yard behind me keeping a sharp look-out to right and left, and Ibbotson a yard behind Tewari to safeguard us against an attack from the rear. In the event of either Ibbotson or I seeing so much as a hair of the tigress, we were to risk a shot.

Cattle had grazed over this area the previous day, disturbing the ground, and as there was no blood and the only indication of the tigress's passage was an occasional turned-up leaf or crushed blade of grass, progress was slow. After carrying the man for 200 yards the tigress had killed and left him, and had returned and carried him off several hours later, when the people of Thak had heard several sambhar calling in this direction. The reason for the tigress not having carried the man away after she had killed him was possibly due to his cattle having witnessed the attack on him, and driven her away.

A big pool of blood had formed where the man had been lying, and as the blood from the wound in his throat had stopped flowing by the time the tigress had picked him up again, and further, as she was now holding him by the small of the back, whereas she had previously held him by the neck, tracking became even more difficult. The tigress kept to the contour of the hill, and as the undergrowth here was very dense and visibility only extended to a few yards, our advance was slowed down. In two hours we covered half a mile, and reached a ridge beyond which lay the valley in which, six months previously, we had tracked down and killed the Chuka man-eater. On this ridge was a great slab of rock, which sloped upwards and away from the direction in which we had come. The tigress's tracks went down to the right of the rock and I felt sure she was lying up under the overhanging portion of it, or in the close vicinity.

Both Ibbotson and I had on light rubber-soled shoes—Tewari was bare-footed—and we had reached the rock without making a sound. Signing to my two companions to stand still and keep a careful watch all round, I got a foothold on the rock, and inch by inch went forward. Beyond the rock was a short stretch of flat ground, and as more of this ground came into view, I felt certain my suspicion that the tigress was lying under the projection was correct. I had still a foot or two to go before I could look over, when I saw a movement to my left front. A golden-rod that had been pressed down had sprung erect, and a second later there was a slight movement in the bushes beyond, and a monkey in a tree on the far side of the bushes started calling.

The tigress had chosen the spot for her after-dinner sleep with great care, but unfortunately for us she was not asleep; and when she saw the top of my head—I had removed my hat—appearing over the rock, she had risen and, taking a step sideways, had disappeared under a tangle of blackberry bushes. Had she been lying anywhere but where she was she could not have got away, no matter how quickly she had moved, without my getting a shot at her. Our so-carefully-carried-out stalk had failed at the very last moment, and there was nothing to be done now but find the kill, and see if there was sufficient of it left for us to sit up over. To have followed her into the blackberry thicket would have been useless, and would also have reduced our chance of getting a shot at her later.

The tigress had eaten her meal close to where she had been lying and as this spot was open to the sky and to the keen eyes of vultures she had removed the kill to a place of safety where it would not be visible from the air. Tracking now was easy, for there was a blood trail to follow. The trail led over a ridge of great rocks and fifty yards beyond these rocks we found the kill.

I am not going to harrow your feelings by attempting to describe that poor torn and mangled thing; stripped of every stitch of clothing and atom of dignity, which only a few hours previously had been a Man, the father of two children and the breadwinner of the wailing woman who was facing—without any illusions—the fate of a widow of India. I have seen many similar sights, each more terrible than the one preceding it, in the thirty-two years I have been hunting man-eaters, and on each occasion I have felt that it would have been better to have left the victim to the slayer than recover a mangled mass of flesh to be a nightmare ever after to those who saw it. And yet the cry of blood for blood, and the burning desire to rid a countryside of a menace than which there is none more terrible, is irresistible; and then there is always the hope, no matter how absurd one knows it to be, that the victim by some miracle may still be alive and in need of succour.

The chance of shooting—over a kill—an animal that has in all probability become a man-eater through a wound received over a kill, is very remote, and each succeeding failure, no matter what its cause, tends to make the animal more cautious, until it reaches a state when it either abandons its kill after one meal or approaches it as silently and as slowly as a shadow, scanning every leaf and twig with the certainty of discovering its would-be slayer, no matter how carefully he may be concealed or how silent and motionless he may be; a one-in-a-million chance of getting a shot, and yet, who is there among us who would not take it?

The thicket into which the tigress had retired was roughly

forty yards square, and she could not leave it without the monkey seeing her and warning us, so we sat down back to back, to have a smoke and listen if the jungle had anything further to tell us while we considered our next move.

To make a machan it was necessary to return to the village, and during our absence the tigress was almost certain to carry away the kill. It had been difficult when she was carrying a whole human being to track her, but now, when her burden was considerably lighter and she had been disturbed, she would probably go for miles and we might never find her kill again, so it was necessary for one of us to remain on the spot, while the other two went back to the village for ropes.

Ibbotson, with his usual disregard for danger, elected to go back, and while he and Tewari went down the hill to avoid the difficult ground we had recently come over, I stepped up on to a small tree close to the kill. Four feet above ground the tree divided in two, and by leaning on one half and putting my feet against the other, I was able to maintain a precarious seat which was high enough off the ground to enable me to see the tigress if she approached the kill, and also high enough, if she had any designs on me, to see her before she got to within striking distance.

Ibbotson had been gone fifteen or twenty minutes when I heard a rock tilt forward, and then back. The rock was evidently very delicately poised, and when the tigress had put her weight on it and felt it tilt forward she had removed her foot and let the rock fall back into place. The sound had come from about twenty yards to my left front, the only direction in which it would have been possible for me to have fired without being knocked out of the tree.

Minutes passed, each pulling my hopes down a little lower from the heights to which they had soared, and then, when tension on my nerves and the weight of the heavy rifle were becoming unbearable, I heard a stick snap at the upper end of the thicket. Here was an example of how a tiger can move through the jungle. From the sound she had made I knew her exact position, had kept my eyes fixed on the spot, and yet she had come, seen me, stayed some time watching me, and then gone away without my having seen a leaf or a blade of grass move.

When tension on nerves is suddenly relaxed, cramped and aching muscles call loudly for ease, and though in this case it only meant the lowering of the rifle on to my knees to take the strain off my shoulders and arms, the movement, small though it was, sent a comforting feeling through the whole of my body. No further sound came from the tigress, and an hour or two later I heard Ibbotson returning.

Of all the men I have been on shikar with Ibbotson is by far and away the best, for not only has he the heart of a lion, but he thinks of everything, and with it all is the most unselfish man that carries a gun. He had gone to fetch a rope and he returned with rugs, cushions, more hot tea than even I could drink and an ample lunch; and while I sat—on the windward side of the kill—to refresh myself, Ibbotson put a man in a tree forty yards away to distract the tigress's attention, and climbed into a tree overlooking the kill to make a rope machan.

When the machan was ready Ibbotson moved the kill a few feet—a very unpleasant job—and tied it securely to the foot of a sapling to prevent the tigress carrying it away, for the moon was on the wane and the first two hours of the night at this heavily wooded spot would be pitch dark. After a final smoke I climbed on to the machan, and when I had made myself comfortable Ibbotson recovered the man who was making a diversion and set off in the direction of Thak to pick up Mrs Ibbotson and return to camp at Sem.

The retreating party were out of sight but were not yet out of sound when I heard a heavy body brushing against leaves, and at the same moment the monkey, which had been silent all this time and which I could now see sitting in a tree on the far side of blackberry thicket, started calling. Here was more luck than I hoped for, and our ruse of putting a man up a tree to cause a diversion appeared to be working as successfully as it had done on a previous occasion. A tense minute passed, a second, and a third, and then from the ridge where I had climbed on to the big slab of rock a kakar came dashing down towards me, barking hysterically. The tigress was not coming to the kill but had gone off after Ibbotson. I was now in a fever of anxiety, for it was quite evident that she had abandoned her kill and gone to try to secure another victim.

Before leaving Ibbotson had promised to take every precaution but on hearing the kakar barking on my side of the ridge he would naturally assume the tigress was moving in the vicinity of the kill, and if he relaxed his precautions the tigress would get her chance. Ten very uneasy minutes for me passed, and then I heard a second kakar barking in the direction of Thak; the tigress was still following, but the ground there was more open, and there was less fear of her attacking the party. The danger to the Ibbotsons was, however, not over by any means for they had to go through two miles of very heavy jungle to reach camp; and if they stayed at Thak until sundown listening for my shot, which I feared they would do and which as a matter of fact they did do, they would run a very grave risk on the way down. Ibbotson fortunately realized the danger and kept his party close together, and though the tigress followed them the whole way—as her pug marks the following morning showed—they got back to camp safely.

The calling of kakar and sambhar enabled me to follow the movements of the tigress. An hour after sunset she was down at the bottom of the valley two miles away. She had the whole night before her, and though there was only one chance in a million of her returning to the kill I determined not to lose that chance. Wrapping a rug round me, for it was a bitterly cold night, I made myself comfortable in a position in which I could remain for hours without movement.

I had taken my seat on the machan at 4 p.m., and at 10 p.m. I heard two animals coming down the hill towards me. It was too dark under the trees to see them, but when they got to the lee of the kill I knew they were porcupines. Rattling their quills, and making the peculiar booming noise that only a porcupine can make, they approached the kill and, after walking round it several times, continued on their way. An hour later, and when the moon had been up some time, I heard an animal in the valley below. It was moving from east to west, and when it came into the wind blowing downhill from the kill it made a long pause, and then came cautiously up the hill. While it was still some distance away I heard it snuffing the air, and knew it to be a bear. The smell of blood was attracting him, but mingled with it was the less welcome smell of a human being, and taking no chances he was very carefully stalking the kill. His nose, the keenest of any animal's in the jungle, had apprised him while he was still in the valley that the kill was the property of a tiger. This to a Himalayan bear who fears nothing, and who will, as I have on several occasions seen, drive a tiger away from its kill, was no deterrent, but what was, and what was causing him uneasiness, was the smell of a human being mingled with the smell of blood and tiger.

On reaching the flat ground the bear sat down on his haunches a few yards from the kill, and when he had satisfied himself that the hated human smell held no danger for him he stood erect and turning his head sent a long-drawn-out cry, which I interpreted as a call to a mate, echoing down into the valley. Then without any further hesitation he walked boldly up to the kill, and as he nosed it I aligned the sights of my rifle on him. I know of only one instance of a Himalayan bear eating a human being; on that occasion a woman cutting grass had fallen down a cliff and been killed, and a bear finding the mangled body had carried it away and had eaten it. This bear, however, on whose shoulder my sights were aligned, appeared to draw the line at human flesh, and after looking at and smelling the kill continued his interrupted course to the west. When the sounds of his retreat died away in the distance the jungle settled down to silence until interrupted, a little after sunrise, by Ibbotson's very welcome arrival.

With Ibbotson came the brother and other relatives of the dead man, who very reverently wrapped the remains in a clean white cloth and, lying it on a cradle made of two saplings and rope which Ibbotson provided, set off for the burning ghat on the banks of the Sarda, repeating under their breath as they went the Hindu hymn of praise 'Ram nam sat hai' with its refrain, 'Satya bol gat hai'.

Fourteen hours in the cold had not been without its effect on me, but after partaking of the hot drink and food Ibbotson had brought, I felt none the worse for my long vigil.

~

After following the Ibbotsons down to Chuka on the evening of the 27th the tigress, some time during the night, crossed the Ladhya into the scrub jungle at the back of our camp. Through this scrub ran a path that had been regularly used by the villagers of the Ladhya valley until the advent of the man-eater had rendered its passage unsafe. On the 28th the two mail-runners who carried Ibbotson's dak on its first stage to Tanakpur got delayed in camp and to save time took, or more correctly started to take, a short cut through this scrub. Very fortunately the leading man was on the alert and saw the tigress as she crept through the scrub and lay down near the path ahead of them.

Ibbotson and I had just got back from Thak when these two men dashed into camp, and taking our rifles we hurried off to investigate. We found the pug marks of the tigress where she had come out on the path and followed the men for a short distance, but we did not see her though in one place where the scrub was very dense we saw a movement and heard an animal moving off.

On the morning of the 29th, a party of men came down from Thak to report that one of their bullocks had not returned to the cattle shed the previous night, and on a search being made where it had last been seen a little blood had been found. At 2 p.m. the Ibbotsons and I were at this spot, and a glance at the ground satisfied us that the bullock had been killed and carried away by a tigress. After a hasty lunch Ibbotson and I, with two men following carrying ropes for a machan, set out along the drag. It went diagonally across the face of the hill for a hundred yards and then straight down into the ravine in which I had fired at and missed the big tiger in April. A few hundred yards down this ravine the bullock, which was an enormous animal, had got fixed between two rocks and, not being able to move it, the tigress had eaten a meal off its hind quarters and left it.

The pug marks of the tigress, owing to the great weight she was carrying, were splayed out and it was not possible to say whether she was the man-eater or not; but as every tigress in this area was suspect I decided to sit up over the kill. There was only one tree within reasonable distance of the kill, and as the men climbed into it to make a machan the tigress started calling in the valley below. Very hurriedly a few strands of rope were tied between two branches, and while Ibbotson stood on guard with his rifle I climbed the tree and took my seat on what, during the next fourteen hours, proved to be the most uncomfortable as well as the most dangerous machan I have sat on. The tree was leaning away from the hill, and from the three uneven strands of rope I was sitting on there was a drop of over a hundred feet into the rocky ravine below.

The tigress called several times as I was getting into the tree and continued to call at longer intervals late into the evening, and the last call coming from a ridge half a mile away. It was now quite evident that the tigress had been lying up close to the kill and had seen the men climbing into the tree. Knowing from past experience what this meant, she had duly expressed resentment at being disturbed and then gone away, for though I sat on the three strands of rope until Ibbotson returned next morning I did not see or hear anything throughout the night.

Vultures were not likely to find the kill, for the ravine was deep and overshadowed by trees, and as the bullock was large enough to provide tigress with several meals we decided not to sit up over it again where it was now lying, hoping the tigress would remove it to a place more convenient and where we should have a better chance of getting a shot. In this however we were disappointed, for the tigress did not again return to the kill.

Two nights later the buffalo we had tied out behind our camp at Sem was killed, and through a little want of observation on my part a great opportunity of bagging the man-eater was lost.

The men who brought in the news of this kill reported that the rope securing the animal had been broken, and that the kill had been carried away up the ravine at the lower end of which it had been tied. This was the same ravine in which MacDonald and I had chased a tigress in April, and as on that occasion she had taken her kill some distance up the ravine I now very foolishly concluded she had done the same with this kill.

After breakfast Ibbotson and I went out to find the kill and see what prospect there was for an evening sit-up.

The ravine in which the buffalo had been killed was about fifty yards wide and ran deep into the foothills. For 200 yards the ravine was straight and then bent round to the left. Just beyond the bend, and on the left-hand side of it, there was a dense patch of young saplings backed by a 100-foot ridge on which thick grass was growing. In the ravine, and close to the saplings, there was a small pool of water. I had been up the ravine several times in April and had failed to mark the patch of saplings as being a likely place for a tiger to lie up in, and did not take the precautions I should have taken when rounding the bend, with the result that the tigress who was drinking at the pool saw us first. There was only one safe line of retreat for her and she took it. This was straight up the steep hill, over the ridge, and into the sal forest beyond.

The hill was too steep for us to climb, so we continued on up the ravine to where a sambhar track crossed it, and following this track we gained the ridge. The tigress was now in a triangular patch of jungle bounded by the ridge, the Ladhya, and a cliff down which no animal could go. The area was not large, and there were several deer in it which from time to time advised us of the position of the tigress, but unfortunately the ground was cut up by a number of deep and narrow rainwater channels in which we eventually lost touch with her.

We had not yet seen the kill, so we re-entered the ravine by the sambhar track and found the kill hidden among the saplings. These saplings were from six inches to a foot in girth, and were not strong enough to support a machan, so we had to abandon the idea of a machan. With the help of a crowbar a rock could possibly have been prised from the face of the hill and a place made in which to sit, but this was not advisable when dealing with a man-eater.

Reluctant to give up the chance of a shot we considered the possibility of concealing ourselves in the grass near the kill, in the hope that the tigress would return before dark and that we should see her before she saw us. There were two objections to this plan: (a) if we did not get a shot and the tigress saw us near her kill she might abandon it as she had done her other two kills, and (b) between the kill and camp there was very heavy scrub jungle, and if we tried to go through this jungle in the dark the tigress would have us at her mercy. So very reluctantly we decided to leave the kill to the tigress for that night, and hope for the best on the morrow.

On our return next morning we found that the tigress had carried away the kill. For 300 yards she had gone up the bed of the ravine, stepping from rock to rock, and leaving no drag marks. At this spot—300 yards from where she had picked up the kill—we were at fault, for though there was a number of tracks on a wet patch of ground, none of them had been made while she was carrying the kill. Eventually, after casting round in circles, we found where she had left the ravine and gone up the hill on the left.

This hill up which the tigress had taken her kill was overgrown with ferns and goldenrod and tracking was not difficult, but the going was, for the hill was very steep and in places a detour had to be made and the track picked up further on. After a stiff climb of a thousand feet we came to a small plateau, bordered on the left by a cliff a mile wide. On the side of the plateau nearest the cliff the ground was seamed and cracked, and in these cracks a dense growth of sal, two to six feet in height, had sprung up. The tigress had taken her kill into this dense cover and it was not until we actually trod on it that we were aware of its position.

As we stopped to look at all that remained of the buffalo there was a low growl to our right. With rifles raised we waited for a minute and then, hearing a movement in the undergrowth a little beyond where the growl had come from, we pushed our way through the young sal for ten yards and came on a small clearing, where the tigress had made herself a bed on some soft grass. On the far side of this grass the hill sloped upwards for twenty yards to another plateau, and it was from this slope that the sound we had heard had come. Proceeding up the slope as silently as possible we had just reached the flat ground, which was about fifty yards wide, when the tigress left the far side and went down into the ravine, disturbing some kaleej pheasants and a kakar as she did so. To have followed her would have been useless, so we went back to the kill and, as there was still a good meal on it, we selected two trees to sit in, and returned to camp.

After an early lunch we went back to the kill and, hampered with our rifles, climbed with some difficulty into the trees we had selected. We sat up for five hours without seeing or hearing anything. At dusk we climbed down from our trees, and stumbling over the cracked and uneven ground eventually reached the ravine when it was quite dark. Both of us had an uneasy feeling that we were being followed, but by keeping close together we reached camp without incident at 9 p.m.

The Ibbotsons had now stayed at Sem as long as it was possible for them to do so, and early next morning they set out on their twelve days' walk to keep their appointment at Askot. Before leaving, Ibbotson extracted a promise from me that I would not follow up any kills alone, or further endanger my life by prolonging my stay at Sem for more than a day or two.

After the departure of the Ibbotsons and their fifty men, the camp, which was surrounded by dense scrub, was reduced to my two servants and myself—my coolies were living in a room in the Headman's house—so throughout the day I set all hands to collecting driftwood, of which there was an inexhaustible supply at the junction, to keep a fire going all night. The fire would not scare away the tigress but it would enable us to see her if she prowled round our tents at night, and anyway the nights were setting in cold and there was ample excuse, if one were needed, for keeping a big fire going all night.

Towards evening, when my men were safely back in camp, I took a rifle and went up the Ladhya to see if the tigress had crossed the river. I found several tracks in the sand, but no fresh ones, and at dusk I returned, convinced that the tigress was still on our side of the river. An hour later, when it was quite dark, a kakar started barking close to our tents and barked persistently for half an hour.

My men had taken over the job of tying out the buffaloes, a task which Ibbotson's men had hitherto performed, and next morning I accompanied them when they went out to bring in the buffaloes. Though we covered several miles I did not find any trace of the tigress. After breakfast I took a rod and went down to the junction, and had one of the best day's fishing I have ever had. The junction was full of big fish, and though my light tackle was broken frequently, I killed sufficient mahseer to feed the camp.

Again, as on the previous evening, I crossed the Ladhya, with the intention of taking up a position on a rock overlooking the open ground on the right bank of the river and watching for the tigress to cross. As I got away from the roar of the water at the junction I heard a sambhar and a monkey calling on the hill to my left, and as I neared the rock I came on the fresh tracks of the tigress. Following them back I found the stones still wet where she had forded the river. A few minutes' delay in camp to dry my fishing line and have a cup of tea cost a man his life, several thousand men weeks of anxiety, and myself many days of strain, for though I stayed at Sem for another three days I did not get another chance of shooting the tigress.

On the morning of the 7th, as I was breaking camp and preparing to start on my twenty-mile walk to Tanakpur, a big contingent of men from all the surrounding villages arrived, and begged me not to leave them to the tender mercies of the man-eater. Giving them what advice it was possible to give people situated as they were, I promised to return as soon as it was possible for me to do so.

I caught the train at Tanakpur next morning and arrived back in Naini Tal on 9 November, having been away nearly a month.

~

I left Sem on the 7th of November and on the 12th the tigress killed a man at Thak. I received news of this kill through the Divisional Forest Officer, Haldwani, shortly after we had moved down to our winter home at the foot of the hills, and by doing forced marches I arrived at Chuka a little after sunrise on the 24th.

It had been my intention to breakfast at Chuka and then go on to Thak and make that village my headquarters, but the Headman of Thak, whom I found installed at Chuka, informed me that every man, woman, and child had left Thak immediately after the man had been killed on the 12th, and added that if I carried out my intention of camping at Thak I might be able to safeguard my own life, but it would not be possible to safeguard the lives of my men. This was quite reasonable, and while waiting for my men to arrive, the Headman helped me to select a site for my camp at Chuka where my men would be reasonably safe and I should have some privacy from the thousands of men who were now arriving to fell the forest.

On receipt of the Divisional Forest Officer's telegram acquainting me of the kill, I had telegraphed to the Tahsildar at Tanakpur to send three young male buffaloes to Chuka. My request had been promptly complied with and the three animals had arrived the previous evening.

After breakfast I took one of the buffaloes and set out for Thak, intending to tie it up on the spot where the man had been killed on the 12th. The Headman had given me a very graphic account of the events of that date, for he himself had nearly fallen a victim to the tigress. It appeared that towards the afternoon, accompanied by his granddaughter, a girl ten years of age, he had gone to dig up ginger tubers in field some sixty yards from his house. This field is about half an acre in extent and is surrounded on three sides by jungle, and being on the slope of a fairly steep hill it is visible from the Headman's house. After the old man and his granddaughter had been at work for some time his wife, who was husking rice in the courtyard of the house, called out in a very agitated voice and asked him if he was deaf that he could not hear the pheasants and other birds that were chattering in the jungle above him. Fortunately for him, he acted promptly. Dropping his hoe, he grabbed the child's hand and together they ran back to the house, urged on by the woman who said she could now see a red animal in the bushes at the upper end of the field. Half an hour later the tigress killed a man who was lopping branches off a tree in a field 300 yards from the Headman's house.

From the description I had received from the Headman I had no difficulty in locating the tree. It was a small gnarled tree growing out of a three-foot-high bank between two terraced fields, and had been lopped year after year for cattle fodder. The man who had been killed was standing on the trunk holding one branch and cutting another, when the tigress came up from behind, tore his hold from the branch and, after killing him, carried him away into the dense brushwood bordering the fields.

Thak village was a gift from the Chand Rajas, who ruled Kumaon for many hundreds of years before the Gurkha occupation, to the forefathers of the present owners in return for their services at the Purnagiri temples. (The promise made by the Chand Rajas that the lands of Thak and two other villages would remain rent-free for all time has been honoured by the British Government for a hundred years.) From a collection of grass huts the village has in the course of time grown into a very prosperous settlement with masonry houses roofed with slate tiles, for not only is the land very fertile, but the revenue from the temples is considerable.

Like all other villages in Kumaon, Thak during its hundreds of years of existence has passed through many vicissitudes, but never before in its long history had it been deserted as it now was. On my previous visits I had found it a hive of industry, but when I went up to it this afternoon, taking the young buffalo with me, silence reigned over it. Every one of the 100 or more inhabitants had fled taking their livestock with them—the only animal I saw in the village was a cat, which gave me a warm welcome; so hurried had the evacuation been that many of the doors of the houses had been left wide open. On every path in the village, in the courtyards of the houses and in the dust before all the doors I found the tigress's pug marks. The open doorways were a menace, for the path as it wound through the village passed close to them, and in any of the houses the tigress might have been lurking.

On the hill thirty yards above the village were several cattle shelters, and in the vicinity of these shelter I saw more kaleej pheasants, red jungle fowl, and white-capped babblers than I have ever before seen, and from the confiding way in which they permitted me to walk among them it is quite evident that the people of Thak have a religious prejudice against the taking of life.

From the terraced fields above the cattle shelters a bird's-eye view of the village is obtained, and it was not difficult, from the description the Headman had given me, to locate the tree where the tigress had secured her last victim. In the soft earth under the tree there were signs of a struggle and a few clots of dried blood. From here the tigress had carried her kill a hundred yards over a ploughed field, through a stout hedge, and into the dense brushwood beyond. The footprints from the village, and back the way they had come, showed that the entire population of the village had visited the scene of the kill, but from the tree to the hedge there was only one track, the track the tigress had made when carrying away her victim. No attempt had been made to follow her up and recover the body.

Scraping away a little earth from under the tree I exposed a root and to this root I tied my buffalo, bedding it down with a liberal supply of straw taken from a nearby haystack.

The village, which is on the north face of the hill, was now in shadow, and if I was to get back to camp before dark it was time for me to make a start. Skirting round the village to avoid the menace of the open doorways, I joined the path below the houses.

This path after it leaves the village passes under a giant mango tree from the roots of which issues a cold spring of clear water. After running along a groove cut in a massive slab of rock, this water falls into a rough masonry trough, from where it spreads onto the surrounding ground, rendering it soft and slushy. I had drunk at the spring on my way up, leaving my footprints in this slushy ground, and on approaching the spring now for a second drink, I found the tigress's pug marks superimposed on my footprints. After quenching her thirst the tigress had avoided the path and had gained the village by climbing a steep bank overgrown with strobilanthes and nettles, and taking up a position in the shelter of one of the houses had possibly watched me while I was tying up the buffalo, expecting me to return the way I had gone; it was fortunate for me that I had noted the danger of passing those open doorways a second time, and had taken the longer way round.

When coming up from Chuka I had taken every precaution to guard against a sudden attack, and it was well that I had done so, for I now found from her pug marks that the tigress had followed me all the way up from my camp, and next morning when I went back to Thak I found she had followed me from where I had joined the path below the houses, right down to the cultivated land at Chuka.

Reading with the illumination I had brought with me was not possible, so after dinner that night, while sitting near a fire which was as welcome for its warmth as it was for the feeling of security it gave me, I reviewed the whole situation and tried to think out some plan by which it would be possible to circumvent the tigress.

When leaving home on the 22nd I had promised that I would return in ten days, and that this would be my last expedition after man-eaters. Years of exposure and strain and long absences from home—extending as in the case of the Chowgarh tigress and the Rudraprayag leopard to several months on end—were beginning to tell as much on my constitution as on the nerves of those at home, and if by the 30th of November I had not succeeded in killing this man-eater, others would have to be found who were willing to take on the task.

It was now the night of the 24th, so I had six clear days before me. Judging from the behaviour of the tigress that evening, she appeared to be anxious to secure another human victim, and it should not therefore be difficult for me, in the time at my disposal, to get in touch with her. There were several methods by which this could be accomplished, and each would be tried in turn. The method that offers the greatest chance of success of shooting a tiger in the hills is to sit up in a tree over a kill, and if during that night the tigress did not kill the buffalo I had tied up at Thak, I would the following night, and every night thereafter, tie up the other two buffaloes in places I had already selected, and failing to secure a human kill it was just possible that the tigress might kill one of my buffaloes, as she had done on a previous occasion when the Ibbotsons and I were camped at Sem in April. After making up the fire with logs that would burn all night, I turned in, and went to sleep listening to a kakar barking in the scrub jungle behind my tent.

While breakfast was being prepared the following morning, I picked up a rifle and went out to look for tracks on the stretch of sand on the right bank of the river, between Chuka and Sem. The path, after leaving the cultivated land, runs for a short distance through scrub jungle, and here I found the tracks of a big male leopard, possibly the same animal that had alarmed the kakar the previous night. A small male tiger had crossed and recrossed the Ladhya many times during the past week, and in the same period the man-eater had crossed only once, coming from the direction of Sem. A big bear had traversed the sand a little before my arrival, and when I got back to camp the timber contractors complained that while distributing work that morning they had run into a bear which had taken up a very threatening attitude, in consequence of which their labour had refused to work in the area in which the bear had been seen.

Several thousand men—the contractors put the figure at 5,000—had now concentrated at Chuka and Kumaya Chak to fell and saw up the timber and carry it down to the motor road that was being constructed, and all the time this considerable labour force was working they shouted at the tops of their voices to keep up their courage. The noise in the valley resulting from axe and saw, the crashing of giant trees down the steep hillside, the breaking of rocks with sledge hammers, and combined with it all the shouting of thousands of men, can better be imagined than described. That there were many frequent alarms in this nervous community was only natural, and during the next few days I covered much ground and lost much valuable time in investigating false rumours of attacks and kills by the man-eater, for the dread of the tigress was not confined to the Ladhya valley but extended right down the Sarda through Kaladhunga to the gorge, an area of roughly fifty square miles in which an additional 10,000 men were working.

That a single animal should terrorize a labour force of these dimensions in addition to the residents of the surrounding villages and the hundreds of men who were bringing foodstuffs for the labourers or passing through the valley with hill produce in the way of oranges (purchasable at twelve annas a hundred), walnuts, and chillies to the market at Tanakpur, is incredible, and would be unbelievable were it not for the historical, and nearly parallel, case of the man-eater of Tsavo, where a pair of lions, operating only at night, held up work for long periods on the Uganda Railway.

To return to my story. Breakfast disposed of on the morning of the 25th, I took a second buffalo and set out for Thak. The path, after leaving the cultivated land at Chuka, skirts along the foot of the hill for about half a mile before it divides. One arm goes straight up a ridge to Thak and the other, after continuing along the foot of the hill for another half-mile, zigzags up through Kumaya Chak to Kot Kindri.

At the divide I found the pug marks of the tigress and followed them all the way back to Thak. The fact that she had come down the hill after me the previous evening was proof that she had not killed the buffalo. This, though very disappointing, was not at all unusual; for tigers will on occasions visit an animal that is tied up for several nights in succession before they finally kill it, for tigers do not kill unless they are hungry.

Leaving the second buffalo at the mango tree, where there was an abundance of green grass, I skirted round the houses and found No. 1 buffalo sleeping peacefully after a big feed and a disturbed night. The tigress, coming from the direction of the village as her pug marks showed, had approached to within a few feet of the buffalo, and had then gone back the way she had come. Taking the buffalo down to the spring I let it graze for an hour or two, and then took it back and tied it up at the same spot where it had been the previous night.

The second buffalo I tied up fifty yards from the mango tree and at the spot where the wailing woman and villagers had met us the day the Ibbotsons and I had gone up to investigate the human kill. Here a ravine a few feet deep crossed the path, on one side of which there was a dry stump, and on the other an almond tree in which a machan could be made. I tied the second buffalo to the stump, and bedded it down with sufficient hay to keep it going for several days. There was nothing more to be done at Thak so I returned to camp and, taking the third buffalo, crossed the Ladhya and tied it up behind Sem, in the ravine where the tigress had killed one of our buffaloes in April.

At my request the Tahsildar of Tanakpur had selected three of the fattest young male buffaloes he could find. All three were now tied up in places frequented by the tigress, and as I set out to visit them on the morning of the 26th I had great hopes that one of them had been killed and that I should get an opportunity of shooting the tigress over it. Starting with the one across the Ladhya, I visited all in turn and found that the tigress had not touched any of them. Again, as on the previous morning, I found her tracks on that path leading to Thak, but on this occasion there was a double set of pug marks, one coming down and the other going back. On both her journeys the tigress had kept to the path and had passed within a few feet of the buffalo that was tied to the stump, fifty yards from the mango tree.

On my return to Chuka a deputation of Thak villagers led by the Headman came to my tent and requested me to accompany them to the village to enable them to replenish their supply of foodstuffs, so at midday, followed by the Headman and his tenants, and by four of my own men carrying ropes for a machan and food for me, I returned to Thak and mounted guard while the men hurriedly collected the provisions they needed.

After watering and feeding the two buffaloes, I retied No. 2 to the stump and took No. 1 half a mile down the hill and tied it to a sapling on the side of the path. I then took the villagers back to Chuka and returned a few hundred yards up the hill for a scratch meal while my men were making the machan.

It was now quite evident that the tigress had no fancy for my fat buffaloes, and as in three days I had seen her tracks five times on the path leading to Thak, I decided to sit up over the path and try to get a shot at her that way. To give me warning of the tigress's approach I tied a goat with a bell round its neck on the path, and at 4 p.m. I climbed into the tree. I told my men to return at 8 a.m. the following morning, and began my watch.

At sunset a cold wind started blowing and while I was attempting to pull a coat over my shoulders the ropes on one side of the machan slipped, rendering my seat very uncomfortable. An hour later a storm came on, and though it did not rain for long it wet me to the skin, greatly adding to my discomfort. During the sixteen hours I sat in the tree I did not see or hear anything. The men turned up at 8 a.m. I returned to camp for a hot bath and a good meal, and then, accompanied by six of my men, set out for Thak.

The overnight rain had washed all the old tracks off the path, and 200 yards above the tree I had sat in I found the fresh pug marks of the tigress, where she had come out of the jungle and gone up the path in the direction of Thak. Very cautiously I stalked the first buffalo, only to find it lying asleep on the path; the tigress had skirted round it, rejoined the path a few yards further on and continued up the hill. Following on her tracks I approached the second buffalo, and as I got near the place where it had been tied, two blue Himalayan magpies rose off the ground and went screaming down the hill.

The presence of these birds indicated (a) that the buffalo was dead, (b) that it had been partly eaten and not carried away, and (c) that the tigress was not in the close vicinity.

On arrival at the stump to which it had been tied I saw that the buffalo had been dragged off the path and partly eaten, and on examining the animal I found that it had not been killed by the tigress but that it had in all probability died of snake-bite (there were many hamadryads in the surrounding jungles), and that, finding it lying dead on the path, the tigress had eaten a meal off it and had then tried to drag it away. When she found she could not break the rope, she had partly covered the kill over with dry leaves and brushwood and continued on her way up to Thak.

Tigers as a rule are not carrion eaters but they do on occasions eat animals they themselves have not killed. For instance, on one occasion I left the carcass of a leopard on a fire track and, when I returned next morning to recover a knife I had forgotten, I found that a tiger had removed the carcass to a distance of a hundred yards and had eaten two-thirds of it.

On my way up from Chuka I had dismantled the machan I had sat on the previous night, and while two of my men climbed into the almond tree to make a seat for me—the tree was not big enough for a machan—the other four went to the spring to fill a kettle and boil some water for tea. By 4 p.m. I had partaken of a light meal of biscuits and tea which would have to keep me going until next day, and refusing the men's request to be permitted to stay the night in one of the houses in Thak, I sent them back to camp. There was a certain amount of risk in doing this, but it was nothing compared to the risk they would run if they spent the night in Thak.

My seat on the tree consisted of several strands of rope tied between two upright branches, with a couple of strands lower down for my feet to rest on. When I had settled down comfortably I pulled the branches round me and secured them in position with a thin cord, leaving a small opening to see and fire through. My 'hide' was soon tested, for shortly after the men had gone the two magpies returned, and attracted others, and nine of them fed on the kill until dusk. The presence of the birds enabled me to get some sleep, for they would have given me warning of the tigress's approach, and with their departure my all-night vigil started.

There was still sufficient daylight to shoot by when the moon, a day off the full, rose over the Nepal hills behind me and flooded the hillside with brilliant light. The rain of the previous night had cleared the atmosphere of dust and smoke and, after the moon had been up a few minutes, the light was so good that I was able to see a sambhar and her young one feeding in a field of wheat 150 yards away.

The dead buffalo was directly in front and about twenty yards away, and the path along which I expected the tigress to come was two or three yards nearer, so I should have an easy shot at a range at which it would be impossible to miss the tigress—provided she came; and there was no reason why she should not do so.

The moon had been up two hours, and the sambhar had

approached to within fifty yards of my tree, when a kakar started barking on the hill just above the village. The kakar had been barking for some minutes when suddenly a scream which I can only very inadequately describe as 'Ar-Ar-Arr' dying away on a long-drawn-out note, came from the direction of the village. So sudden and so unexpected had the scream been that I involuntarily stood up with the intention of slipping down from the tree and dashing up to the village, for the thought flashed through my mind that the man-eater was killing one of my men. Then in a second flash of thought I remembered I had counted them one by one as they had passed my tree, and that I had watched them out of sight on their way back to camp to see if they were obeying my instructions to keep close together.

The scream had been the despairing cry of a human being in mortal agony, and reason questioned how such a sound could have come from a deserted village. It was not a thing of my imagination, for the kakar had heard it and had abruptly stopped barking, and the sambhar had dashed away across the fields closely followed by her young one. Two days previously, when I had escorted the men to the village, I had remarked that they appeared to be very confident to leave their property behind doors that were not even shut or latched, and the Headman had answered that even if their village remained untenanted for years their property would be quite safe, for they were priests of Purnagiri and no one would dream of robbing them; he added that as long as the tigress lived she was a better guard of their property—if guard were needed—than any 100 men could be, for no one in all that countryside would dare to approach the village for any purpose, through the dense forests that surrounded it, unless escorted by me as they had been.

The screams were not repeated, and as there appeared to be nothing that I could do I settled down again on my rope seat. At 10 p.m. a kakar that was feeding on the young wheat crop at the lower end of the fields dashed away barking, and a minute later the tigress called twice. She had now left the village and was on the move, and even if she did not fancy having another meal off the buffalo there was every hope of her coming along the path which she had used twice every day for the past few days. With finger on trigger and eyes straining on the path I sat hour after hour until daylight succeeded moonlight, and when the sun had been up an hour, my men returned. Very thoughtfully they had brought a bundle of dry wood with them, and in a surprisingly short time I was sitting down to a hot cup of tea. The tigress may have been lurking in the bushes close to us, or she may have been miles away, for after she had called at 10 p.m. the jungles had been silent.

When I got back to camp I found a number of men sitting near my tent. Some of these men had come to inquire what luck I had the previous night, and others had come to tell me that the tigress had called from midnight to a little before sunrise at the foot of the hill, and that all the labourers engaged in the forests and on the new export road were too frightened to go to work. I had already heard about the tigress from my men, who had informed me that, together with the thousands of men who were camped round Chuka, they had sat up all night to keep big fires going.

Among the men collected near my tent was the Headman of Thak, and when the others had gone I questioned him about the kill at Thak on the 12th of the month when he so narrowly escaped falling a victim to the man-eater.

Once again the Headman told me in great detail how he had gone to his fields to dig ginger, taking his grandchild with him, and how on hearing his wife calling he had caught the child's hand and run back to the house—where his wife had said a word or two to him about not keeping his ears open and thereby endangering his own and the child's life—and how a few minutes later the tigress had killed a man while he was cutting leaves off a tree in a field above his house.

All this part of the story I had heard before, and I now asked him if he had actually seen the tigress killing the man. His answer was, no; and he added that the tree was not visible from where he had been standing. I then asked him how he knew the man had been killed, and he said, because he had heard him. In reply to further questions he said the man had not called for help but had cried out; and when asked if he had cried out once he said, 'No, three times,' and then at my request he gave an imitation of the man's cry. It was the same—but a very modified rendering—as the screams I had heard the previous night.

I then told him what I had heard and asked him if it was possible for anyone to have arrived at the village accidentally, and his answer was an emphatic negative. There were only two paths leading to Thak, and every man, woman, and child in the village through which these two paths passed knew that Thak was deserted and the reason for its being so. It was known throughout the district that it was dangerous to go near Thak in daylight, and it was therefore quite impossible for anyone to have been in the village at eight o'clock the previous night.

When asked if he could give any explanation for screams having come from a village in which there could not—according to him—have been any human beings, his answer was that he could not. And as I could do no better than the Headman it were best to assume that neither the kakar, the sambhar, nor I heard those very real screams—the screams of a human being in mortal agony.

~

When all my visitors, including the Headman, had gone, and I was having breakfast, my servant informed me that the Headman of Sem had come to the camp the previous evening and had left word for me that his wife, while cutting grass near the hut where his mother had been killed, had come on a blood trail, and that he would wait for me near the ford over the Ladhya in the morning. So after breakfast I set out to investigate this trail.

While I was fording the river I saw four men hurrying towards me, and as soon as I was on dry land they told me that when they were coming down the hill above Sem they had heard a tiger calling across the valley on the hill between Chuka and Thak. The noise of the water had prevented my hearing the call. I told the men that I was on my way to Sem and would return to Chuka shortly, and left them.

The Headman was waiting for me near his house, and his wife took me to where she had seen the blood trail the previous day. The trail, after continuing along a field for a short distance, crossed some big rocks, on one of which I found the hairs of a kakar. A little further on I found the pug marks of a big male leopard, and while I was looking at them I heard a tiger call. Telling my companions to sit down and remain quiet, I listened, in order to locate the tiger. Presently I heard the call again, and thereafter it was repeated at intervals of about two minutes.

It was the tigress calling and I located her as being 500 yards below Thak and in the deep ravine which, starting from the spring under the mango tree, runs parallel to the path and crosses it at its junction with the Kumaya Chak path.

Telling the Headman that the leopard would have to wait to be shot at a more convenient time, I set off as hard as I could go for camp, picking up at the ford the four men who were waiting for my company to Chuka.

On reaching camp I found a crowd of men round my tent, most of them sawyers from Delhi, but including the petty contractors, agents, clerks, timekeepers, and gangmen of the financier who had taken up the timber and road construction contracts in the Ladhya valley. These men had come to see me in connexion with my stay at Chuka. They informed me that many of the hillmen carrying timber and working on the road had left for their homes that morning and that if I left Chuka on 1st December, as they had heard I intended doing, the entire labour force, including themselves, would leave on the same day; for already they were too frightened to eat or sleep, and no one would dare to remain in the valley after I had gone. It was then the morning of 29th November and I told the men that I still had two days and two nights and that much could happen in that time, but that in any case it would not be possible for me to prolong my stay beyond the morning of the 1st.

The tigress had by now stopped calling, and when my servant had put together something for me to eat I set out for Thak, intending, if the tigress called again and I could locate her position, to try to stalk her; and if she did not call again, to sit up over the buffalo. I found her tracks on the path and saw where she had entered the ravine, and though I stopped repeatedly on my way up to Thak and listened I did not hear her again. So a little before sunset I ate the biscuits and drank the bottle of tea I had brought with me, and then climbed into the almond tree and took my seat on the few strands of rope that had to serve me as a machan. On this occasion the magpies were absent, so I was unable to get the hour or two's sleep the birds had enabled me to get the previous evening.

If a tiger fails to return to its kill the first night it does not necessarily mean that the kill has been abandoned. I have on occasions seen a tiger return on the tenth night and eat what could no longer be described as fresh. On the present occasion, however, I was not sitting over a kill, but over an animal that the tigress had found dead and off which she had made a small meal, and had she not been a man-eater I would not have considered the chance of her returning the second night good enough to justify spending a whole night in a tree when she had not taken sufficient interest in the dead buffalo to return to it the first night. It was therefore with very little hope of getting a shot that I sat on the tree from sunset to sunrise, and though the time I spent was not as long as it had been the previous night, my discomfort was very much greater, for the ropes I was sitting on cut into me, and a cold wind that started blowing shortly after moonrise and continued throughout the night chilled me to the bone. On this second night I heard no jungle or other sounds nor did the sambhar and her young one come out to feed on the fields. As daylight was succeeding moonlight I thought I heard a tiger call in the distance, but could not be sure of the sound or of its direction.

When I got back to camp my servant had a cup of tea and a hot bath ready for me, but before I could indulge in the latter—my 40-lb. tent was not big enough for me to bathe in—I had to get rid of the excited throng of people who were clamouring to tell me their experiences of the night before. It appeared that shortly after moonrise the tigress had started calling close to Chuka, and after calling at intervals for a couple of hours had gone off in the direction of the labour camps at Kumaya Chak. The men in these camps hearing her coming started shouting to try to drive her away, but so far from having this effect the shouting only infuriated her the more and she demonstrated in front of the camps until she had cowed the men into silence. Having accomplished this she spent the rest of the night between the labour camps and Chuka, daring all and sundry to shout at her. Towards morning she had gone away in the direction of Thak, and my informants were surprised and very disappointed that I had not met her.

This was my last day of man-eater hunting, and though I was badly in need of rest and sleep, I decided to spend what was left of it in one last attempt to get in touch with the tigress.

The people not only of Chuka and Sem but of all the surrounding villages, and especially the men from Talla Des where some years previously I had shot three man-eaters, were very anxious that I should try sitting up over a live goat, for, said they, 'All hill tigers eat goats, and as you have had no luck with buffaloes, why not try a goat?' More to humour them than with any hope of getting a shot, I consented to spend this last day in sitting up over the two goats I had already purchased for this purpose.

I was convinced that no matter where the tigress wandered to at night her headquarters were at Thak, so at midday, taking the two goats, and accompanied by four of my men, I set out for Thak.

The path from Chuka to Thak, as I have already mentioned, runs up a very steep ridge. A quarter of a mile on this side of Thak the path leaves the ridge, and crosses a more or less flat bit of ground which extends right up to the mango tree. For its whole length across this flat ground the path passes through dense brushwood, and is crossed by two narrow ravines which run east and join the main ravine. Midway between these two ravines, and a hundred yards from the tree I had sat in the previous two nights, there is a giant almond tree; this tree had been my objective when I left camp. The path passes right under the tree and I thought that if I climbed half-way up not only should I be able to see the two goats, one of which I intended tying at the edge of the main ravine and the other at the foot of the hill to the right, but I should also be able to see the dead buffalo. As all three of these points were at some distance from the tree, I armed myself with an accurate ·275 rifle, in addition to the 450/400 rifle which I took for an emergency.

I found the climb up from Chuka on this last day very trying, and I had just reached the spot where the path leaves the ridge for the flat ground, when the tigress called about 150 yards to my left. The ground here was covered with dense undergrowth and trees interlaced with creepers, and was cut up by narrow and deep ravines, and strewn over with enormous boulders—a very unsuitable place in which to stalk a man-eater. However, before deciding on what action I should take it was necessary to know whether the tigress was lying down, as she very well might be, for it was then 1 p.m., or whether she was on the move and if so in what direction. So making the men sit down behind me I listened, and presently the call was repeated; she had moved some fifty yards, and appeared to be going up the main ravine in the direction of Thak.

This was very encouraging, for the tree I had selected to sit in was only fifty yards from the ravine. After enjoining silence on the men and telling them to keep close behind me, we hurried along the path. We had about 200 yards to go to reach the tree and had covered half the distance when, as we approached a spot where the path was bordered on both sides by dense brushwood, a covey of kaleej pheasants rose out of the brushwood and went screaming away. I knelt down and covered the path for a few minutes, but as nothing happened we went cautiously forward and reached the tree without further incident. As quickly and as silently as possible one goat was tied at the edge of the ravine, while the other was tied at the foot of the hill to the right; then I took the men to the edge of the cultivated land and told them to stay in the upper verandah of the Headman's house until I fetched them, and ran back to the tree. I climbed to a height of forty feet, and pulled the rifle up after me with a cord I had brought for the purpose. Not only were the two goats visible from my seat, one at a range of seventy and the other at a range of sixty yards, but I could also see part of the buffalo, and as the ·275 rifle was accurate I felt sure I could kill the tigress if she showed up anywhere on the ground I was overlooking.

The two goats had lived together ever since I had purchased them on my previous visit, and, being separated now, were calling lustily to each other. Under normal conditions a goat can be heard at a distance of 400 yards, but here the conditions were not normal, for the goats were tied on the side of a hill down which a strong wind was blowing, and even if the tigress had moved after I had heard her, it was impossible for her not to hear them. If she was hungry, as I had every reason to believe she was, there was a very good chance of my getting a shot.

After I had been on the tree for ten minutes a kakar barked near the spot the pheasants had risen from. For a minute or two my hopes rose sky-high and then dropped back to earth, for the kakar barked only three times and ended on a note of inquiry; evidently there was a snake in the scrub which neither he nor the pheasants liked the look of.

My seat was not uncomfortable and the sun was pleasingly warm, so for the next three hours I remained in the tree without any discomfort. At 4 p.m. the sun went down behind the high hill above Thak and thereafter the wind became unbearably cold. For an hour I stood the discomfort, and then decided to give up, for the cold had brought on an attack of ague, and if the tigress came now it would not be possible for me to hit her. I retied the cord to the rifle and let it down, climbed down myself and walked to the edge of the cultivated land to call up my men.

~

There are few people, I imagine, who have not experienced that feeling of depression that follows failure to accomplish anything they have set out to do. The road back to the camp after a strenuous day when the chukor (hill partridge) bag is full is only a step compared with the same road which one plods over, mile after weary mile, when the bag is empty, and if this feeling of depression has ever assailed you at the end of a single day, and when the quarry has only been chukor, you will have some idea of the depth of my depression that evening when, after calling up my men and untying the goats, I set off on my two-mile walk to camp, for my effort had been not of a single day or my quarry a few birds, nor did my failure concern only myself.

Excluding the time spent on the journeys from and to home, I had been on the heels of the man-eater from 23rd October to 7th November, and again from 24th to 30th November, and it is only those of you who have walked in fear of having the teeth of a tiger meet in your throat who will have any idea of the effect on one's nerves of days and weeks of such anticipation.

Then again my quarry was a man-eater, and my failure to shoot it would very gravely affect anyone who was working in, or whose homes were in, that area. Already work in the forests had been stopped, and the entire population of the largest village in the district had abandoned their homes. Bad as the conditions were they would undoubtedly get worse if the man-eater was not killed, for the entire labour force could not afford to stop work indefinitely, nor could the population of surrounding villages afford to abandon their homes and their cultivation as the more prosperous people of Thak had been able to do.

The tigress had long since lost her natural fear of human beings as was abundantly evident from her having carried away a girl picking up mangoes in a field close to where several men were working, killing a woman near the door of her house, dragging a man off a tree in the heart of a village, and, the previous night, cowing a few thousand men into silence. And here was I, who knew full well what the presence of a man-eater meant to the permanent and to the temporary inhabitants and to all the people who passed through the district on their way to the markets at the foothills or the temples at Purnagiri, plodding down to camp on what I had promised others would be my last day of man-eater hunting; reason enough for a depression of soul which I felt would remain with me for the rest of my days. Gladly at that movement would I have bartered the success that had attended thirty-two years of man-eater hunting for one unhurried shot at the tigress.

I have told you of some of the attempts I made during this period of seven days and seven nights to get a shot at the tigress, but these were by no means the only attempts I made. I knew that I was being watched and followed, and every time I went through the two miles of jungle between my camp and Thak I tried every trick I have learnt in a lifetime spent in the jungles to outwit the tigress. Bitter though my disappointment was, I felt that my failure was not in any way due to anything I had done or left undone.

~

My men when they rejoined me said that, an hour after the kakar had barked, they had heard the tigress calling a long way off but were not sure of the direction. Quite evidently the tigress had as little interest in goats as she had in buffaloes, but even so it was unusual for her to have moved at that time of day from a locality in which she was thoroughly at home, unless she had been attracted away by some sound which neither I nor my men had heard; however that may have been, it was quite evident that she had gone, and as there was nothing further that I could do I set off on my weary tramp to camp.

The path, as I have already mentioned, joins the ridge that runs down to Chuka a quarter of a mile from Thak, and when I now got to this spot where the ridge is only a few feet wide and from where a view is obtained of the two great ravines that run down to the Ladhya river, I heard the tigress call once and again across the valley on my left. She was a little above and to the left of Kumaya Chak, and a few hundred yards below the Kot Kindri ridge on which the men working in that area had built themselves grass shelters.

Here was an opportunity, admittedly forlorn and unquestionably desperate, of getting a shot; still it was an opportunity and the last I should ever have, and the question was, whether or not I was justified in taking it.

When I got down from the tree I had one hour in which to get back to camp before dark. Calling up the men, hearing what they had to say, collecting the goats and walking to the ridge had taken about thirty minutes, and judging from the position of the sun which was now casting a red glow on the peaks of the Nepal hills, I calculated I had roughly half an hour's daylight in hand. This time factor, or perhaps it would be more correct to say light factor, was all-important, for if I took the opportunity that offered, on it would depend the lives of five men.

The tigress was a mile away and the intervening ground was densely wooded, strewn over with great rocks and cut up by a number of deep nullahs, but she could cover the distance well within the half-hour—if she wanted to. The question I had to decide was, whether or not I should try to call her up. If I called and she heard me, and came while it was still daylight and gave me a shot, all would be well; on the other hand, if she came and did not give me a shot some of us would not reach camp, for we had nearly two miles to go and the path the whole way ran through heavy jungle, and was bordered in some places by big rocks, and in others by dense brushwood. It was useless to consult the men, for none of them had ever been in a jungle before coming on this trip, so the decision would have to be mine.

I decided to try to call up the tigress.

Handing my rifle over to one of the men I waited until the tigress called again and, cupping my hands round my mouth and filling my lungs to their utmost limit, sent an answering call over the valley. Back came her call and thereafter, for several minutes, call answered call. She would come, had in fact already started, and if she arrived while there was light to shoot by, all the advantages would be on my side, for I had the selecting of the ground on which it would best suit me to meet her. November is the mating season for tigers and it was evident that for the past forty-eight hours she had been rampaging through the jungles in search of a mate, and that now, on hearing what she thought was a tiger answering her mating call, she would lose no time in joining him.

Four hundred yards down the ridge the path runs for fifty yards across a flat bit of ground. At the far right-hand side of this flat ground the path skirts a big rock and then drops steeply, and continues in a series of hairpin bends, down to the next bend. It was at this rock I decided to meet the tigress, and on my way down to it I called several times to let her know I was changing my position, and also to keep in touch with her.

I want you now to have a clear picture of the ground in your mind, to enable you to follow the subsequent events. Imagine then a rectangular piece of ground forty yards wide and eighty yards long, ending in a more or less perpendicular rock face. The path coming down from Thak runs on to this ground at its short or south end, and after continuing down the centre for twenty-five yards bends to the right and leaves the rectangle on its long or east side. At the point where the path leaves the flat ground there is a rock about four feet high. From a little beyond where the path bends to the right, a ridge of rock, three or four feet high, rises and extends to the north side of the rectangle, where the ground falls away in a perpendicular rock face. On the near or path side of this low ridge there is a dense line of bushes approaching to within ten feet of the four-foot-high rock I have mentioned. The rest of the rectangle is grown over with trees, scattered bushes, and short grass.

It was my intention to lie on the path by the side of the rock and shoot the tigress as she approached me, but when I tried this position I found it would not be possible for me to see her until she was within two or three yards, and further, that she could get at me either round the rock or through the scattered bushes on my left without my seeing her at all. Projecting out of the rock, from the side opposite to that from which I expected the tigress to approach, there was a narrow ledge. By sitting sideways I found I could get a little of my bottom on the ledge, and by putting my left hand flat on the top of the rounded rock and stretching out my right leg to its full extent and touching the ground with my toes, retain my position on it. The men and goats I placed immediately behind, and ten to twelve feet below me.

The stage was now set for the reception of the tigress, who while these preparations were being made had approached to within 300 yards. Sending out one final call to give her direction, I looked round to see if my men were all right.

The spectacle these men presented would under other circumstances have been ludicrous, but was here tragic. Sitting in a tight little circle with their knees drawn up and their heads together, with the goats burrowing in under them, they had that look of intense expectancy on their screwed-up features that one sees on the faces of spectators waiting to hear a big gun go off. From the time we had first heard the tigress from the ridge, neither the men nor the goats had made a sound, beyond one suppressed cough. They were probably by now frozen with fear—as well they might be—and even if they were I take my hat off to those four men who had the courage to do what I, had I been in their shoes, would not have dreamt of doing. For seven days they had been hearing the most exaggerated and blood-curdling tales of this fearsome beast that had kept them awake the past two nights, and now, while darkness was coming on, and sitting unarmed in a position where they could see nothing, they were listening to the man-eater drawing nearer and nearer; greater courage, and greater faith, it is not possible to conceive.

The fact that I could not hold my rifle a D.B. 450/400, with my left hand (which I was using to retain my precarious seat on the ledge) was causing me some uneasiness, for apart from the fear of the rifle slipping on the rounded top of the rock—I had folded my handkerchief and placed the rifle on it to try to prevent this—I did know what would be the effect of the recoil of a high velocity rifle fired in this position. The rifle was pointing along the path, in which there was a hump, and it was my intention to fire into the tigress's face immediately it appeared over this hump, which was twenty feet from the rock.

The tigress however did not keep to the contour of the hill, which would have brought her out on the path a little beyond the hump, but crossed a deep ravine and came straight towards where she had heard my last call, at an angle which I can best describe as one o'clock. This manoeuver put the low ridge of rock, over which I could not see, between us. She had located the direction of my last call with great accuracy, but had misjudged the distance, and not finding her prospective mate at the spot she had expected him to be, she was now working herself up into a perfect fury, and you will have some idea of what the fury of a tigress in her condition can be when I tell you that not many miles from my home a tigress on one occasion closed a public road for a whole week, attacking everything that attempted to go along it, including a string of camels, until she was finally joined by a mate.

I know of no sound more liable to fret one's nerves than the calling of an unseen tiger at close range. What effect this appalling sound was having on my men I frightened to think, and if they had gone screaming down the hill I should not have been at all surprised, for even though I had the heel of a good rifle to my shoulder and the stock against my cheek I felt like screaming myself.

But even more frightening than this continuous calling was the fading out of the light. Another few seconds, ten or fifteen at the most, and it would be too dark to see my sights, and we should then be at the mercy of a man-eater, plus a tigress wanting a mate. Something would have to be done, and done in a hurry if we were not to be massacred, and the only thing I could think of was to call.

The tigress was now so close that I could hear the intake of her breath each time before she called, and as she again filled her lungs, I did the same with mine, and we called simultaneously. The effect was startlingly instantaneous. Without a second's hesitation she came tramping with quick steps through the dead leaves, over the low ridge and into the bushes a little to my right front, and just as I was expecting her to walk right on top of me she stopped, and the next moment the full blast of her deep-throated call struck me in the face and would have carried the hat off my head had I been wearing one. A second's pause, then again quick steps; a glimpse of her as she passed between two bushes, and then she stepped right out into the open, and, looking into my face, stopped dead.

By great and unexpected good luck the half-dozen steps the tigress took to her right front carried her almost to the exact spot at which my rifle was pointing. Had she continued in the direction in which she was coming before her last call, my story—if written—would have had a different ending, for it would have been as impossible to slew the rifle on the rounded top of the rock as it would have been to lift and fire it with one hand.

Owing to the nearness of the tigress, and the fading light, all that I could see of her was her head. My first bullet caught her under the right eye and the second, fired more by accident than with intent, took her in the throat and she came to rest with her nose against the rock. The recoil from the right barrel loosened my hold on the rock and knocked me off the ledge, and the recoil from the left barrel, fired while I was in the air, brought the rifle up in violent contact with my jaw and sent me heels over head right on top of the men and goats. Once again I take my hat off to those four men for, not knowing but what the tigress was going to land on them next, they caught me as I fell and saved me from injury and my rifle from being broken.

When I had freed myself from the tangle of the human and goat legs I took the ·275 rifle from the man who was holding it, rammed a clip of cartridges into the magazine and sent a stream of five bullets singing over the valley and across the Sarda into Nepal. Two shots, to the thousands of men in the valley and in the surrounding villages who were anxiously listening for the sound of my rifle, might mean anything, but two shots followed by five more, spaced at regular intervals of five seconds, could only be interpreted as conveying one message, and that was, that the man-eater was dead.

I had not spoken to my men from the time we had first heard the tigress from the ridge. On my telling them now that she was dead and that there was no longer any reason for us to be afraid, they did not appear to be able to take in what I was saying, so I told them to go up and have a look while I found and lit a cigarette. Very cautiously they climbed up to the rock, but went no further for, as I have told you, the tigress was touching the other side of it. Late in camp that night, while sitting round a camp-fire, and relating their experiences to relays of eager listeners, their narrative invariably ended up with, 'and then the tiger whose roaring had turned our livers into water hit the Sahib on the head and knocked him down on top of us and if you don't believe us, go and look at his face.' A mirror is superfluous in camp and even if I had one it could not have made the swelling on my jaw, which put me on milk diet for several days, look as large and as painful as it felt.

By the time a sapling had been felled and the tigress lashed to it, lights were beginning to show in the Ladhya valley and in all the surrounding camps and villages. The four men were very anxious to have the honour of carrying the tigress to camp, but the task was beyond them; so I left them and set off for help.

In my three visits to Chuka during the past eight months I had been along this path many times by day and always with a loaded rifle in my hands, and now I was stumbling down in the dark, unarmed, my only anxiety being to avoid a fall. If the greatest happiness one can experience is the sudden cessation of great pain, then the second greatest happiness is undoubtedly the sudden cessation of great fear. One short hour previously it would have taken wild elephants to have dragged from their homes and camps the men who now, singing and shouting, were converging from every direction, singly and in groups, on the path leading to Thak. Some of the men of this rapidly growing crowd went up the path to help carry in the tigress, while others accompanied me on my way to camp, and would have carried me had I permitted them. Progress was slow, for frequent halts had to be made to allow each group of new arrivals to express their gratitude in their own particular way. This gave the party carrying the tigress time to catch us up, and we entered the village together. I will not attempt to describe the welcome my men and I received, or the scenes I witnessed at Chuka that night, for having lived the greater part of my life in the jungles I have not the ability to paint word-pictures.

A hayrick was dismantled and the tigress laid on it, and an enormous bonfire made from driftwood close at hand to light up the scene and for warmth, for the night was dark and cold with a north wind blowing. Round about midnight my servant, assisted by the Headman of Thak and Kunwar Singh, near whose house I was camped, persuaded the crowd to return to their respective villages and labour camps, telling them they would have ample opportunity of feasting their eyes on the tigress the following day. Before leaving himself, the Headman of Thak told me he would send word in the morning to the people of Thak to return to their village. This he did, and two days later the entire population returned to their homes, and have lived in peace ever since.

After my midnight dinner I sent for Kunwar Singh and told him that in order to reach home on the promised date I should have to start in a few hours, and that he would have to explain to the people in the morning why I had gone. This he promised to do, and I then started to skin the tigress. Skinning a tiger with a pocket-knife is a long job, but it gives one an opportunity of examining the animal that one would otherwise not get, and in the case of man-eater enables one to ascertain, more or less accurately, the reason for the animal having become a man-eater.

The tigress was a comparatively young animal and in the perfect condition one would expect her to be at the beginning of the mating season. Her dark winter coat was without a blemish, and in spite of her having so persistently refused the meals I had provided for her she was encased in fat. She had two old gunshot wounds, neither of which showed on her skin. The one in her left shoulder, caused by several pellets of homemade buckshot, had become septic, and when healing the skin, over quite a large surface, had adhered permanently to the flesh. To what extent this wound had incapacitated her it would have been difficult to say, but it had evidently taken a very long time to heal, and could quite reasonably have been the cause of her having become a man-eater. The second wound, which was in her right shoulder, had also been caused by a charge of buckshot, but had healed without becoming septic. These two wounds received over kills in the days before she had become a man-eater were quite sufficient reason for her not having returned to the human and other kills I had sat over.

After having skinned the tigress I bathed and dressed, and though my face was swollen and painful and I had twenty miles of rough going before me, I left Chuka walking on air, while the thousands of men in and around the valley were peacefully sleeping.

I have come to the end of the jungle stories I set out to tell you and I have also come near the end of my man-eater hunting career.

I have had a long spell and count myself fortunate in having walked out on my own feet and not been carried out on a cradle in the manner and condition of the man of Thak.

There have been occasions when life has hung by a thread and others when a light purse and disease resulting from exposure and strain have made the going difficult, but for all these occasions I am amply rewarded if my hunting has resulted in saving one human life.

www.ingramcontent.com/pod-product-compliance
Lightning Source LLC
Chambersburg PA
CBHW052045220426
43663CB00012B/2452